Social History of Africa

AFRICAN WORKERS AND COLONIAL RACISM

Social History of Africa
Series Editors: Allen Isaacman and Jean Hay

African Workers and Colonial Racism: *Mozambican Strategies and Struggles in Lourenço Marques, 1877–1962*   Jeanne Marie Penvenne

Burying SM: *The Politics of Knowledge and the Sociology of Power in Africa* David William Cohen and E. S. Atieno Odhiambo

Colonial Conscripts: *The* Tirailleurs Sénégalais *in French West Africa, 1875–1960* Myron Echenberg

Cutting Down Trees: *Gender, Nutrition, and Agricultural Change in the Northern Province of Zambia, 1890–1990*   Henrietta L. Moore and Megan Vaughan

Feasts and Riot: *Revelry, Rebellion and Popular Consciousness on the Swahili Coast, 1856–1888*   Jonathon Glassman

Insiders and Outsiders: *The Indian Working Class of Durban, 1910–1990* Bill Freund

Law in Colonial Africa: Kristin Mann and Richard Roberts (editors)

Money Matters: *Instability, Values and Social Payments in the Modern History of West African Communities*   Jane I. Guyer (editor)

The Moon Is Dead! Give Us Our Money!: *The Cultural Origins of an African Work Ethic, Natal, South Africa, 1843–1900*   Keletso E. Atkins

Peasants, Traders, and Wives: *Shona Women in the History of Zimbabwe, 1870–1939* Elizabeth Schmidt

"We Spend Our Years as a Tale That is Told": *Oral Historical Narrative in a South African Chiefdom*   Isabel Hofmeyr

Women of Phokeng: *Consciousness, Life Strategy, and Migrancy in South Africa, 1900–1983*   Belinda Bozzoli (with the assistance of Mmantho Nkotsoe)

Work, Culture, and Identity: *Migrant Laborers in Mozambique and South Africa, 1860–1910*   Patrick Harries

AFRICAN WORKERS AND COLONIAL RACISM

Mozambican Strategies and Struggles in Lourenço Marques, 1877–1962

Jeanne Marie Penvenne

HEINEMANN
Portsmouth, NH

WITWATERSRAND
UNIVERSITY PRESS
Johannesburg

JAMES CURREY
London

Heinemann
A division of Reed Elsevier Inc.
361 Hanover Street
Portsmouth, NH 03801-3912

James Currey Ltd.
54b Thornhill Square,
Islington
London N1 1BE

Witwatersrand University Press
University of Witwatersrand
Johannesburg
PO Wits 2050
South Africa

Offices and agents throughout the world

Photo credits: pages 21, 31, and 77, Eliza McClennen, cartographer; Pages 35, 36, 38, 39, 46, 48, 53, 55, 56, 81, 119, 121, 144, 145, 149, and 150, Archívo Histórico de Moçambique; pages 66 and 67, *Brado Africano*.

ISBN 0-435-08952-8 (Heinemann cloth)
ISBN 0-435-08954-4 (Heinemann paper)
ISBN 0-85255-664-0 (James Currey cloth)
ISBN 0-85255-614-4 (James Currey paper)
ISBN 1-86814-268-X (Witwatersrand University Press paper)

Library of Congress Cataloging-in-Publication Data
Penvenne, Jeanne
    African workers and colonial racism : Mozambican strategies and struggles
in Lourenço Marques, 1877–1962 / Jeanne Marie Penvenne.
        p.   cm. — (Social History of Africa)
    Includes bibliographical references and index.
    ISBN 0-435-08952-8. — ISBN 0-435-08954-4 (pbk.)
    1. Labor—Mozambique—Maputo—History.   2. Working Class—
Mozambique—Maputo—History.   3. Labor disputes—Mozambique—
Maputo—History.   4. Labor laws and legislation—Mozambique—
Maputo—History.   5. Portuguese—Mozambique—Maputo—History.
6. Maputo (Mozambique)—Colonial influence.   7. Maputo (Mozambique)—
Race relations.   I. Title.   II. Series.
HD8798.Z8M325   1994
331'.09679'—dc20   94-10574
                                                                            CIP

British Library Cataloguing in Publication Data
Penvenne, Jeanne Marie
    African workers and colonial racism: Mozambican Strategies and
    Struggles in Lourenço Marques, 1877–1962. — (Social History of Africa Series)
    I. Title II. Series
    331.109679

Cover design by Jenny Greenleaf.
Printed in the United States of America.
99 98 97 96 95 BB 1 2 3 4 5 6 7 8 9

To
Passion, Hope, Mischief
Johnny, Ruth, Mussongueia, and Meke

CONTENTS

PREFACE

This book has taken too long. I once thought that I could write this manuscript in stolen moments amidst a too-full life centered upon my children, my family, my community, and my students. I could not. The manuscript had to become the central focus with life lived around it. I once thought I would not begin my book with an apology and thanks to the people and tasks I ignored and abused in order to complete the task. I was wrong. So I begin with a sincere thanks to the intimates—family, colleagues and friends—who received much less of my time and who often found me looking at them, but clearly thinking about chapter whatever. As it turns out I really like being squirreled away in a quiet office with this nifty machine, my notes, books, and disks. I aspire to continue to neglect tasks, family, community, and friends and write much more.

I was able to research and write the book with funds, technical help, and collaboration from many people and institutions. The Fulbright-Hays doctoral research program for Portugal, the Social Science Research Council's International Doctoral Fellowship program, and the Fundação Calouste Gulbenkian's International Fellow program all funded the original field and archival research. Several subsequent trips to Portugal were partly subsidized by Norman R. Bennett's book business, *Livros*, and a National Endowment for the Humanities Grant through James McCann and Margaret Jean Hay at the Boston University African Studies Center.

The staff at several very diverse archive and library facilities served me well. My presence as a foreigner was tolerated at the Arquivo Histórico Ultramarino in Lisbon. I received computer instruction and a functioning beeper at the Public Record Office in the United Kingdom. In Maputo labor relations became more personalized. I was allowed to spend days on end, without regard for scheduled office hours, working my way through piles of unclassified documentation sitting in a dusty attic at the former municipal labor office. Sr. Alexandre Veloso and his staff watched in awe as I rose and descended like a chimney sweep, but they cheerfully and generously shared their space with me for months. Also in Maputo, the National Archive director, Maria Inês Nogueira da Costa, graciously allowed me to continue my research despite the fact that a cyclone had made the archive roof look like Swiss cheese and the boxes and papers were being moved out from under me to the new archive. The entire staff at Arquivo Histórico de Moçambique has always been unfailingly helpful and made me feel quite at home. António Sopa helped extensively with photographs and final details.

Research clearance and support from the Centro de Estudos Africanos, Universidade Eduardo Mondlane, the Administração dos Portos, Caminhos de Ferro e Transportes, and the Câmara Municipal de Maputo allowed me to structure and conduct oral interviews. Gaspar Salamão Guevende, Alexandre Vitor Santos, Isaíahs Muhate, Gabriel Mabunda, Sr. Serra-Ventosa, Alpheus Manghezi, Saul Tembe, Paulo Zombole, Ruth First, Aquino Bragança, and Fernando Ganhão all supported that effort. Prof. Dr. Bento Sitoe and Prof. Dr. José Mateus Katupha assisted with orthographic and linguistic problems. Obviously the most important collaboration came from the Mozambicans who shared their experience with me and my unfamiliar tape recorder. They are named in Annex I. After my return to the United States, the African Studies Center at Boston University supported the presentation of my research at national conferences. It became my intellectual home, and a fine one at that. The manuscript was prepared on the Center's computer equipment, and I thank Shawn Dennard, Karen Keller-Heybey, and Joanne Hart for helping me work out technical glitches.

Many, many people have inspired this work by their ideas, their support, the material they brought to my attention, and their example. I include them in no special order: my extended Penvenne, Shugg, Bennett, and Darey families, Lydia Dana, Nancy Warner, Jean Hay, Sara Berry, Michael and Mary Beth Feldman, Frederick Cooper, Douglas Wheeler, Robbie Walsh, Polly Lanman, Leroy Vail, Landeg White, James McCann, José Soares Martins, Norman R. Bennett, John and Louis Bennett, Sherilynn Young, Patrick Harries, Jill and Alberto Dias, David and Elizabeth Birmingham, Jacques Depelchin, Carlos Serra, Kathleen E. Sheldon, António Nogueira da Costa, Nadine DeLew, Shirley Penvenne, colleagues at Departamento de História, Universidade Eduardo Mondlane, and James C. Armstrong. The Heinemann Social History of Africa series editors Allen Isaacman, Luise White, Jean Hay, and their excellent critical readers gave me the invaluable perspective I needed to present this material in more effective form. I am most grateful for the intellectual investment they made in earlier drafts of this manuscript. Thanks to their suggestions, it is a much better study. The remaining weaknesses reflect my limits, not their efforts.

Four people floated in and out of my consciousness as I wrote this manuscript. Johnny Penvenne, António [Meke] Nogueira da Costa, and Ruth First lived intense, passionate lives and died so tragically and so young. Mussongueia Samuel Mussona sparkled with mischief, zest for life, and spiritual freedom in 1977 when he was by all accounts more than one hundred years old. I was privileged to work with Mozambicans in the intense and passionate period of the new nation's youth, and it has been most painful to witness the country's subsequent tragic struggles. My sincere hope is that Mozambicans will survive this tragic youth and move toward the joyous, confident maturity that Mussongueia seemed to personify.

Jeanne Penvenne
Boston / Duxbury, MA

GLOSSARY

a bem da nasão: "for the good of the nation," motto of the early New State
afilhado/a: godchild or person who enjoyed partronage protection or promotion in his or her job
anda procura: door-to-door or person-to-person job search
assimilado/a: assimilated person, or person of "of the Negro race or descendant therefrom" who was suppposed to enjoy full citizen rights
álvara de assimilação: assimilation document
bairros: neighborhoods/planned municipal housing areas
baixa: the central business district of Lourenço Marques/Maputo
brancos da terra: "whites of the land," a nineteenth-century term for politically well-connected mulattos
caça de quinhenta: the hunt for the fifty-cent registration fee
cantina: trade store
cantineiro: shopkeeper of trade store
cartões de efectividade: attendance cards used for day labor at the port
centavo: a cent, see Currency Note below
chapa: labor registration tag
chefe de posto: lowest-level Portuguese rural administrator
conto: a thousand units of currency, see Currency Note below
contribuição predial: building tax
cunha: "wedge," or patron in the bureaucracy who could help with promotions
desemprego: unemployment
encarregado: supervisor
escudo: currency denomination, see Currency Note below
grupo dinimizador: group political leader under the Frelimo government
indigenato: the legal system that defined separate and subordinate citizen status for "people of the Negro race or descendant therefrom"
kubvana: common Portuguese immigrant
liberto: freed person
lobolo: bridewealth
magaiça: returned mine migrant
mainato/a: laundry person
matadouro: slaughterhouse
milreis: a thousand *reis*, see Currency Note below
mudende: personal tax on urban Africans including women

mumaji: common Portuguese immigrant

mwamu cholo: Mozambican who worked repeated forced labor contracts

não-indígena: non-native status, including Europeans, Asians, and Africans who held assimilation status

padrinho: godfather or personal patron

palmatória: paddle with five holes used to beat Africans

pancada da graça: a gratuitous beating

pantano: the swamp

para o Inglês ver: For the English to see, or window dressing

pequeno funcionário: petty bureaucrat, term used to designate the majority, lowest-ranking Portuguese civil servants

Português do quintal: backyard (or kitchen) Portuguese

procurador: attorney or agent

quintal: term for backyard, common synonym for domestic service

reis: currency denomination, see Currency Note below

régulo: designated African political authority or chief

rusga: roundup or raid for forced laborers

sertanejo: backwoodsman or itinerant trader

servente: entry-level civil servant position for Africans

shibalo: conscripted contract labor, forced labor (alternative spellings *chibalo, xibalo, chibaro*)

sopé: alcoholic drink made from sugar cane

sumpango: honeywagon, or sewage disposal wagon

uputsu: millet beer

CURRENCY NOTE

The basic currency unit in nineteenth-century colonial Mozambique was the *reis*, designated as follows:

one *reis*, $001
one *milreis* = a thousand reis, 1$000
one *conto* = one thousand *milreis*, 1,000$000.

With the overthrow of the monarchy and establishment of the Republic in 1910, the *reis* was replaced with the *escudo*, and the entire currency system shifted from a base of one thousand to a base of one hundred. *Escudo* designation was as follows:

one *centavo*, $01
one hundred *centavos* = one *escudo*, 1$00
one *escudo*, 1$00, replaced one *milreis*, 1$000
one *conto* = one thousand *escudos*, 1,000$00.

Introduction: African Workers and Colonial Racism

"The Portuguese who were here thought that the black man
did not have two legs like they did."

Sianai Lakene Chichongo[1]

Work: Images and Meaning

This is a study of the struggle between Mozambican men, their employers, and the Portuguese colonial administration over Chichongo's metaphor of anatomy. From the end of the nineteenth century, the Portuguese promulgated a body of labor legislation and developed personal and labor relations with Africans that cumulatively came to be called the *indigenato*. Under the *indigenato* a whole range of regulations and sanctions applied only to people who were classified as *indígenas* or "natives." "Native" was articulated as an essentially masculine concept, while women comprised the sub-category of "native women." The *indigenato* was created and extended to define and treat Africans as fundamentally lesser beings, particularly in the workplace.

How did the labor controls and relations embodied in the *indigenato* come into being, and what role did they play in the labor history of colonial Mozambique? What were the costs of this coercive and pervasive system? Who paid those costs, and how? Who cooperated, who resisted, who accommodated, who suffered, and who benefited from the *indigenato*? This study considers the dialectic of labor relations between Africans and Europeans in the port capital of colonial Mozambique, Lourenço Marques (today Maputo), from the origins of the modern city in the late 1870s to the transformation of labor relations with the end of the *indigenato* in the early 1960s. It explores how forced labor, called *shibalo*,[2] which was the essential underpinning of the *indigenato*, shaped the formation of the largely male African work force. Lourenço Marques was built and serviced with the tax money, sweat,

I

skills, laughter, and patience of African workers, both independent laborers and *shibalo*. The study seeks to convey and analyze this process as much as possible from the workers' perspectives.

Informant testimony was replete with animal imagery. Men angrily recalled being reprimanded for speaking their mother tongue, "the language of dogs."[3] The Portuguese denied them meaningful speech; their mouths were merely "beaks." They were allowed to say, "Yes, sir; yes, sir," but nothing else.[4] Employers housed their African workers in stables and hay wagons, dressed them in used animal fodder sacking and provided them with food "not even a dog would eat."[5] Mozambican men courted deportation for daring to reveal that they were clever, confident, skilled, or sexually mature human beings. They were often severely beaten for testing the unspoken limits of European power or for triggering underlying European fears. African men and women working in Lourenço Marques struggled to sustain their confidence and pride as adults against a humiliating system of domination, which treated them at worst like animals and at best like incompetent children—but never like full adult human beings with two legs.

In individual exchanges with Europeans, African mouths were indeed mere "beaks," but some forms of speech enjoyed a modicum of protection. Adulthood and masculinity could be asserted and powerful people could be mocked through song conventions.[6] Thus the cruelly powerful "little white man" was mocked for the insecurity and fear that fueled much of colonial policy. The "crazy little white man" was always seeing ghosts. He was pathetic, haggard, and cross because he dared not let down his guard in Africa, where he was so vastly outnumbered:

> You crazy little white man, you are seeing ghosts, little whiteman.
> We've worked for you a long time, but you don't dare trust us, little whiteman.[7]

Manuel Mendes, the most important Portuguese planter in the Xai-Xai[8] region of Gaza, humiliated his workers by dressing them in used pig fodder sacks. His workers taunted: did such a powerful and wealthy settler have to confirm his own manhood by humiliating others? Was that what the pitiful Mendes had to do to enjoy himself?

> Oh Manuel Mendes dresses us in pig sacks.
> Ah Mendes, old boy, you enjoy doing it, don't you Mendes!
> You enjoy it! Enjoy it! Manuel Mendes, you enjoy it![9]

Although worksongs addressed expressions of resistance, complaint, lament, sarcasm, and anger to the oppressor, the communication among co-workers was also important.[10] The songs obviously helped coordinate a work rhythm and break the tedium. They also conveyed mutual encouragement, punctuated with both warnings and restraints. Working in the hundreds of landfill, quarry, and roadwork gangs, experienced men sang to calm and soothe the anger of the inexperienced youth:

> Be calm my son. . . . You will see, you are shoveling sand my son. . . . you will see.
> Shovel sand, since you are here my son. . . . be calm my son![11]

Their soothing cadences were periodically interrupted by sharp, frightening interjections warning of the deadly presence of the overseer:

Get going! Get Going! . . . Devil snake Ndziwena!
Work! Work! Die! Work to death. . . . ![12]

The most familiar worksong, "*Shibalo* muni Magandana, ho . . ." echoed danger, but also incorporated a genuine puzzlement:

What kind of *shibalo* is this of Magandana, ho . . . ?
It catches everyone, even the women . . . , ho . . . .
It catches even the grandparents [mothers, parents, children, sisters, etc.]
They don't even let us rest, ho. . . .
What kind of *shibalo* is this of Magandana, ho . . . ?[13]

The ways of the whiteman, the ways of Magandana, did not make sense. His greed and demands were excessive to the point of foolishness. An often-quoted lyric from the musical repertoire of the Chopi-speaking people of southern Mozambique suggested the essential contradiction. The crazy Portuguese were not satisfied with just eating eggs, they ate the chickens too, thus killing the source of future eggs.[14] What kind of labor exploitation was this that burned up the labor force to the point of threatening its reproduction? Indeed, "What kind of *shibalo* was this of Magandana?"

Labor relations emerged in worksongs and interviews in stark terms of humans and animals, power and perversion—and generational survival against forces of death and deviation. African fathers, sons, daughters, mothers, grandparents, all faced Magandana, who worked people without rest, even the old and the young. Devil snake Ndziwena whipped up the pace of production with "Work! Die! Work to death!" The whiteman made himself sick and crazy keeping watch, day and night, over those he worked to death. Even Manuel Mendes, with all his power and wealth, seemed only to find his manhood and pleasure in humiliating his workers, treating them like animals. The labor system emerged with little respect for African dignity and humanity, thus the actors who developed it were perceived as sinister.

Labor Policy and Practice

Clearly Portuguese colonial legislation and policy statements did not articulate labor relations in such terms. African labor was recognized throughout this period as the colony's principal resource, the key to Portugal's ability to realize wealth from her holdings. Portugal's colonial ideology was patronizing and cloaked in self-serving protectionism. Africans were to be protected from one another and from exploitation by "superior races," but it was also Portugal's duty as the beacon to civilization to instruct them in their "moral obligation to work."[15] The policy behind the *indigenato* was as "protective" and "instructive" as the practice was harsh and exploitative. Nobody was more aware of the chasm between policy rhetoric and practice than the Portuguese administration charged with implementing policy. Research confirmed James Duffy's classic observation about Portuguese labor policy for the period well beyond the closing date of Duffy's study (1920): "reformist aspirations of Portuguese governments would be contained in legislation and decrees. Most of these failed in their purpose, and where they succeeded they led to the perverted continuation of traditional practices."[16]

This book argues that colonial labor legislation and relations were certainly about productivity, time, wages, and benefits, but they were also about authority, respect, and dignity. Throughout the study, the articulation of the *indigenato* is juxtaposed with its application—through legislation, policy statements, internal correspondence, informant testimony, the press, and international exposés of the Portuguese system. The justification for poor wages, long hours, no benefits, and no security for African workers emerges in sharp contrast with discourse around wages and working conditions for Portuguese workers. The difference between "workers" and "natives" was not simply a matter of semantics; it was a fundamental distinction carrying its own coding of authority and respect.

In his important study of Mozambican labor in the 1950s, Marvin Harris recognized that familiar terms of labor market analysis did not fit the colonial situation. The situation of African colonial labor did not emerge from market conditions, it was consciously and painstakingly constructed. In places where European workers as well as European employers participated in the colonial economy, that construction took on special textures to buffer competition and comparisons between African and European workers. African workers were not permitted the opportunity to train and compete for higher wages or added benefits:

> it has been the historical function of colonial governments to force Africans into European employment without paying the price which the Africans could have obtained had free market conditions prevailed. To call Africans "vagrants" is only justified if it is recognized that in the wage labor frame of reference, the Europeans are "thieves."[17]

It is hardly surprising that Africans who were seized for *shibalo* by the colonial government and put to work shoveling coal on the Lourenço Marques waterfront shared Harris's analysis. They paced their shoveling to the chorus:

> The Portuguese live by stealing our wages,
> Heave that shovel, heave. . . .[18]

It is surprising that the man who presided over the *shibalo* system in the late 1950s when Harris conducted his research, and who described Harris as "one of our most persistent detractors," also strongly corroborated Harris's analysis.[19] The administrative inspector of native affairs, Sr. Pinto de Fonseca, described the *indigenato* and its key underpinning, *shibalo*, as "obnoxious," "inefficient," "unjust," and at times "intolerable."[20] He echoed Harris and corroborated extensive informant testimony to the effect that the *indigenato* specifically undermined pressure to bid up wages or improve working conditions. Rather, Pinto da Fonseca acknowledged, the *shibalo* system enabled "the worst employers [to] pay the absolute minimum, requisition the most labor and make the loudest fuss when their workers resist such poor conditions."[21]

Mozambicans used the term *shibalo* to designate a whole range of work relations, including unpaid labor, coerced labor, ill-paid labor, and slavery. Their broad usage suggests both their sense of history and their awareness of the system's broader implications. *Shibalo* and the "moral obligation to work" revealed the fundamental role of the *indigenato* in making the transition from slaves to *libertos* (or freedmen), and from *libertos* to *indígenas*. Each civil status incorporated claims on the individual's labor. *Shibalo*, the claim that could be made on an *indígena*'s labor, was an important sanction to discipline and intimidate the labor force. While it was a sanction for Africans, it was a boon for Portuguese settlers, ensuring them a steady supply of labor without improved wages and working conditions. *Shibalo* was as fundamental an explanation of the plight of an ill-paid urban volunteer worker as it was of the unpaid conscripted worker. Each condition was rooted in the fettered, unequal situation imposed by the *indigenato* system. Europeans were correctly perceived as "stealing" the value of African labor through *shibalo*, whether it was unpaid or ill paid. The Portuguese coerced the provision of services they refused to buy at the offering price.

The *indigenato* obviously carried recruitment and management costs, but it also eroded the ability of the majority labor force to challenge wages. Shortly before the *indigenato* was legally abolished in the early 1960s, Pinto de Fonseca frankly confirmed that people subject to the *indigenato* were condemned to "enormous moral and material prejudice."[22] The pay scales established for municipal workers in Lourenço Marques in the 1950s make nonsense of the familiar excuse that low wages for Africans merely reflected their low productivity. The annual salary of European municipal drivers was nearly three times that of equally qualified "native" drivers—33,000$00 *escudos*[23] as opposed to 12,000$00.[24] All drivers passed the same examination, held the same license, and presumably obeyed the same traffic codes. "Native" drivers resented their inability to organize collectively under labor laws and demand equal pay, but they were even more indignant about their differential legal treatment as "irresponsible children."[25] Despite the fact that "native" drivers earned less than half the salaries of whites for equal work, their salaries were among the highest paid to anyone subject to the *indigenato*. Ordinary municipal "native" laborers earned 5,260$00 a year, and municipal *shibalo* labor earned less than half that amount, 2,160$00.[26]

An African Working Class

Definitions and Contradictions

Although the *indigenato* privileged social relations based on colonial definitions of race over class relations, it could not fully eclipse class relations that developed from production, waged work, workplace relations, and working conditions. Waged labor was largely restricted to males throughout most of the period considered. Contract and *shibalo* labor directed males to workplaces separate from their female family members; class formation was thus a specifically gendered process. From at least the 1920s, Lourenço Marques was home to thousands of Mozambican men who had worked for wages full time, or nearly full time, for their entire adult lives. Their fathers' and grandfathers' adult lives had been regularly punctuated by labor contracts, but they had seen themselves predominantly as farming, herding, rural people. The generations from the 1920s, however, increasingly saw themselves as workers.[27] They developed mutual support, credit, intelligence, and friendship networks around their workplace and urban neighborhood acquaintances, and they are the principal focus of the study.

African workers in Lourenço Marques clearly formed a class in relation to capital, and developed strategies to protect and advance their interests. The dialectic of colonial class struggle was skewed because the *indigenato* imbued the fundamental opposition of labor and capital with a racial overlay. White labor, employers, and capitalists commanded special authority and privilege, whereas Africans in all three categories were hampered by special constraints. A conversation manual in African and European languages, written in Lourenço Marques at the turn of the century by the famous missionary ethnographer Henri A. Junod, suggests the nature of these constraints.[28] The dialogues referred to all African males, regardless of age, as "boys," and advised them about "proper behavior" toward an implicitly European employer. The "boys" were instructed to respond with immediate and "respectful" attention to the demands of the their "master," the "whiteman." In the colonial setting, white employers felt entitled to prompt attention and deference, not merely an honest day's labor.[29]

This study argues that, although an African working class developed in Lourenço Marques, forming itself and being formed, the dynamic behind the process was often not the alienation of the labor force from the means of production. A great many of the African men working in the city, perhaps the majority, came to see themselves as workers and to develop their futures as workers in Lourenço Marques despite their continued access to land, small stock, tools, and family labor. The essential dynamic in the formation of an African working class was the *indigenato*, which prevented most Africans from developing their rural holdings. The *indigenato* physically removed men from their rural holdings through *shibalo*, and it ensured that African farmers, cattlemen, merchants, and artisans were severely compromised in their efforts to compete with Portuguese whites. The *indigenato* cast the majority male population of Mozambique as minimum wage and condition contract laborers.

Since many urban African workers maintained at least some rural-based social investments, their networks were often closely interwoven with family and rural acquaintance networks. Many if not most workers' wives, daughters, sisters and mothers continued to live, farm, trade, and develop support relationships outside the city. The familial overlay and integration of male urban workplace networks and female farming and rural networks shaped the socioeconomic position of the urban African working class. Why were Mozambican workers who continued to hold viable claims to land and rural labor increasingly concerned with workplace issues and with their futures as workers? The development of an African working class in Lourenço Marques was both contradictory to and a direct result of colonial labor policy. This labor policy consistently opposed the development of communities of urban African families who lived predominantly and generation after generation from the sale of male labor or from urban-based enterprise. Again, labor policy was gendered. Males were ideally supposed to fulfill the "moral obligation to work" required by the *indigenato* through a labor contract with a white employer. They were simultaneously supposed to retain their rural base in small-scale family agriculture as heads of household through the labor and management capacity of their wives. Labor policy indirectly recognized African women as the principal producers in family agriculture, and increasingly constrained their ability to leave rural areas. African males were not supposed to be deprived of their access to land, labor, and factors of production. They were just supposed to take half a year or more away from it to fulfill their "moral obligation to work."

Yet, as so often happened, policy ideals were in sharp contrast with the dynamic of practice. The "moral obligation to work" too often threatened male well-being in rural areas. Colonial reports, from Governor Freire de Andrade in the first decade of the century to Pinto de Fonseca a half-century later, revealed the extreme vulnerability of rural males to ill-paid, unpaid, poor condition *shibalo*. Pinto de Fonseca explained:

In rural areas where [wage] employment opportunities are limited, the "moral obligation to work" promotes a system of contracts for men who become automatically considered "lazy" [and thus vulnerable to *shibalo*] every six months. . . .

Employers can depend upon the "moral obligation to work" to provide them with a regular cyclical supply [of labor]. . . .

They do not have to improve or maintain conditions and they still have labor.[30]

Although the intensity of *shibalo* recruitment varied through time, it was much more consistent in rural districts south of the Save River, the area called Sul do Save. Recruitment peaked in response to agricultural demand in the early 1920s and mid to late 1940s, but even in the 1930s when planters elsewhere cut severely back on labor supplies, Sul do Save settlers tried to raise production to accommodate for falling prices, and they did it on the backs of *shibalo* workers. Farmers who did not have to "improve or maintain conditions" overworked, underfed, and failed to pay their workers. Such jobs were very dangerous to people's health and well-being. The best long-term protection against such cyclical *shibalo* was a full-time job that paid enough to survive and to cover one's tax burden. Such jobs were largely restricted to towns and cities.

An African working class developed in Lourenço Marques in part because some men in southern Mozambique were unable to make a livelihood and pay their taxes from rural production and income opportunities, but in much larger part because African males were prevented from developing their rural holdings and were driven to urban employment by the chronic threat of *shibalo*. Thus, one pillar of labor ideology, the "moral obligation to work," undermined the other pillar, the essential rural and agricultural nature of the African population. The upshot was that committed African workers in Lourenço Marques were not necessarily proletarians.

Individuals, Structures, and Groups

Mozambicans negotiated social and work space for themselves and their families in Lourenço Marques. The task called for courage, luck, cleverness, and perseverance. Informants for this study were those who survived. We do not have the perspective of those who fled or were defeated by the formidable control structure embedded in the *indigenato*. The survivors regarded any open or direct individual challenge to the colonial structure as a foolish invitation "to bring trouble upon oneself and one's family."[31] The labor control structures prescribed claims or exemptions on Mozambicans according to their individual and group identity. From the opportunities of labor migration to the textures of urban struggles, people's ability to make a life and a livelihood was shaped in important ways by the parameters of their personal and group identity. The key shaping factors were sex, age, education, and ethnicity. They are highlighted here, but developed in greater detail as appropriate in the following chapters.

Sex and age were the most important determinants, because they were clearly linked to labor claims through the *indigenato*. Men between fourteen and sixty-five were obliged to fulfill their "moral obligation," whereas most women, young men, and older males were either excluded or partially exempted. Until the forced cultivation schemes of the late 1930s, women were most often forced to labor as surrogates for their spouses or male relatives. The majority of Lourenço Marques wage earners and *shibalo* were men from rural districts of Sul do Save—Gaza, Inhambane and Lourenço Marques. Sul do Save migrants developed their life and work strategies in a regional context. The focus here is Lourenço Marques, but many workers spent part of their lives working in the South African mining industry, the agricultural economy of Sul do Save, and the city of Lourenço Marques.

By the 1870s voluntary labor migration from Sul do Save was strongly influenced by men's efforts to accumulate capital for specific social and economic investments linked with the life cycle. The accumulation of bridewealth, or *lobolo*, which confirmed marriage, adulthood, and the full participation of men and women in community affairs, was a major consideration. The higher wages and eventually the contract payment system available at the South African mines facilitated capital accumulation for *lobolo*. Unskilled mine labor, however, was only open to healthy adult males. Men unfit for the mines frequently had to fulfill their "moral obligation" via *shibalo*. Returning miners, or *magaiça* as they were called, returned with money in their pockets, but *shibalo* were often lucky to return with a tax receipt stamped paid.

Shibalo and mine contracts were important markers in the lives of all Mozambicans in Sul do Save. The relationship between them contributed to specific patterns of migration and employment in Lourenço Marques. Some men came to Lourenço Marques to earn a *lobolo* because they were unfit for the mines. Some earned *lobolo* at the mines, but then settled for work in Lourenço Marques because they were too "tired" to sustain the physical rigor of mine labor or the chronic flight from *shibalo* between mine contracts. About half the informants for this study settled in Lourenço Marques to escape the chronic threat of *shibalo*. Some came to Lourenço Marques as boys because they were too young to work a mine contract. Others came seeking an education which might qualify them for a position that would protect them from *shibalo*, and perhaps even enable them to accumulate capital without resort to a mine contract. Some women came to the city because the men who had formerly provided them with access to land, physical protection, and claims on cash income had failed to return from a *shibalo* or mine contract—leaving them to fend for themselves and their children in desperate circumstances. In periods of peak labor demand, conscription for roadwork, portage, and plantation labor was extended to women. At such times both men and women fled to the city to escape *shibalo*.

Within Lourenço Marques, older people and those with health handicaps might slide cautiously into minimum-wage, poor-condition employment, seemingly grateful for the wage and temporary security. Healthy, bright young men with some education might daringly risk working their way along the margins and through the loopholes of the tightly coercive system to their best advantage. Women of all ages negotiated much narrower spaces. Sometimes they benefited from gender biases that tolerated their activity as inconsequential, and sometimes they were heavily encumbered by layers of discrimination as poor, black females.

Although African workers in and around the city confronted many common barriers because of their race, divisions within the African community could be as significant at certain junctures as divisions separating Africans and Europeans. The *indigenato* applied to all "people of the Negro race or descendants therefrom," but divided them into two categories.[32] The vast majority were considered "natives," but in the second decade of the century an honorary "non-native" status was articulated to incorporate wealthy educated Africans under *indigenato* controls. To be considered "non-native," Africans had to go through the bother, expense, and humiliation of applying for a certificate of assimilation (*álvara de assimilação*). If the certificate was granted, she or he would become an *assimilado/a*. Everyone realized that the crucial distinction was not between "native" and "non-native," but between white and non-white. *Assimilados* were sometimes taunted as "pocket whites"—brown people who carried a document in their pocket that claimed they were white people.[33]

Finally, ethnicity emerged as a relational base from which individuals negotiated identities, interests, and advantage in the competition for claims on valued resources. The knowledge and deployment of language, protocol, and symbols figured in any individual's ability to negotiate claims on resources.[34] In the urban context market intelligence, capital, shelter, and, most of all, good jobs were valued resources. Claims of "belonging" to the specific group or "relationship" to the specific individual who controlled such resources were often the key to access. Sometimes shared language, protocol, and symbols emerged from childhood experience in rural Sul do Save—that kind of sharing is familiarly associated with ethnicity. But shared language, protocol, and symbols also developed around workplace experience among urban groups from diverse rural backgrounds. Membership in sports groups, social and church associations, or mutual aid and savings groups at the workplace could also foster claims of "belonging," and provide avenues of information, assistance, and dependency.

The historical process through which Mozambicans came to Lourenço Marques, managed to find and keep employment, and promote and protect their developing interests is explored here through a series of case studies in the three dominant areas of urban employment, two public and one private: the port and railway complex, the municipality, and domestic service.[35] Throughout the century the port and rail complex was the largest single employer in the city. By mid-century the port and railway complex employed about the same number of Africans as the domestic service sector. The municipality was the largest employer outside the port zone. These three groups encompassed a great range of skills, mobility patterns, and income levels. The necessarily intimate interaction of employer and employee in domestic service promoted systems of labor control and work relationships which, with some specific exceptions, were qualitatively different from those prevailing in the public sector. The development of the larger system designed to engineer labor control on the basis of race, the emergence of specific groups with distinct interests within the labor force, and finally patterns of workers' strategies to make their way in, around, and through the larger system are explored through the case studies.

Voices and Historians

The question of resistance among colonial peoples has inspired a large and impressive literature. In the past decade, the focus in resistance literature has shifted from revolts and revolution to what James C. Scott has aptly christened *Weapons of the Weak: Everyday Forms of Resistance.*[36] Mozambicans working in Lourenço Marques periodically did revolt, and such incidents were important markers. With every lost battle, however, open confrontation not only lost its efficacy, it became counterproductive. The cost for "any little thing" ranged from *shibalo* to a beating to deportation. This study support's Scott's position that, although "the weapons of the weak" seem subdued in relation to the level of exploitation suffered, they were viewed by the participants as appropriate to the situation at hand. The participants' judgments of what was and was not appropriate and their construction of the context have been privileged here.

Once the *indigenato*'s central mechanisms were in place, ordinary Mozambican men and women found it much more costly to escape government impositions. In that situation, they judged that the most appropriate strategy was protecting oneself—one's body, spirit, family, and good nature—from excessive abuse. The materialist bent of labor history has sometimes undervalued people's attention to their social and spiritual needs as well as their stomachs. Insultingly low wages were an important grievance, but insulting attitudes and treatment could be equally important. Humor and satire figured strongly in day-to-day survival strategies because they fed people's spirits in the face of demeaning treatment. Risks taken to see one's family and share a meal with colleagues spoke to such social and spiritual needs. It was a challenge for many to feed their stomachs, but if people lost their spirit, their bodies would easily follow.

A survey of African social and labor history literature reveals a broad range of emphasis. Some scholars emphasize the power of states or companies to hold their African labor force to the straight and narrow, while others stress the ability of African workers to identify and manipulate niches amid state- and company-dominated structures in which they managed to sustain power and independence, and a good deal of work fits in between. Scholarship has also ranged from concern with relations among labor unions, leadership, companies, and government to concern with relations among workers and between workers and their families and neighbors. The general trend has been away from a focus on employer power and labor union politics toward worker experience in the workplace and their relations with fellow workers and neighbors.[37] The trend away from structures and leaders toward relationships and groups has also fostered the "engendering" of labor history, by introducing women as friends, family members, neighbors, and businesspeople in relation to the predominantly male wage labor force and by expanding appreciation of what comprises commoditized work. 38

Africanist labor historians have been inspired to test insights from comparative historical and social science literature in the African context and have advanced arguments and contributed original insights in the process.[39] Some of this literature is particularly important here. Patrick Harries, inspired by questions raised in the French anthropology debates, has firmly located analysis of the origins of labor migration from southern Mozambique to South Africa in the culture, economy, and politics of the societies from which they were drawn or sent. His important essays urge us away from the perspective that accords disproportionate agency to the groups that commoditize labor relations, and thereby facilitate our understanding of a process of transformation that grew out of complex relationships in areas giving up the labor as well as in the receiving areas.[40] Charles van Onselen's work *Chibaro* marked the shift in the labor literature to closer attention to worker strategies and options within the mine migrant and compound arena, and his subsequent *Studies in the Social and Economic History of the Witwatersrand* worked the same magic for urban areas.[41] Part of the great value of the latter is its firm location of African labor and entrepreneurial strategies in dialectic with those of other urban groups.

The History Workshop at University of the Witwatersrand has underscored the importance of careful and active oral collection in combination with archival materials, and has pioneered the use of individual testimony to enrich and deepen our understanding of general trends.[42] In an equally important if contrasting way, Frederick Cooper's study of Mombasa's dockworkers has underscored the need to focus on the organization of work and the employer's sense of Africans as actors as revealed in archival evidence.[43] Luise White, Sharon Stichter, Iris Berger, and others have facilitated the incorporation of work done by women into the analysis of urban labor history by following the process of commoditization, sustaining the link between commoditized and non-commoditized labor; and refusing to be bound by narrow definitions of work or wage.[44] Leroy Vail and Landeg White have pursued a quest for the least accessible African voices. Their exploration of song, performance, and praise poems has revealed a complex range of previously underappreciated voices in southern African history.[45] Incorporating such voices in historical analysis presents its own challenge. To what extent are worksongs, laments, or praise poems specifically local or individual? Historians have asked similar questions of interview testimony. To what extent can individual testimony, personal or group "protected" or unprotected speech be taken as collective or corporative?[46] Finally, the Personal Narratives Group at Indiana University has focused attention on key methodological problems in the use of individual oral testimony, whether in interview, song, performance, storytelling, or any other mode, and on the relationship between historian and informant. They challenge us to examine the practice of history as critically as the production of historical literature.[47] The shift in emphasis from state and company action to the actions and intentions of African workers, farmers, traders, artisans, brewers, and thieves confirms Africans as historical actors, enriches the record of contending actors, and allows analysis and meaning to reach beyond the fairly narrow categories of resistance, consciousness, and expression predicted for a generic international working class. This study has attempted to assess the relationships between structures, individuals, and groups, confirming the power and relevance of structures without diminishing individual and group agency. The study contrasts the perspectives of ordinary unskilled laborers with those of the elite leadership, seeking to draw out points of coincidence and divergence. It highlights patterns in Mozambican strategies to make a life and livelihood in Lourenço Marques, and draws out differences correlated with age, education, luck, and, to a lesser extent, gender. The study opens with songs that highlight and question the basic inhumanity of colonial labor relations and closes with the confirmation that Mozambicans across the class structure perceived the exploitative base of the system as one group being privileged to "drink the blood" of the other.

The labor history of Lourenço Marques developed from struggles between and within colonially defined racial categories. This work is principally concerned with struggles between Europeans and Africans and among different groups of Africans. It privileges African imagery of that process and the meaning they assigned to it. But since it is an historian who selects and manipulates the voices, that historian must explain something of the process at the outset.

African workers were no more free to shape the circumstances of their economic and social world than were the Portuguese bureaucrats, South African shipping and forwarding agents, or Indian and Chinese merchants who competed for their services and wages. They were, nonetheless, independent historical actors. Like the others, they had an essential voice in their own destiny. To date we have a fairly well developed understanding of the agency, strengths, limitations, and interests among various groups of European actors in twentieth-century Lourenço Marques.[48] The role of the diverse Asian community has barely been addressed as yet, and this study contributes little to that important task. To date the contributions and voices of Lourenço Marques's African population remain muted. The task here is to develop them as fully as possible.

Some African voices were much more accessible than others. The voices of African men who wrote and spoke the colonizer's language and published their images and messages in formats that eventually ended up in libraries and archives were the most accessible. From as early as 1908, Lourenço Marques had an African-owned and -edited newspaper, which appeared more or less regularly through to the 1970s. It published the usual news, editorials, and letters to the editor, as well as occasional series of stories, interviews, and investigative reports. The newspapers, O Africano (1908–1920) and O Brado Africano (1918–1974), were published under the auspices of the Grêmio Africano. The Grêmio, which changed its name in the late 1930s to the Associação Africana da Colónia de Moçambique (AACM), was comprised of some of the city's best-educated and most prosperous Africans and mulattos.[49] Although the Grêmio membership was hardly representative of the urban population as a whole, many of the editors and writers were gifted observers and compassionate allies of the urban labor force. The newspapers are an invaluable source for the social history of the complex urban African community.[50] European voices emerged, in large part, from the city's many newspapers.[51]

The voices of ordinary Africans were less accessible. A portrait of the men building the port and railway complex and moving goods along their way in Lourenço Marques was captured in turn-of-the-century photography. Those photographs revealed the men's straining bodies, clothed in used fodder sacks, and their faces variously displayed fatigue, anger, humor, and even a hint of mischief, but they carried no names and no words. The voices of ordinary workers were sought for this project through an extensive interview program conducted among elderly urban workers in Maputo in 1977 and among Mozambicans resident in Portugal and the United States between 1978 and 1989.[52] The vast majority of Africans who worked for wages prior to the early 1960s were men, and the informant sample reflects that bias. Although informants were asked about families and urban networks, and many discussed the importance of women in their mobility and settlement patterns, this is a study of male experience and a collage of male voices. Research conducted in 1992-1993 focused on the history of women workers, and those women will be the focus of another book.

Most of the interviews were conducted among two groups of workers, one at the port and railway complex, the other at City Hall. These informants, all of whom were men, ranged in age from 30 to 103. Port interviews were conducted exclusively by the author, but the City Hall interviews were organized in cooperation with an assistant, Gaspar Salamão Guevende. Mr. Guevende, who was one of the many *grupo dinimizadores* (political advocates) among the municipal work force in 1977, collaborated in approximately one-third of the municipal interviews. His youth, geniality, and obvious respect for the workers, most of whom were twice or three times his age, strongly outweighed any influence his political role might have had on the nature of testimony. The majority of interviews were conducted in Portuguese, but moved into Tsonga, Chopi and Bitonga when convenient or necessary.[53]

Informants were questioned about why they came to work in the city and how they marketed their labor upon arrival. Each informant recounted his entire employment history, whether in Lourenço Marques or not. Informants also responded to standard questions that collected comparable data on education, mother tongue, migration history, personal and family-controlled resources, material possessions, and families. When these questions were completed, each informant was encouraged to raise any issues or stories we had overlooked, to elaborate on any issue or contribute a song or any testimony that might be valuable to the project.

The port and railway informants included well-educated men in top positions as tally clerks, office workers, supervisors, and also unskilled hod carriers who could not write or read any language. Some informants had worked *shibalo* gang labor, some had supervised it, and some had been displaced by it. The port and rail complex was not only the largest single employer in the city and in Sul do Save, it also boasted some of the best and worst jobs.

The municipal group was much larger, including workers from five divisions: the slaughterhouse, construction depot, municipal gardens, central market, and a contingent of skilled artisans and professionals who floated among the various divisions. The fifty-nine workers in this contingent provided an exceptional diversity of generational, educational, regional, and personal experience. The slaughterhouse workers provided a window into the life, personal networks, and work relations among men who had little formal education and skill, but who occupied a stable and comparatively comfortable niche. The garden, market, and construction workers, in contrast, had almost no formal education, worked unskilled manual jobs, seemed much less well off, and had much more experience with *shibalo* in both rural and urban situations. Finally, the skilled artisans and professionals were predominantly local men, part of a very small group of informants who did not personally know people who had worked *shibalo*. They and the small group of highly skilled workers at the port were also the most likely to have been members, or personally known members, of the Grêmio Africano or the Instituto Negrófilo (later named the Centro Associativo dos Négros de Moçambique, or CANM), a comparable elite urban group formed in the early 1930s.

No interview program was undertaken among people working as domestic servants in the independence era, but the majority of port and municipal informants had spent some of their urban employment in domestic service. It was clearly an important occupation in any quantitative or qualitative assessment of the urban labor force. Archival and newspaper sources contained material on domestics, and informant testimony offered an interesting foil to the written perspective. Analysis of urban registration records discussed below also provided an excellent overview of wages and mobility for different categories of domestic employees for the last decade of the study.

Informants thus provided a rich and varied overview of life and work in Lourenço Marques and the larger region. They helped delineate material differences within the urban labor force and helped relate such differences to employment and viewpoint. Although a great range of viewpoints emerged, ordinary workers usually conveyed a striking counterpoint to official colonial sources, and also often tempered the views of the African elite as expressed in *O Africano* and *O Brado Africano.*

Historians who engage in oral collection are midwives in the creation of documentation. Extended testimony, songs, and stories were taped. Tapes, transcripts, and notes were reproduced and deposited at the Arquivo Histórico de Moçambique and at Harvard University. Stories, songs, and performance are particularly challenging texts with value well beyond the straightforward information they convey. They have been used here in the most limited sense and beg further exploitation.

The municipal archive (Administração do Concelho de Lourenço Marques, ACLM) and the Native Affairs Archive (Secretaria de Negócios Indígenas, SNI) contained formal, paternalistic policy statements but also confidential circulars that "reinterpreted" formal policy into practice to meet the demands of the Portuguese colonial population. These records clearly revealed the duplicity of the colonial state. Pinto de Fonseca was merely one of a long line of high-level administrators whose published and confidential texts corroborated the most serious international critiques of Portuguese colonialism. These administrators provided some of the most damning evidence of racist, patronizing, and crushingly bureaucratic rule.[54]

The final source base is the urban employment registration archive, which covered the entire urban African labor force for the period 1950 to 1962. The municipal labor office was an albatross around the neck of every African who wished to work and live in Lourenço Marques, but it is a treasure chest for historians seeking to recapture their struggle. By 1950, all Africans who worked for wages in Lourenço Marques, regardless of age or sex, had to register at the municipal office. Self-employed males between fourteen and sixty also had to register. Most workers had to renew their contracts annually and all had to change them if they changed jobs. Each worker's employment history was contained on an individual record card with his or her photo. Each card listed the worker's name, date (if known) and place of birth, employer's name, job category, and wage for each job held for every year the worker remained in the city. Home visits, out-migration, arrests, shibalo contracts, labor discipline, and any other "irregularities" were also recorded on the back of the card. A 5 percent systematic sample of those records was taken, programmed, and analyzed.[55] The sample permitted linkage of variables such as sex and birthplace with job category. It allowed one to chart mobility patterns, out-migration, and wage increments and ranges for different jobs across the entire labor force and over a twelve-year period.

Data generated by the sample also provided a quantitative context for more qualitative informant testimony. It enabled the historian to evaluate just how representative an individual informant's experience was. For example, many informants emphasized that shibalo was a pervasive and costly sanction that could be quite arbitrarily applied to discipline any African worker. The sample corroborated that claim. It also confirmed that, although unskilled migrants and casual laborers were the most often seized for shibalo, local men in the best-paid jobs were also sentenced to shibalo quite arbitrarily for offenses such as "breach of trust." Although this systematic overview of wages, conditions, out-migration, and mobility covered only the last twelve years of the study, it so strongly corroborated oral testimony for that period that it enhanced the weight assigned to the overall body of oral data.

These are rich and suggestive sources, although some are clearly much stronger for some periods and topics than for others. The oral sources are almost exclusively male and are richest for the 1930s through the 1960s. The African press is also androcentric, elitist, and most revealing between 1910 and 1926. The utility of administrative published and archival sources varied greatly depending upon the administrator. The quantitative sample contributes an even-handed portrait of immigration, mobility, and employment patterns for women, which helped compensate for the informants' male bias, but only for just over a decade. What follows is an effort to draw together these uneven sources to explore African labor experience in the context of a labor-coercive colonial system and a labor-competitive regional economy.

Chapter 1 explains the chronological framework for the study and introduces key elements of the broader context within which Mozambicans developed their life strategies. Chapter 2 considers the creation of a white man's town in Lourenço Marques and its implications for future social and labor relations. Chapter 3 explores labor relations in the developing city on the threshold of the implementation of the *indigenato*, and experiments with early voices and images. Chapter 4 explains the articulation and imposition of the various components of the *indigenato*, and Chapter 5 is a case study of that process in the strategic port and railway complex. Chapters 6 and 7 consider continuity and change in labor policy and practice during the New State era. Finally, Chapters 8 through 10 develop case studies in the port complex, the municipality, and domestic service to explore individual and group strategies in the context of changing economic and political conditions. The brief Conclusion seeks to generalize about images and individuals and to assess the overall relationship between coercive colonial labor policies and the history of the African working class in Lourenço Marques.

1

Context and Chronology: The Metropole, the Hinterland, and the Region

Chronology—The Metropole

Portuguese labor policy and practice in Lourenço Marques define the chronological framework for this study, but both were shaped by developments in the regional economy centered upon the mining industry of the neighboring Transvaal and by social institutions and natural resources in the Sul do Save hinterland. This chapter explains the chronology and introduces essential elements of the regional and hinterland context. Those elements are more fully explored where appropriate in subsequent chapters.

The study opens with the large-scale and sustained recruitment of *shibalo* labor for the city and closes at the point when *shibalo* labor had diminished economic attraction and counterproductive political implications. In 1877, Portuguese public works employees arrived in Lourenço Marques to undertake a series of municipal infrastructure projects. Those projects triggered the first sustained demand for unskilled local labor, and led to the first widespread requisitions of *shibalo* labor for the town. Portugal decided to invest in the infrastructure of Lourenço Marques because the alluvial gold strikes to the west in Lydenburg in the 1870s enhanced the city's potential as a port of access . By the 1870s Mozambicans were already an important component of the labor force in the neighboring areas from Cape Town and Kimberley to Natal and the Transvaal. With the major gold strike at Witwatersrand in the 1880s, the importance of both the port and the region's labor resources increased dramatically. Portugal could neither develop the port nor broker access to migrant labor unless she could control Mozambique's labor resources.

Although Portugal could requisition labor and claim the allegiance of African leadership in various pockets of Sul do Save, the watershed in her quest to control the hinterland's labor resources was her defeat of the major African polity in Sul do Save, the Gaza state. The Luso-Gaza wars that culminated in 1897 marked the beginning of the implantation of the colonial state in southern Mozambique.[1] Roberto Mashaba, an important Mozambican clergyman who was deported during those wars, captured the meaning of that defeat for many Mozambicans. He observed that the Gaza military leaders should put away the spears, guns, and shields: "these things were unnecessary now that times had changed. The leader's duty now was to send men to work when the [Portuguese] government needed them."[2] Gaza military leaders would no longer control the region's labor resources, the Portuguese would.

On the one hand, the Portuguese needed sufficient labor to construct the port and railway facilities that would enable her to handle and tax the import and export trade with the Transvaal—the so-called transit trade. On the other hand, they were eager to harness recruitment revenues from the already well-developed migration flows. By the turn of the century Portugal was able to claim control over the region's labor force in her negotiations with the newly formed representative of the Witwatersrand mining industry, the Chamber of Mines. The Chamber eventually agreed to ship almost half the region's transit trade through the port at Lourenço Marques in exchange for Portugal's agreement to allow the recruitment of a fixed maximum of Mozambican contract workers by the Chamber's recruiting arm—the Witwatersrand Native Labour Association, known as Wenela.[3]

From 1877 until the overthrow of the Portuguese monarchy in 1910, the city grew in response to Portugal's open trade policies and the development of the Transvaal mining industry. Mozambique's foreign trade increased 300 percent between 1877 and 1892, driven largely by trade through the port at Lourenço Marques.[4] Although the British controlled the lion's share of the port's import/export trade, Portugal's revenues from customs duties and handling fees were sufficient to convince her to exempt the port from the higher duties imposed throughout her overseas empire in 1892. Customs revenues in Lourenço Marques climbed from 47,000 *milreis* in 1888 to 600,000 *milreis* in 1895, the year the rail line to South Africa opened.[5] Trade at Lourenço Marques was then up and down due to the South African War and the economic cycles of the gold industry.

Up to 1910, Portuguese and South African interests competed intensely in Lourenço Marques, but South African interests clearly dominated key sectors—utilities, shipping and handling, insurance, and banking.[6] With the declaration of the First Republic (1910-1926), Portuguese local entrepreneurs moved aggressively against foreign interests. The state quickly displaced foreign investment in utilities, rail yard handling, and banking during the first few years of the Republican era.[7] With the extension of state control over the economy came the expanded use of *shibalo* gangs, thus enhancing *shibalo*'s insidious drag on wages and conditions for the volunteer labor force as well.

Successive changes of Republican governments in Portugal, the disastrous policies of the colony's bank of issue, Banco Nacional Ultramarino, and Portugal's involvement in World War I led to chaos and paralysis in Lourenço Marques. The ineffectiveness of Lisbon's colonial leadership in the Republican era permitted the emergence of more powerful local interests. Wartime inflation and currency instability contributed to a steady fall in real wages from 1914 to the early 1930s. The sharpest decline in real wages coincided with the period from the end of World War I to the mid-1920s. An increase in transit traffic and a short-lived boom in sugar prices

spiked labor demand in the area. When volunteer labor did not respond to the flag-
ging wage rates, the state responded by permitting employers to overwork their
employees and by greatly expanding conscription. Heightened levels of exploitation
generated extensive labor resistance, including strikes, work stoppages, labor exodus
to South Africa, and thousands of local escapes. The strikes were put down with
increasing force, culminating with the defeat of the 1925–1926 strike by the powerful
Portuguese railway workers union.[8]

A military coup in 1926 ended the First Republic and set the so-called New State
(1926–1974) into motion. The New State's impact on life in Lourenço Marques does
not follow the same chronology as its articulation in Portugal. It developed its agenda
and structures in stages between 1926 and 1933. With the promulgation and ratification of the *Acto Colonial* and the *Carta Orgánica do Império Colonial Português* in 1933,
the structures were essentially in place in the overseas colonies.[9]

This study divides the New State period into two stages, subdivided into three
phases. The first phase dates from the coup in 1926 to the watershed of 1933. The
second phase, 1933 to 1946, develops with fiscal reform, coordination of the colonial
and metropolitan economies, and the tentative economic recovery that was stalled by
World War II. The third phase, 1946 to 1962, covers postwar economic growth and
renewed Portuguese investment to the end of the *indigenato*. The labor case studies
take 1933, the end of the first phase, as their dividing marker because the early 1930s
emerged in both interviews and the African press as a key turning point. The early
1930s marked the formal ratification of New State policy and legal structures in
Mozambique, but moreover 1933 was the turn-around year for the depressed economy, the breaking point for the first generation of the urban elite leadership, and the
nadir of African labor's power during the twentieth century. In a series of confrontations, culminating with the so-called *quinhenta* strike of 1933, African casual workers
lost virtually all the gains they had made through labor action over the past
generation.[10] The once-confident and articulate mature leadership was either silent or
obsequiously thankful for the crumbs tossed in their direction. Mozambicans who
lived through the hard times of the early 1930s were transformed by the experience.[11]

The first phase of New State policy reflected the economic situation from 1926 to
1946. Portugal met the economic crisis with tight fiscal policies and strong protectionist legislation. In Lourenço Marques, unemployed Portuguese workers won quota
legislation designed to force most of the remaining non-European workers out of
upper- and mid-level positions in state and municipal employment.[12] Portugal sustained the fiscal and protectionist policies despite the slowly improving economy
until the post–World War II era. By 1946, however, both labor demand and resistance had rebounded with the regional economy. The New State's economic policies
and her neutrality in World War II allowed Portuguese business groups to emerge
from the war quite strong. By 1946 businesses had successfully lobbied the state to
begin loosening constraints on growth in the colonies.

The regime's response to such pressure defines the second stage of New State
policy and practice, from 1946 to 1962.[13] White immigration increased sharply, fiscal
constraints were somewhat relaxed, and Portugal undertook a series of development
plans. The first projects in the early 1950s targeted expansion of Mozambique's transportation, communication, and energy infrastructure. Although state development
projects employed *shibalo* labor, the expanded infrastructure they created encouraged
private investment, and that eventually increased demand for volunteer labor.[14]

By the late 1950s contradictions began to emerge in the less-constrained system. Portuguese businesses that had prospered from the features of the earlier era (the monopolies, protectionism, and *shibalo* supplies), diversified into manufacturing and industry. When they began to seek the more skilled, settled labor force necessary for such endeavors, they were frustrated by the heritage of other features of the earlier era (such as rudimentary educational facilities, poor housing, and nonexistent services in African urban neighborhoods). Portugal's second development package included a social investment component, but, much to the dismay of the urban African community, the fruits of that investment were largely absorbed by the burgeoning white population. The developing labor surplus in Lourenço Marques, combined with Portugal's decision to pursue closer links with western Europe and international organizations, hastened the pace of labor reform. The formal structure of the *indigenato* was abolished in the early 1960s to bring Portugal into compliance with international standards for labor relations.

Those reforms, however incomplete and inadequate they may have been (particularly in rural areas), removed many impediments to African labor mobility in Lourenço Marques. The *indigenato* had tied most workers to contracts and provided dozens of opportunities for arrest, *shibalo*, and fines. With the reform legislation of this era, Africans were not subject to penal sanctions for breach of contract. Abolition of the *indigenato* greatly enlarged the economic space available to urban Africans. Deeply embedded social constraints, such as sanctions on Africans who competed directly or aggressively with Europeans, continued to weigh heavily on many sections of the labor force. On the whole, however, it became much easier for urban Africans to change jobs, work several part-time jobs, bid up their wages among competing employers, and engage in independent trade, service, and commodity production.

That largely positive set of changes in the day-to-day experience of African workers in Lourenço Marques, however, paled in comparison with the profoundly negative implications of a second set of changes that occurred at the same point. The Portuguese could not block the continental assertion of African political rights at their borders. The political uprisings in Angola in early 1961 and the formation of the Front for the Liberation of Mozambique (Frelimo) in Tanganyika in 1962 brought the already growing political and racial tension to a peak. The resultant political crisis transformed urban labor relations throughout the colony.

The crisis provoked a two-pronged response by the Portuguese state.[15] One prong was a counterinsurgency program of the "hearts and minds" variety. The abolition of the *indigenato* was clearly a component of that prong. In her anxiety to foster the rapid development of an African middle class with vested economic interests in the colonial system, Portugal also strongly encouraged African advancement throughout the civil service. Africans who were in the position to take advantage of that policy could ride the political tide to rapid promotion. The other prong was of the "mailed fist" variety. It was always dangerous for Africans to challenge European authority, but the growing tension sharply increased the likelihood that any confrontation would have serious, even deadly consequences.

The legislative reforms and political insurgence of the early 1960s placed Africans living and working in Lourenço Marques in a qualitatively different situation. The closing years of colonialism with their heightened mix of economic opportunity and political repression require a separate study. Malyn Newitt correctly argued that events of the early 1960s were both less and more than previously argued.[16] This study takes 1962 as its closing date, but recognizes that key changes were brewing as early as the 1950s and that many practices endured into the 1970s.[17] In the most general terms, the study opens with Portugal's first sustained recruitment of *shibalo* for Lourenço Marques, and closes with the formal and practical acknowledgment that *shibalo* had outlived its utility in that city.

The Hinterland Textures

Weather, Women, and Wealth

The goals, strategies, and necessities of Lourenço Marques workers reflected the social institutions, economy, and resources of the communities from which they came. The varied and fragile environment of Sul do Save, the institution of *lobolo* (bridewealth), the competence of women in agricultural food production, and the early and forceful penetration of merchant capital along trade and migration routes all contributed to the pace, patterns, and sustainability of the male movement into wage labor. This section introduces basic concepts regarding the population of Sul do Save and particularly the importance of male access to and control over women in relation to patterns of migration and wage labor.[18]

Elizabeth Colson's classic essay on African communities at the threshold of conquest emphasized the fluidity, adaptation, and limitations of African social units and cautioned against cataloguing them into distinct, static, ahistorical groups with linguistic labels.[19] Indeed, descriptions of Sul do Save societies during the first half of the twentieth century complement Colson's insights. Observers remarked that Sul do Save incorporated "a crossroad[s] of peoples" comprising a most interesting "ethnographic puzzle."[20] Words like "complexity" and "fluid" punctuate most descriptions.[21]

Leroy Vail and Patrick Harries similarly emphasize language adaptation and symbol manipulation as situational and as part of a larger process of negotiating and mediating changes in social identities.[22] All of these scholars identify people by language, yet all emphasize that such identities are dynamic, historically developed, and partial. Within these firm cautions, Sul do Save was home to two broadly defined groups and several subgroups. Tsonga speakers and Chopi speakers comprised the two broadly distinct groups.[23] Tsonga speakers inhabited the Lourenço Marques hinterland and most of Sul do Save. They commonly differentiated themselves into Ronga-speaking clans of the immediate Lourenço Marques area, Tswa speakers of the northern Inhambane district, and Shangaan speakers of Gaza District. Shangaan speakers include Tsonga speakers, who were most influenced by the penetration and conquest of Nguni-speaking people in the nineteenth century and became the nucleus of the so-called Gaza state.[24] Chopi speakers, a much smaller group, cluster to the south and southwest of Inhambane along the coast to the Limpopo River valley. Bitonga speakers are classified in the same linguistic group as Chopi, but they live along the coast north of Inhambane and have closer cultural links with northern coastal people than with Chopi speakers to the south.[25]

The historically fickle rainfall, sandy soils, and diverse vegetation zones of Sul do Save strongly shaped migration patterns among these various groups.[26] Average annual rainfall in the area varies: the narrow coastal plain enjoys between 800 and

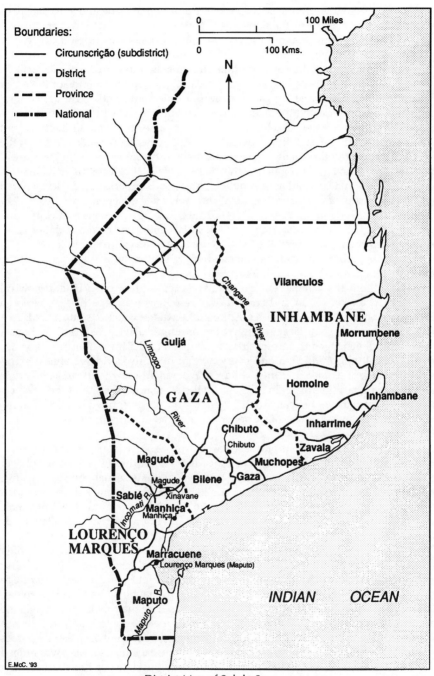

Boundaries:

——— Circunscrição (subdistrict)

- - - - - District

— — — Province

—·—·— National

0   100 Miles

0   100 Kms.

N

Vilanculos

INHAMBANE

Morrumbene

Changane River

Limpopo

Guijá

GAZA

Homoine

Inhambane

River

Chibuto

Chibuto

Inharrime

Zavala

Magude

Muchopes

Magude

Bilene

Gaza

Sabié

Xinavane

Manhiça

Manhiça

Incomati

LOURENÇO

MARQUES

Marracuene

Lourenço Marques (Maputo)

Maputo

Maputo R.

INDIAN   OCEAN

E.McC. '93

District Map of Sul do Save.

1,000 millimeters annually, but some pockets around Inhambane and Xai-Xai experience as much as 1400 to 1600 millimeters.[27] Most of Sul do Save, however, receives only 400 to 600 millimeters in normal years and is classified as tropical dry. A few pockets are tropical semi-arid.[28]

The riverine soils of the Limpopo, Maputo, Umbeluzi, and Incomati river valleys, and the scattered deposits of water-retentive "Nhaca" soil west and southwest of Inhambane and Inharrime are the only areas in the south with great agricultural potential. The promise of those river valleys is compromised by periodic flood losses. Some steppe areas provide excellent pasturage for game and domestic livestock, but complex tse-tse fly infestation tempers the region's pastoral potential. In short, the region's resource endowment is mixed and frequently subject to ecological stress. Societies of Sul do Save struggled within these ecological constraints to maintain a proper balance and circulation of producers and goods produced. People prepared for periodic stress by cultivating personal and family ties of dependency in a variety of ecozones.[29] The wealthier the household, the greater the possibility for cultivating debts that could be called in during a crisis. If social coping and accommodation strategies broke down, males with the least secure access to resources could migrate in search of wage labor. The women and children they left behind, however, were the most likely to perish.[30]

Throughout the colonial era, Sul do Save's typical unit of social and political mobilization for claims on and control over resources was a patrilineal, virilocal, extended household.[31] Senior males aspired to control polygamous households that might eventually become large enough to be considered a village. Sul do Save households typically engaged in agro-pastoral production under the authority of a senior male. Agricultural production and everything to do with food were almost exclusively the task of women and their children. Women also saw to the basic domestic and nurturing tasks. Partially in response to the ecological strength of their respective areas, Tsonga men typically contributed to food stores through hunting, fishing, and livestock management, while Chopi men engaged in agriculture as well as hunting and gathering.[32]

Elder males were responsible for social control, resource management, organization of agricultural production, and product distribution through their control over ritual, trade, military activity, and ideologically legitimate sexual and reproductive relations. As the spiritual link between the living and dead, senior males benefited from the wisdom and experience of those who passed before. The balance of female cultivators to arable land, of cattle to pasturage, and of productive and fallow lands to water supply was all the responsibility of elder males.[33]

Ideologically legitimate access to women's labor, sexual services, and fertility was articulated and adjudicated by senior males through exchange of *lobolo*. *Lobolo* accrued to the lineage that gave up a bride so that it might bring in another bride to maintain lineage strength. The accumulation and exchange of *lobolo* were ideologically essential for men and women to marry and assume the privileges of legitimate adult status in the lineage. It was also essential for the lineage to reproduce itself. A familiar saying in Sul do Save holds that "A woman who has not been 'loboloed' does not build the village."[34] A marriage confirmed by the exchange of *lobolo* was indeed the base for a future village, whereas without *lobolo* the status of a woman and her children within the lineage building the village could always be challenged. That is not to deny that many couples (particularly Christians) lived together, had children, and perhaps even built their own village without the requisite exchange of *lobolo*, but the dominant social protocol viewed marriage as socially legitimate only when confirmed by a completed *lobolo* payment. Acquisition of *lobolo* figured strongly into which men went into wage labor and when, and *lobolo* negotiations and challenges were a dominant feature of elder adjudications.[35]

Young men could accumulate a bridewealth in a number of ways. They could inherit sufficient wealth when they became the eldest in the primary lineage; they could be assigned the *lobolo* from a sister's marriage; they could appeal to the elders to allocate *lobolo* from group resources, or they could accumulate wealth independently as hunters, traders, craftsmen, and, eventually, as wage laborers. Since the authority and inheritance structure limited the ability of some men (younger brothers, men without sisters, sons of junior wives, and men from families with little influence) to accumulate *lobolo*, those were the most likely to seek the alternative of wage labor.[36]

Although *lobolo* reproduced the material base of male domination, it also served women who wished to mediate the tensions of that domination. Women negotiated their positions within their own lineage or their husband's lineage through their powers of fertility, spirituality, and healing. Those powers were enhanced or diminished by the conditions of a woman's marriage. Women married with *lobolo* were in a much stronger position to advocate and defend their individual interests than women married without *lobolo*. Women who were married with *lobolo* "belonged to the *lobolo*" that frequently served the bride's brother for his marriage. The brother who claimed his sister's bridewealth assumed a special relationship toward her and her offspring. He became the socially appropriate person to intercede on his sister's behalf in any controversy between her and her in-laws or her husband.[37]

In the late nineteenth century, the expanding demand for labor from the nascent mining industry coincided with the Gaza state's decision to relocate from the northern reaches of Sul do Save to the lower Limpopo river at Manjacaze. The Gaza leadership controlled trade and hunting in their areas and collected tribute from or raided neighboring people. Gaza leaders thus came to control wealth, and therefore a disproportionate number of brides.[38] The Chopi, who were frequently raided by the Gaza during this period, recalled their situation in songs recorded in the 1940s:

We fought but we were conquered
We were without women
Because the Vátuas [Gaza] carried them off
We were a village of bachelors.[39]

The concentration of wealth and brides in the era of peak Gaza prosperity led to the inflation of *lobolo*. Social differentiation in areas under Gaza state control and the accompanying *lobolo* inflation throughout the region further encouraged the movement of young men into wage labor.[40]

The social institutions and patterns of production in Sul do Save were capable of absorbing a great deal of stress due to the absence of young men, whether for hunting, trading, military encounters, herding, or wage labor. Food production and most household reproduction tasks were accomplished by women under the protection, management, and jurisdiction of elder males. Production and reproduction were not severely compromised in the short run by periodic absences of young males, especially if those absences suited the agricultural year. Sul do Save men played an important role in the construction of social dependency relations. They completed household and tool construction and repair, opened new lands, and cared for livestock.[41] Their extended absence jeopardized the well-being of both their immediate families and the larger community.

The Regional Textures—Wenela Without/*Shibalo* Within

The Developing Wenela Option

In those days, those who were fit walked to South Africa to the mines.
You would carry dry maize; eat a little and drink a lot of water so that you felt full.
It was hard. It was dangerous. We walked for the money.[42]

The mineral strikes of the late nineteenth century put into motion a wide range of regional changes. By the turn of the century, the development of the mining industry transformed social and economic relationships throughout much of the region south of the Zambezi River. Some communities were displaced by the mines; some sent their sons to dig the minerals; some planted to feed the burgeoning labor force; and some handled the trade that kept the mine areas supplied daily. Communities experienced the changes differently, but virtually everyone within the region experienced altered options, opportunities, and constraints. Some men set out independently to sell their labor, while others were seized or coerced to build the related road, rail, and capital infrastructure, but most people remained in rural villages and faced the challenge of adjusting to the increasingly familiar absence of young men.

Prior to the South African War (1899–1902), Mozambicans comprised 60 percent of the Transvaal mine labor force. At the turn of the century mines tried to force a substantial wage cut for African labor. When workers failed to respond to the diminished wage packet, the mines turned to the importation of Chinese labor. By 1906 Mozambican workers had returned to the mines in sufficient numbers to facilitate the end of the Chinese experiment. That year Mozambicans again comprised 60 percent of the mine labor force. From that point until 1920 they generally contributed about 40 percent. From 1920 until Mozambican independence in 1975, the percentage of Mozambicans at the mines varied a great deal, but averaged about 25 percent.[43] As early as the 1920s, however, many Sul do Save families already had two generations with mine labor experience.[44]

By the first decade of the twentieth century, thousands more Mozambicans worked in the mines than in Lourenço Marques.[45] Access to mine labor had complex implications for Mozambican labor history. In terms of "native policy," mine migration was always a major concern to the Portuguese colonial government. It was regularly blamed for every ill the colony and its population experienced. The handful of programs formulated by the Native Affairs Department during the twentieth century designed to do more than simply control labor movement and collect taxes among the African population were explicitly articulated as attempts to remedy the outflow of Mozambicans to labor in neighboring countries.[46] Most importantly the colonial government chronically legitimated its resort to *shibalo* conscription within Mozambique in terms of accommodating the labor drain to South Africa.

In terms of the regional movement into wage labor, the mining industry acted as a pump primer. Men who worked mine contracts returned with information, networks, and experience that facilitated the migration of subsequent waves of Mozambicans. They also brought back commodities and cash wages that greatly stimulated consumer demand, retail commerce, and the development of transportation networks. The extensive penetration of merchant capital in pursuit of mine wages promoted further commoditization and industry replacement. Again, Henri Junod's conversation manual clearly reflected contemporary merchants' concerns and agenda. The trade store dialogue is a classic:

Metal spoons are better than those which are carved.
If you are hungry, buy bread, biscuits, and sardines.
If you are thirsty, buy rum by the glass.[47]

Junod, true to his Presbyterian missionary convictions, was careful to have his Ronga character respond that he preferred millet beer (*uputsu*) to rum because it was better for his health. Such commercialization eventually encouraged reliance upon wage savings and purchased foods.[48] Social support networks remained fundamental to family survival strategies, however, and mine migrants frequently invested their earnings in parties that courted social indebtedness. Such debts could be called in during a crisis and make the difference between a family's starvation and survival.[49]

Southern Mozambique increasingly lived from the earnings of returned mineworkers (or *magaiça*), both directly and indirectly. Magaiça paid their own taxes and those of their families. Commerce was supported in large part by repatriated earnings. The state received a bonus per migrant contracted by Wenela, collected handling fees, licenses, and taxes on both commerce and migration. In short, even though *magaiça* worked outside Mozambique, the state, the merchants, and Mozambican families lived from the revenues their migration generated.

The Wenela system was well developed in Sul do Save by 1910. Mozambicans were recruited, examined, transported, distributed, paid, and repatriated through the extensive Wenela bureaucratic network. The Wenela system furnished the Chamber of Mines members with contract labor to do the jobs that would otherwise go begging. The Wenela and *shibalo* systems were similar in that both provided contracted, lower-wage workers for distribution to employers whose wages and conditions of labor were insufficient to attract sufficient volunteers. Whereas Wenela was very large scale, well funded, reliable, and relatively efficient by 1910, *shibalo* was still localized, inefficient, corrupt, and arbitrary.[50] At that time there were approximately 2,500 men from Sul do Save working *shibalo* contracts in Lourenço Marques out of a labor force of about 10,100. Approximately one-quarter of the urban labor force was conscripted.[51] Between 91,000 and 92,000 Mozambicans were working Wenela contracts in South Africa at that time.[52] In short, *shibalo* was clearly significant in relation to labor relations in Lourenço Marques, but it was dwarfed in the regional context by the various options of mine labor.

Mine labor in South Africa soon became a familiar and accessible option for Mozambicans. Mozambican men could generally count upon employment in South Africa to enable them to accumulate cash wages for the bridewealth necessary to enter adult status. Families could try to tap a relative's repatriated wages for tax money or famine stores in a crisis. The dialectic between Wenela and *shibalo* recruitment was varied and complex. Although the Portuguese argued that *shibalo* was a necessary counterweight to legal and clandestine migration to South Africa, many Mozambicans argued that the arbitrary abuse of the *shibalo* system drove them to work in South Africa as an escape.

Shibalo—Implanting the System

> People were seized in their homes at night. We were like dogs fleeing into the bush. The police seized many people. You worked, you went hungry and you were paid nothing.[53]

People walked to the mines, worked hard, and lived in dangerous situations. They did it for the money. People walked to *shibalo*, worked hard, and lived in dangerous situations. They were paid "nothing." Sometimes their payment was a *pancada de graça*, a free beating.[54] Indeed, nothing distinguished work within and outside Mozambique more than the issue of payment. Payment, again, was a concept beyond mere money. It involved value. Was payment in money or in kind? If it was in kind, was it appropriate for human beings or for animals—rotten peanuts and insect-infested flour for food and fodder sacking for clothing were inappropriate payments. Finally, what was the probability of being paid the full amount one earned when it was due?

In 1906 the governor of Inhambane District reported that "unfortunately" most Inhambane Africans chose to work in South Africa rather than Mozambique because Wenela's 750 uniformed recruiters were "well received" by Africans, whereas Portugal's 240 shabby police enjoyed little prestige because they harassed people for taxes and seized them for unpaid labor on plantations, road clearing, and bridge building. He concluded, "The English give and the Portuguese take. . . . Whether underground in the mines or under the hot December sun with a hoe in Inhambane, what matters to Africans is that the English pay 3£ (a month) and the Portuguese 3$000 [less than 14 shillings]."[55] He was right, but it also mattered that Wenela contracts were paid on time, in full, and in a currency that had value. Mozambicans working for the Portuguese could not be sure they would ever see any of their payment. Non-payment, unjustified discounts, skimmed benefits, and scams to avoid payment were chronic complaints against Portuguese employers from oral, newspaper, and internal government sources throughout the colonial era.

The *shibalo* system grew out of earlier practices of simply commandeering labor. In the late nineteenth century, Africans in areas under Portuguese control were commandeered for military assistance and portage.[56] As the demand for labor became more sustained, commandeering was found inadequate. The shift from commandeering to a system of requisitioning, transporting, employing, servicing, paying, and repatriating labor developed piecemeal, but again conquest was the watershed. Junod's conversation manual echoed Roberto Mashaba's advice to the Gaza leadership at conquest: "The chief has given notice that there will be a work to be done for the government."[57]

Shibalo was first systematized in areas firmly under Portuguese control, like Inhambane, and subsequently spread to hinterland areas like Chibuto and Bilene.[58] Even during peak periods of demand for *shibalo* labor, such as the early 1920s and late 1940s, however, the *shibalo* net was always cast unevenly. The ideal combination for the government was cooperative African leadership with access to large groups of exploitable workers. In the early twentieth century, for example, Tsonga leaders in Inhambane cooperated with the government demands for *shibalo* by requisitioning Chopi groups, whom they considered more expendable than their relatives and supporters.[59]

The chain of command was from the Native Affairs Department, or SNI,[60] which received requisitions for labor from state, municipal, and private employers. The SNI then notified circumscription administrators of the numbers and conditions for recruitment. The circumscription administrators could either send out their own police force to the local designated authorities (or *régulos*) whose duty it was to supply labor, or they could send that information through the lowest-level administrator, the *chefe de posto*. The *régulos* in turn used either their own retainers or the administrative police force to round up conscripts. The rural *rusgas*, as these round-ups were called, were invariably described as above—night assaults from which families fled into the bush.

Although the *régulo's* continued recognition depended upon his cooperation in *shibalo* recruitment, there was room to maneuver. Not all *régulos* were willing collaborators in the exploitation of Mozambican labor, and most who were enjoyed little respect locally.[61] Some *régulos* indeed sent anyone who was not a relative off to *shibalo* and took no responsibility for the abuse of their undisciplined retainers.[62] Others, however, were broadly credited with sheltering their people from the worst abuses of *shibalo*. Augusto Nhaposse of Inhambane explained that in his area the Portuguese were too well established for people simply to withdraw until *shibalo* harassment passed. One régulo in his area always urged people to pay their taxes, or if they did not have the money to bribe the administrative police to let them go. That usually cost less than paying one's taxes. It did not yield a receipt, which would help protect against conscription for tax default, but it bought people some time to seek a mine contract or another job. If people simply had no money, "The *régulo* would warn you. Hide when the police come. Sleep in the top of a coconut tree with your knife. Sleep in the bush or walk with a gun."[63]

The lure of consumer goods, the dynamic of bridewealth acquisition, the sturdy socioeconomic structures, the fragile environment, social differentiation, and conquest followed by enhanced *shibalo* requisitions all contributed to the instigation and accommodation of migrant labor flows from Sul do Save. Mozambican men were likely to travel several of those flows during their lifetime. People were aware of the opportunities and constraints in the regional mining economy, the Sul do Save hinterland, and Lourenço Marques. Workers and work in Lourenço Marques were strongly influenced by relations and conditions in the larger context. Between 1877 and 1910 Lourenço Marques also changed dramatically. The rapid physical transformation of Lourenço Marques from a small town to the capital city, boasting one of the region's most modern ports, was accompanied by a social transformation in labor relations and conditions for Africans. The physical and social transformation of Lourenço Marques and its implications for African labor are the topics of Chapters 2 and 3.

2

Creating a White Man's Town Xilunguine, Lourenço Marques, Delagoa Bay

When wage labor first became significant in the 1870s, the town was known to some people as Xilunguine, the white man's place. It was also the land of the Mpfumo, Maxaquene, Polana, and other Ronga-speaking people of the bay area. English speakers called the settlement Delagoa Bay, and Portuguese speakers called it Lourenço Marques. White women and men were a minority, even within the community of foreign traders, travelers, and workers at the port. Europeans were outnumbered three to one by Asians and hundreds to one by Africans.[1] In the 1870s the town was a place where some "white men" lived, but by 1910 it was fast becoming a "white man's town."

Before the mineral revolution, a small group of Portuguese competed to make a profit as planters, traders, and labor agents in the port town. In that era, people prospered if they enjoyed good relations with African political authorities, raftsmen, porters, and caravan guides. The mineral revolution, however, introduced a whole new cast of characters. These people encouraged both conquest and large-scale foreign and Portuguese investment in railways and port works. They also promoted development of a "native affairs" bureaucracy to generate and control the African labor force necessary to build and maintain the growing port city. After conquest, the colonial government was recognized as the dominant power. Power shifted from those who had influence with African leadership to those who had access to government concessions, monopolies, or influence with the bureaucracy.

The creation of a "white man's town" was both a physical and a social phenomenon. The shifting social order, business protocol, and labor relations required the creation and reproduction of a specifically disadvantaged social strata. People who could not escape classification as "natives" would be the "white man's" workers, not his colleagues or competitors.[2] This chapter introduces the changing cast of characters, explores the physical transformation of Xilunguine, and discusses the specific forms of transformation as a metaphor of the larger process of domination, accommodation, and dispossession. It closes with a focus on the implications of shifting protocol for African labor in the city.

The Contenders and the Stakes

Many people arrived in town over this period. The different names they had for the town reflected their different ideas about doing business in it. Portuguese *sertanejos* (backwoods hunter-traders), African and Asian traders, hunters, and transport workers came to Xilunguine and worked within African protocol. *Sertanejo* Diocleciano Fernando das Neves, for example, was comfortable working with African leadership and within their concept of law and business. He was known in Sul do Save as Mafambacheca, he who greets you with a quick smile or easy laughter.[3] His correspondence with Governor Augusto de Castilho revealed the spirit behind the nickname:

> do you want to know why they [African leaders] admired me and also respected me? It was because I admired them too. . . .
> I spoke to important blacks and ordinary folks with equal attention as I would anyone of my own race.[4]

Jim Ximungana was a prosperous trader from Catembe, with family ties to Tembe royalty. He enjoyed a reputation as a keen businessman, a pillar of the Swiss Mission church, and a just and kind person in Xilunguine. He and his family worked comfortably with local people and foreigners. He was able to straddle competing concepts of law and business. His credit was good all over town. He acquired property through trade and marriage, but realized the benefit of securing it in the freehold form of tenure recognized by Portuguese law.[5]

António Gabriel Gouveia, a Goanese trader and transporter, was another familiar figure in Xilunguine. He married a prosperous mulatto woman named Gravata, whose father was a prominent Portuguese military figure. Their daughter Especiosa da Conceição, familiarly known as Bengalena, owned "a fortune in properties" in freehold in the city. When she died in 1907, her funeral was a major social event for the town's African and Afro-Portuguese community. An island beach resort in Marracuene and a public fountain in Maputo still carry her name.[6] Mafambacheca, Jim Ximungana, Gouveia, Gravata, and Bengalena all traded and negotiated with the various people in town, moving easily among the population's different approaches to law and business. They married and lived in extended families that incorporated European, African, Indian, and mulatto members. These were the dominant people in Xilunguine.[7]

Another group of people arrived in town in the last few decades of the century. They called the place Delagoa Bay and had quite different plans for it. Their plans required an altered and uniform approach to law and business, and hinged upon the construction of a railway to the Transvaal. They expected to develop their claims

through European colonial laws. British businessmen such as Charles Wack and Benjamin and Leon Cohen were among the first to form the Câmara do Comércio de
Lourenço Marques to lobby politicians to shape laws and business contracts to suit
their interests.[8]

These businessmen were well aware of their status as foreigners, and many cultivated Portuguese counterparts as agents and front men. Francisco de Melo Breyner
was the archetype of such compradores. He arrived in Lourenço Marques in the late
1880s and held Portuguese citizenship. He was clearly a sharp operator. For example,
he won the city's tramway concession in 1902 against a British competitor. Within a
year he undertook the tramway construction with British capital and equipment as
the agent of that same British competitor. By 1905 Melo Breyner was not only a member of the Câmara de Comércio de Lourenço Marques, he was the Portuguese agent
for the two most important foreign concerns in the city, the Delagoa Bay Development Corporation, which held the water, electricity, and tramway concessions, and
Breyner and Wirth, the local representative of Wenela.[9] Although the Portuguese
workers' press was clearly antagonistic to foreign capital in the city, the Portuguese
compradore elite prospered in this period.

British and South African interests were prominent on the waterfront and
remarkable for the sums of capital they controlled. It was not unusual for English or
South African residents to acknowledge their business in the city as "speculation."
By the turn of the century, property on the healthy and scenic bluffs overlooking the
city enjoyed a brisk market among this group. English-speaking shipping and handling agents, insurance agents, and large-scale importers interacted with Africans as
employer to employee, not as colleagues. They were remembered by Africans as the
important capitalists of the era. Indeed, informants did not assert that Africans workers had built Lourenço Marques, but rather recognized the key role of British capital
in their claim that: "The English built all this!"[10] They were also remembered as fair
employers who paid competitive wages but seldom if ever interacted with Africans
as individuals.[11] Jobs at Charles Wack's firm (Allen, Wack and Cia) were considered
good jobs, but he did not deign to include the names of African employees alongside
those of white colleagues in the company photograph.[12]

The majority of merchants in the city throughout this period were Indians who
held British passports. They were often envied and feared as fierce competitors by
European and African merchants alike. European wholesale merchants ultimately
depended upon Indians to develop the most difficult markets in the interior. Despite
their important role in the development of regional commerce, periodic anti-Indian
outbursts bear witness to the tension their energy and success generated among customers and competitors alike. Indian merchants employed very few Africans, and
had almost no role in the development of labor policies and protocols prejudicial to
African interests. They had their hands full trying to defend and advance their own
interests against Portuguese commercial licensing policies.

The Portuguese public works and railway contract workers of the 1870s and
1880s and the soldiers who fought the successful campaigns of the 1890s were
embraced as the city's "pioneers." By the early twentieth century they, and a new
group of Portuguese settlers, colonial administrators, bureaucrats, and workers considered the city properly their own. Like their English-speaking competitors, they
tried to write, interpret, ignore, and cash in on laws and business practices to suit
their interests. State contracts, sinecures, and monopolies were their chief concerns,

and political influence was their capital. Paulino dos Santos Gil was the archetype of this genre. He arrived in Lourenço Marques in 1903 at the age of nineteen and began work as an accountant for the public sanitation contractor. By 1909 he was director of the Republican association "Couceiro da Costa," and his career took off when the Republicans came to power in 1910.[13] As we shall see, his name became associated with quite contradictory meanings within the urban African community.

Portuguese-speaking residents bitterly protested the "denationalization" of the economy by such a "powerful octopus" as the Delagoa Bay Development Corporation.[14] English speakers, for their part, complained that politically important Portuguese received government contracts and monopolies in unfair competition. Historians find their petitions in consular despatches under the heading, "pervasive corruption in Lourenço Marques."[15] Periodically sharp competition among the Portuguese themselves erupted into public charges of corruption and scandal. During the tumultuous urban and waterfront expansion at the turn of the century, government employees were particularly generous with state funds and then at pains to account for them.[16]

Merchants, state contractors, compradores, bureaucrats, and speculators were not the only groups seeking to shape the transformation of Lourenço Marques. European laborers, artisans, and ne'er-do-wells arrived independently and as contract workers, often en route to the gold fields. Local Africans and hundreds of migrants also swelled the town's population as in-transit miners, forced laborers, petty commodity producers, casual day laborers, domestic servants, and entrepreneurs attracted by the town's growing market. Although African laborers built and serviced the white man's town, they were a diverse lot and fitted differently into relationships with other groups in town.

Contending views regarding land tenure, land use, commerce, business protocol, and labor allocation were echoed in the contending names for the town. Each group was well aware of the potential gains to be made from lobbying for political favor and playing sets of interests off one another. Everyone had a considerable stake in which views and protocol became ascendant. Again, although conquest was a watershed in Portuguese political and economic ascendance, it was only part of a larger process.

Xilunguine, Lourenço Marques, Delagoa Bay

The Transformation

Portugal's developing strategy in the city was shaped by both metropolitan and settler contenders. Some metropolitan groups had high stakes in the colonies. The Geographical Society of Lisbon, which played an important role in Portuguese colonial policy during the last quarter of the nineteenth century, was dominated by "a nationalist bourgeoisie formed predominantly by a middle level merchant bourgeoisie, intellectuals, and military officials."[17] The soldiers, intellectuals, and bureaucrats all had careers to build in Africa. The Oporto viticulture bourgeoisie and Lisbon commercial and shipping bourgeoisie also hoped African markets could compensate for their declining fortunes in Europe and Brazil.[18] Each of these groups cultivated its interests close to the centers of power.

The Portuguese made their decisive move to develop Xilunguine into Lourenço Marques in 1877. In 1875 Portugal's claim to southern Mozambique was secured in international arbitration over British counter-claims through the so-called MacMahon decision.[19] The next year alluvial gold strikes in the hinterland fueled increased interest in the port. The arrival of J. J. Machado's public works expedition aboard the ship *Africa* on 7 March 1877 marked the beginning of the end for *sertanejos* and many independent African traders and transporters.[20] From then on, the raft and caravan trades would be displaced by port and railway traffic. The decision also had ominous implications for the Ronga groups, since the city's transformation would take place in their midst and at their expense.

Machado's mandate contained important clues about the nature of that transformation. He was to undertake what were defined as "public works": a hospital, church, military barracks, ammunition dump, and jail. Obviously conquest and conversion were envisioned from the outset, but a sweeping physical transformation of the city soon became a priority. Machado realized that if his Portuguese contract crews were to survive to complete any project at all, he would have to address health concerns immediately. Judging from contemporary descriptions of the town, Machado had his work cut out for him.

Lourenço Marques became a town in 1876, a city in 1887, and the colonial capital in 1898.[21] Throughout the transformation from town to city to capital, travelers contrasted the natural beauty and commercial potential of the site with the unhealthy, grim condition of the town and its residents. In 1860 Lyons McLeod remarked, "The town is filthy in every sense, even the Governor's quarters being so surrounded by filth and dirt of all sorts that none but the Portuguese and natives . . . can approach it without being attacked by fits of vomiting."[22] A decade later, but prior to the mineral boom, St. Vincent Erskine suggested the sluggish economy was a metaphor for the town's overall sense of decay:

> The future of Delagoa Bay under Portuguese rule can be but decay and death. . . . This mass of grass huts, reed fences, decayed forts . . . and stench is enclosed by a wall about 6 feet high. At one time the slave and ivory trade must have made this an important station, but the abolition of the former and failure of the other . . . have reduced the place to a most miserable condition.[23]

Despite the economic upswing fueled by the gold rush, Wallis Mackay echoed St. Vincent Erskine in the 1880s: "set in a land of loveliness, surrounded by rich luxuriant vegetation [Lourenço Marques] is cursed with malaria and given over to lazy people who wallow in their filth. . . ."[24] Mackay described the population as a "dissolute, immoral and useless" collection of sickly soldiers, money lenders, liquor sellers, tedious bureaucrats, and self-important overseers.[25] Even Portuguese residents, administrators, and military officers of the era had little good to say about the people who represented Portugal in Mozambique.[26]

By the first decade of the twentieth century, however, the town was no longer a backwater. The city's transformation was most strikingly expressed by George Chamberlain, a frequent visitor. In 1899 when he arrived in town by steamer he recalled coming ashore, "on the neck of a kaffir, who puts you down in eighteen inches of sand, eighteen inches deep and fifty miles wide. . . . You climb into a rickshaw with a boy pulling and another pushing, and you go anywhere you like at a mile an hour."[27]

When he disembarked in 1909, however, his ocean liner docked directly at the concrete wharf. He found hydraulic cranes unloading numerous ships, a dozen taxis working the streets, some forty miles of macadam roadway, trams, and hotels and homes with their verandahs "thoroughly mosquito proofed."[28] Quite a contrast from the spit of sand of the previous decade.

The transformation of the city from the pestiferous, depressed trading post of the 1870s, to the rough-and-tumble boom town of the 1890s, to the comparatively sedate and tidy modern port of 1910, has implications that went beyond mere appearance. Xilunguine of the 1870s was shabby and smelly for most of the residents most of the time. By the first decade of the twentieth century, different residents experienced different cities. One Lourenço Marques was "very clean." The city that extended from one side of the central square, Praça Sete de Março, was "a continental city with beautifully paved streets, precise avenues of fine trees, . . . uniformed police, comfortable trams, and all the signs of modern prosperity."[29] The city stretching out from the "other" side of the Praça, however, was "dirty, muddled, chaotic, all dust and disorder, with sandy tracks for roads adorned by empty bottles, tins and old paper."[30] That was the visual reflection of the process of social differentiation that accompanied the city's development into sectors that were rich and poor, big and small, tidy and dirty.

Sculpting the City's Main Lines

The Port, the Railway, and Public Works

Smart investors understood that there were many opportunities to develop profitable businesses in the niches and interstices among large-scale enterprises. Large-scale state and private-funded enterprise set the pace of development in Lourenço Marques, but the interests of small business people shaped the living conditions for Mozambican laborers in the city. Private capital, usually linked with South African mining interests, was invested in groups like the Delagoa Bay Land Syndicate or the Delagoa Bay Development Corporation. They purchased strategic tracks of land and undertook most of the essential infrastructure.[31] State projects such as the railway, the port complex, and enormous landfills controlled huge sums of money. The state could assign lucrative contracts or concessions to Portuguese client entrepreneurs. These areas, whether Portuguese or foreign, were not easily penetrated by people without substantial capital or political connections.

Ordinary Portuguese, Indians, Africans, and others without substantial connections or cash maneuvered in the niches of opportunity created by state projects and the foreign syndicates. They became the city's *cantineiros*, petty proprietors, bureaucrats, *procuradors* (proxies hired to get around the bureaucrats), and petty business people of every description. Large- and small-scale businesses flourished both within and without the developing legal system. Graft, kickbacks, speculation, embezzlement, and skimping on contracts were common strategies for capital accumulation in the large-scale state and private enterprises. Bribery and the evasion of licenses, taxes, and legal minimums of quality controls significantly subsidized the incomes of people in the bureaucracy and small-scale enterprises.

Most big businesses promoted their claims on resources through the Chamber of Commerce and Association of Proprietors. All investors lobbied to initiate "public" projects that would enhance the value of their speculatory, residential, or business properties. Access roads, tramways, power lines, and piped water and sewerage were coveted and sharply contested resources. Although such facilities and utilities were often termed "public" works and "public" utilities, they were mostly about private gain.[32]

The port and railway complex would clearly be the linchpin facility for both public and private interests. As early as the 1880s, Municipal President Augusto de Castilho complained he was under constant pressure from foreign investors to upgrade port and municipal facilities. The town government, he claimed, was "enslaved by the foreign community."[33] Castilho may have felt himself "enslaved" by demands to develop the city, but Africans throughout Sul do Save could certainly have made a better case. They built the port, the railway, the roadways, and landfills that comprised the burgeoning municipality. Castilho acknowledged that the construction of the railway was central to all future investment:

> Lourenço Marques without the railway will get no further than it has over the last three hundred years; not because it does not have the resources for its own development, but because we do not have the spirit of the capitalist—there is no initiative. There is no capital.[34]

Whatever Castilho's judgment about Portugal's particular spirit, he was certainly right about the money. Construction of the city's major facilities was driven by the tense interaction of the colonial state, foreign investors, and Portuguese contractors. Investment capital was introduced through private, largely foreign concessions.[35] Even the railway was originally undertaken on a concession basis and funded by foreign shareholders.[36] The Portuguese hoped to generate capital for major undertakings with concessions and promises of cheap labor supplies. Foreign investors banked on the rapid valuation of their marginally improved concessions as the town prospered. Portuguese contractors hoped to broker their ability to cut through government roadblocks to secure projects from the concessionaires. Each group had its distinct capital and goals, and each counted on access to African labor to realize those goals.

Contractors for strategic concessions and public works projects were entitled to requisition conscript labor. The railway was the region's strategic project, and it eventually took related projects such as port and landfill construction under its massive wings. It was the largest employer of African labor throughout this period. Patterns of labor conscription, housing, and work conditions adopted by the railway provided a model for both public and private employers that endured into the second decade of the century. It was on the whole a sorry precedent.

After several false starts, Edward McMurdo was awarded a concession to build a rail line from the port to the border with the South African Republic in 1883. McMurdo contracted about two hundred British, Dutch, Italian, and Irish workmen and was allowed to conscript and hire about three thousand Mozambicans. Historians have referred to the railway's labor foremen as "scoundrels."[37]

> It was probably an inevitable evil; certainly only with men of this caliber would it have been possible to realize this hard work of transporting mountains, spreading rocks and dynamite loads and imposing on locally recruited native labor the most severe discipline for the roughest work, and to survive in spite of it. . . .[38]

Opening the rail line.

The McMurdo concession stipulated completion of the line to the border by June 1889. On 26 June 1889 the rail line was still several kilometers short of the border. The Portuguese claimed the contract was in non-compliance, seized the line, and canceled the concession. McMurdo's shareholders sued and the matter went into international arbitration. Just as the MacMahon decision confirmed Portugal's possession of southern Mozambique a quarter-century earlier, the Bern decision of 29 March 1900 legitimated Portugal's seizure of the railway and set a payoff figure for the shareholders.[39]

Portugal moved quickly to consolidate her gains by negotiating a loan to construct extensive port works. The town's only existing dock facility at the time was a private deep-water pier owned by the Netherlands Corporation, called Netherlands's pier. In 1900 Portugal began construction of Gorjão wharf, and subsequently built warehouses and extended the original wharf. A port improvement commission had been formed in 1895 based on close cooperation between private British shipping and forwarding companies and the state. By 1905, however, the state merged the port and railway administrations and eliminated formal collaboration with the private sector. The newly established port and railway administration soon bought out Netherlands's pier. In short, between the 1880s and 1910, the key port and railway facilities that were built with foreign capital came under direct state control.[40]

State expansion and consolidation of the port and railway complex was accomplished hand in hand with the massive landfills. For Lourenço Marques to develop into a white man's town, it would have to overcome its stubborn reputation as a

Expanding the docks.

white man's grave. White businessmen lobbied for major allocations of African-generated tax money and labor to accomplish the task. They were also quite willing to sacrifice African-held lands to the endeavor. Their lobby was framed as a public health crisis. Public interest and public health were frequently invoked in colonial Africa to justify alienating African land and investing African tax money and labor in facilities designed to serve the health and well-being of only the palest public. Lourenço Marques's landfills provide a classic example of that process.

J. J. Machado's swamp drainage and landfill was the first of a series of projects designed to remove the malarial swamps that surrounded the trade post. The town's health records indicated that malaria was at the heart of the town's insalubrious reputation, and at the heart of the malaria problem was the *pantano*, the swamp.[41] The town plan drawn up in 1876 clearly shows that the commercial district and fortifications at the waterfront were indeed situated on "a spit of sand surrounded by marsh."[42] Beyond the marsh the land sloped steeply upward, forming bluffs to the north of the commercial district. As the town spread up the surrounding slopes, the core of the trade post came to be called the lower city or the *baixa*.

Machado organized swamp drainage and construction of a 1,200-meter seawall to prevent tidal flooding of the drained areas. By 1880 the seawall was in place and some 555,000 square meters of swampland had been filled. Africans living in the area had been expelled and eucalyptus trees planted to aid in the desiccation process. By 1904 over 800,000 cubic meters of sand and rock had been hauled into the swamp and

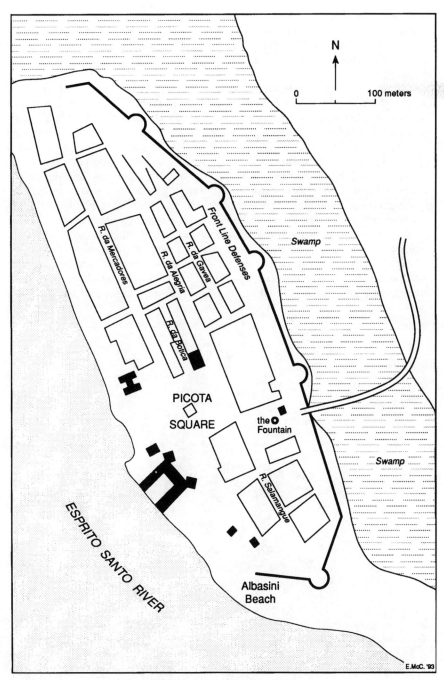

Map of Lourenço Marques, 1876.

over the next three years Africans shoveled in another 90,000 cubic meters.[43] The landworks were all accomplished by *shibalo* working in appalling conditions. A local woman described the landworks undertaken as part of the railway projects as "a sea of black stinking mud, with three hundred kafirs working in it, digging trenches and throwing up banks."[44]

Although the original swamp fill was directly related to health concerns, subsequent equally large landfills served speculators and South African investors in the fast-developing tourist industry. Parks, beaches, and a seaside boulevard, all built by *shibalo* crews conscripted under the rubric of public works, were important attractions for the South African tourists who came to count on Lourenço Marques beaches, campgrounds, casinos, and "continental" flavor for their vacations.[45]

Avenida Marginal was the elaborate crown on the group of landfill, drainage, and waterfront projects that transformed the city's physical space. It embellished the upper city residential areas, bolstered tourism, and completed plans for the city's coastline. Built in the tradition of Lisbon's famous *marginal*, it runs along the bay from the *baixa* in the southwest to the Polana beach resort in the northeast. It required nearly five kilometers of fill and construction of a sea wall three meters high.[46]

The landfills comprised a massive subsidy to the resident and seasonal European community of Lourenço Marques. They were part of the bargain struck between the colonial state and private capital for investment in the city. In that bargain Ronga-

Working in a sea of mud.

speaking groups were displaced and their lands were marred.[47] Earth and rock taken from Ronga lands filled malarial lowlands increasingly claimed by Europeans. Fill removal left open pits in Ronga areas. The pits soon filled with water and the still water encouraged mosquito breeding.[48] Thus the malarial threat was diminished in the European-claimed area at the expense of the health of African-claimed areas.

Prison and *shibalo* labor built virtually all the landfills. *Shibalos* worked the quarries that rendered the fill. They hauled, loaded, unloaded, and graded the fill and finally planted the grass and tree cover that held it in place. Dozens of *shibalo* workers were buried in landslides, explosions, and cave-ins on the these projects.[49] The port and railway complex and landfills not only transformed the city's physical space, they shaped labor relations and work conditions throughout the city and region. Those relations and conditions are the topic of Chapter 3.

The transformation of the city may have been designed and urged by large-scale state and private investment, but it was facilitated and shaped by small-scale businesses. The African labor force drawn into town by the major projects interacted more intensely with and created a market for the small-scale businesses. Those businesses lobbied hard to guarantee their share of the developing prosperity. The political and social relationship among large-scale employers and the small-scale businesses within the Portuguese community significantly shaped social conditions for African workers in Lourenço Marques.

Shaping the Citys Characteristic Textures

Cantineiros and Bureaucrats

In the bustling era of port, railway, and landfill construction, thousands of African workers had to eat, drink, check in and out of work, socialize, and eventually be paid something. Eating, drinking, gambling, sex, and song were all commoditized to capture wage packets and sustain the urban labor force. Daily reproduction for most African workers centered around the *cantina*, a combination trade store, bar, brothel, and rooming house.[50] *Cantinas* were comparatively simple, secure low-investment businesses. Portuguese owned two-thirds of the *cantina* licenses in the city at the turn of the century, but Chinese, Indians, and a small group of Eastern European women competed with the Portuguese for alcohol sales to Africans.[51]

Despite Junod's promotion of low-alcohol local brews like *uputsu* over the more potent range of drinks, the alcohol trade shaped regional labor migration and the experience of African workers in Lourenço Marques in important ways. Well before imported and European introduced brews were consumed in significant quantities, Sul do Save people brewed and distilled juices from an enormous variety of local fruits and vegetables. Alcoholic drink was familiar, and the traders who lined migrant routes with their *cantinas* found it to be among the most marketable commodities in Sul do Save.[52]

Commerce in Sul do Save was forged by British Indians, Chinese, Portuguese, and a few Africans, but Portuguese traders specialized in alcoholic drink. From the late nineteenth century they aggressively sought to capture a larger market share with "colonial wine," imported from Portugal specifically for the colonies.[53] Portuguese traders, or *cantineiros*, came to be called "*mumaji*." "*Mumaji*" was the man who always offered his customers more (*mais*)—more rum, more wine. He asked "Quer mais? Quer mais?" (Would you like more? Would you like more?). Given the Ronga lilt the man who always asked "Quer mais (maji)?" became *mumaji*.[54] *Mumaji*'s customers were increasingly wage laborers.

Late nineteenth-century sources invariably remark on the area's brisk trade in alcohol. English writers, who seldom missed an opportunity to scorn the Portuguese, remarked that "Lourenço Marques lives by grog and by natives in search of work and the money they earn when they come back."[55] The extent and variety of Portuguese investment in alcohol sales and its insidious impact on the region, however, was also frankly admitted at the highest levels of the colonial government. A Portuguese royal commissioner in the 1890s, António Enes, observed that "the exploitation of native drunkenness is the principal object of agricultural, commercial and industrial activity in the province."[56]

Mozambicans may not have been any more inclined to drink than any other groups in Southern Africa, but from the turn of the twentieth century, they had easier access to highly alcoholic beverages than did their neighbors.[57] For some workers, at least, that seems to have made a difference. Labor recruiters and managers attributed the repeat migration of Mozambicans to alcohol addiction. One recruiter observed:

> Their earnings were spent, not on cattle but on whisky and gin. Thus, a period of work, instead of supplying them with the means of settling down, only gave them a period of drink and idleness. Afterwards they had to return to work in order to earn the coin wherewith to gratify their culti-

vated tastes. In this way they have come nearer than any of the other South African races to supplying the material of an industrial as distinguished from an agricultural population.[58]

Portuguese wine sellers failed in their attempt to develop a market in South Africa among Mozambicans working in the South African mines. The mining companies successfully resisted vigorous efforts to tie wine sales to recruitment accords. But in Lourenço Marques alcohol interests significantly shaped both labor controls and life in African neighborhoods.[59]

Wine exports from Portugal to her colonies increased sharply in the last quarter of the nineteenth century. Mozambique's wine imports, most of which went to Lourenço Marques, increased 350 percent between 1890 and 1905 to about 11 million liters per year.[60] Liquor licenses, excluding those in the heavily populated urban outskirts, increased from 175 in 1895 to 678 by 1907. If one believes the census statistics, that meant one cantina for every twenty people in 1899 and one for every fourteen by 1907.[61]

In southern Mozambique, as elsewhere in Africa, competition among liquor distillers, wine importers, and brewers of all sorts of indigenous plant life was intense. Sul do Save sugar planters (concentrated around Inhambane) produced and sold an alcoholic drink called *sopé*. Mozambican women brewed *uputsu* beer and a variety of other fruit- or grain-based alcoholic drinks for consumption and sale. Portuguese wholesale and retail merchants imported and sold Portugal's so-called colonial wine. The planters, brewers, and merchants competed to capture Mozambican wages through alcohol sales. Portuguese *cantineiros* also counted on wine sales to draw in customers for their less competitive trade goods.

Charles van Onselen analyzed the complex and changing role of alcohol sales in the overall mix of competing interests in the Witwatersrand mining area of the Transvaal.[62] Much of that fascinating story is irrelevant to our purposes, but some elements of the Witwatersrand case contrast strikingly with the situation that developed in Lourenço Marques. For a time Afrikaner farmers' and politicians' interests in Hatherley Distillery's grain alcohol sales dovetailed with the British mine owners' strategy of using alcohol as a lure to attract and hold African labor. Eventually, however, amidst a myriad of other tensions between the two groups, contradictions arose between the mine owners' desire to attract labor with alcohol and their frustration with trying to manage the effects of alcohol on their labor force. Eventually mine owners' growing interest in worker sobriety combined with declining political influence of Hatherley supporters to facilitate the legal prohibition of sales of grain alcohol and other highly alcoholic drinks to Africans. Although alcohol sales were never completely eliminated, the closure of Hatherley, destruction of much of the illegal supply network, and the industry's commitment to controlled sales of low-alcohol beer eventually brought the balance of alcohol sales and worker sobriety closer to the satisfaction of the ascendant classes.

In Lourenço Marques the constellation of employers, alcohol producers, consumers, and sellers worked out quite differently. Those differences had important implications for Africans working and living in the city. Metropolitan wine importers were important political figures throughout the period, and wine was a critical export for Portugal. In 1908, for example, eleven of the twelve members of the municipal commercial council were liquor dealers.[63] Employers, including the state, had to contend with work time lost to alcohol-related problems, but employers and alcohol sellers were more often on the same side of the political fence. The combined political influence of Portugal's viticulture and commercial bourgeoisie, the local petite bourgeoisie, state and municipal bureaucracy, and the hundreds of Portuguese *cantineiros* ensured that alcohol sales would not be significantly curbed.

The mining industry's concern with safety, productivity, and efficiency reflected the more specialized and dangerous nature of the work and workplace. Lourenço Marques's state and municipal unskilled gang laborers did not necessarily have to be sober to shovel, sweep, and tote. The mines' commitment to compound housing with adjacent beer halls, offering low-alcohol beer, also contrasted sharply with the situation in Lourenço Marques. The only building in the city that really qualified as a compound was owned and run by Wenela. Municipal and state *shibalo* workers were housed in make-shift shacks, hay wagons, stables, and a half-dozen wood and zinc sheds. The city's migrant volunteer labor force constructed their own housing, and ate, drank, and socialized in *cantinas* when they could afford it. Local casual workers lived with their families in the suburbs. Throughout the century, initiatives to force African workers to live in South African style compounds or township-like neighborhoods never materialized. First, the state and municipality were not willing either to spend the considerable sums necessary to build such housing or to increase wages or subsidize transportation fares to enable workers to live further outside the city. Compounds and distant neighborhoods (*bairros*) were also sharply contested by the influential *cantineiro* lobby, which protected its stake in worker consumption and housing patterns.[64]

Interest in worker-generated alcohol revenues went well beyond *cantineiros*. At the turn of the century the municipal and colonial treasuries depended heavily on alcohol revenues. Customs and license income from alcohol contributed about 3,000,000$00 *milreis* per year between 1899 and 1901. Fines and correctional labor for public drunkenness increased from about 60,000$00 in 1901 to 101,000$00 in 1904. In 1903 drunkenness fines were the city's largest single source of income, more than double the next largest source.[65]

Drunkenness fees provided the resources necessary for the creation of a police and administrative bureaucracy capable of implementing a firm labor control system. Police and the burgeoning cadres of petty bureaucrats developed both direct and indirect interests in worker drinking patterns. They were well aware that alcohol resources contributed a large portion of their budgets. Police and petty bureaucrats could also subsidize their own salaries by accepting money to overlook a drunkenness fee or labor sentence. Once the control system was in place, it not only generated substantial revenues in recruitment fees, registration fees, and fines for infractions of the labor code, but also a myriad of opportunities for bribe income. Workers paid for the implantation and expansion of the very structures that oppressed them.

State and municipal departments also had a stake in the health, sobriety, and discipline of their workers, but alcohol revenues were too important and too evenly distributed among politically influential groups to seriously consider the Transvaal's municipal beer system. An alternative solution developed to cope with the contradiction between alcohol sales and incapacitated laborers. The solution hinged upon the relationship among returning mine migrants, volunteer urban labor, *shibalo*, and prison labor.

Mine migrants returning from South Africa through Lourenço Marques stayed in Wenela's compound in the Malanga section of the city. Local *cantineiros* knew they had money to spend, and all vied for space closest to the compound. The Malanga compound was literally encircled with *cantinas*, and further encroachment was only prevented by laws that required commercial establishments to keep a specific distance away from the compound. Since the miners were waiting for transportation home, not working in the city, their drinking habits were of no concern to urban employers. Breyner and Wirth, the compound management firm, however, fought a chronic battle with City Hall regarding the lure of the neighboring *cantinas*. Breyner and Wirth claimed that drunken miners destroyed compound property and tried to hold the *cantineiros* liable for the damage.[66]

Casual laborers were also free to drink their wages, and the South African firms that depended upon their labor frequently complained of "sodden stevedores." [67] The state and municipality, however, depended upon *shibalo* gangs for the backbone of their labor force in this period. Since a large portion of *shibalo*'s scant wage packet was paid in kind (room and board) and part of the rest deferred for payment upon repatriation to the area of recruitment, they had very little money to spend on drink. Summary convictions for public drunkenness often provided the turnstile through which casual labor with money to spend was transformed into prison or *shibalo* labor with empty pockets.[68]

In short, vested interests in alcohol linked a whole range of politically important groups, including the state and the municipality, and alcohol-related revenues fueled accumulation in the private and state sectors of the urban economy. The interplay of characters and of relationships among alcohol revenues, unpaid municipal labor, and the development of a bureaucracy and police sufficient to control and direct urban labor shaped both the demand for labor and the context within which Africans struggled to build their lives and livelihoods.

The port, the railway, the landfills, tramways, *cantinas*, and *shibalo* sheds provided physical evidence of the emergence of a "white man's town." They were all built, serviced, and sustained by African labor and African money. What was it like for Africans to work in the developing "white man's town"? What was their perspective on Junod's dialog heading: "Work for the white people, you will be able to get money."[69] Chapter 3 introduces a range of African worker strategies and attitudes toward the early experience of urban wage labor, labor conscription, and strategies to cope with enhanced labor control.

3

"Work for the White People, You Will Be Able To Get Money"[1] African Perspectives on Changing Labor Relations

With the advent of railway, wharf, landfill, and roadway construction, the demand for unskilled labor in Lourenço Marques soared.[2] The port and railway complex absorbed the largest portion of the urban labor force, with hod carrying, stevedoring, and manual labor at the wharves leading the way. Public works employment comprised a second large and diverse area, including road building, sanitation, landfill, and the construction of municipal and state buildings. The developing port and railway complex, landfills, parks, and avenues all encouraged European settlement and investment in commerce and tourism, which increased demand for service labor: cleaning, laundry, cooking, running errands, and waiting table. Domestic service was the most common service position. Throughout the twentieth century most wage employment for urban Africans fell into one of these three sectors: port complex, public works, and service labor.[3] Although service workers were almost all volunteer, Africans working in other sectors of the white man's town could be either volunteers or *shibalo*. For most of the colonial period, however, the distinction between those two categories was slight.

This chapter suggests African strategies for living and laboring in the developing "white man's town" before 1933 through a series of brief studies: a turn-of-the-century collage of labor relations at the waterfront, the narrative of an elderly Mozambican, a speculative study of the possibilities of *shibalo* entrepreneurship, and an exploration of the peculiar risks and benefits implicit in domestic service. Each brief section seeks to

44

reconstruct shifting labor relations and highlight African perspectives on the process. Chapter 4 details the articulation and implementation of the *indigenato*'s component parts, and the ideological and practical contradictions that developed in the process. Chapter 5 then develops a more detailed case study of labor in the key port and railway sector to highlight the multi-layered challenges to the labor control and systemic racism embedded in the *indigenato*.

Worker Attitudes and Strategies

A Waterfront Collage

Most written documents for this period treat Africans like just so many workers, contributing just so much tax money, and earning just so much in total wages. Africans were clearly historical actors who had an impact contending for their own space and interests in the fast-changing city, but their views are more challenging to reconstruct. Although some oral testimony is available for the turn of the century, the contending strategies and attitudes of most ordinary workers toward the changing protocol must be sought through a kind of collage of primary sources, photographs, stories, quotes, and dialogues.

Since the port and railway complex was the core of the city's development at the turn of the century, it provides the most promising focus for such a collage. Henri Junod tells us that "Thousands of natives are employed in discharging the large steamers which arrive by the hundreds. . . . at this work a native can earn fifteen shillings a week." Although he judged these tasks to be "much easier than collecting [oilseeds], wax or tapping rubber,"[4] he also confirmed that discharging steamers was not without its risks:

> It's a real spectacle to see these natives, dressed in sacks, working away twenty or thirty at a time around a heavy piece of machinery, destined for the Johannesburg gold mines. . . . They sing to give themselves strength. . . . If they lose their grip and the piece falls, they jump aside with the agility of cats to avoid being crushed.[5]

Junod's written description echoed the visual portrait provided by photographs appended to port documents of that era. The Lourenço Marques waterfront indeed was a beehive of African gang laborers, dressed in used feed sack cloths, struggling with a whole range of heavy tasks.

Junod's conversation manual allows us to eavesdrop on contemporary labor negotiations at the waterfront, and glimpse a typical exchange regarding the emerging protocol of "proper behavior":6

> Good morning.
>   Good morning, Sir.
> What are you doing?
>   I am not doing anything.
> Do you want to work for me?
>   I should like to work. . . . What work shall I have to do?
> You will carry boxes.
>   Where must I carry them?
> You will take them from the customs house and carry them to my store.

Waterfront landfill labor, Lourenço Marques, 1914.

Let us go then!
Carry this box.
   It is heavy for me.
Trust yourself. It is not very heavy.
   Oh, it is heavy; I can't.
You are simply lazy.
   It would be good if you could find somebody to help me.
What shall we do? All right, go and fetch another man.
   Here he is. I have found him.
Lift up, both of you.
   We shall not get there.
Non sense [sic]! Show your strength. . . . Look, all these boxes here, you will
carry them home.
   Hold fast, it is falling.
Take care, it will hurt you.
   Ho! It has fallen on my foot.
No matter. I will give you some medecine [sic]. . . . When you have finished,
you will come to my house. I shall pay you.
   How much will you pay us?
I shall give you one shilling a day.
   It is too little; we will not agree. We want two shillings a day.

That is not right; you are not behaving properly. I shall give you twenty *reis* each time. You will get three pence for three journeys. Two three penny bits make six pence. Two six pence make a shilling. You shall get much money.

All right, white man! Let us work, boys! . . . The sun has set. We have not had anything to eat yet. We are hungry. . . . I am going to rest. The boxes of to day [sic] were big. They were not very big. We shall see each other to-morrow [sic].

Very good, we shall come to finish up.

The conversation between Junod's fictitious importer and hod-carriers was strikingly similar to the recollections of men who began work at the waterfront slightly later. Workers tried to shape the organization of tasks and payment. In order to earn the two shillings they wanted, they had to make the journey from waterfront to warehouse eight times. They negotiated piecework against flat rates, and struggled constantly to protect their safety, strength, and health against employer demands for increased production. The dialectic between employer and worker interests could not be clearer; it was expressed as: "It is heavy! I can't" vs. "They are not very big . . . You are simply lazy." The money "is too little," vs. "You will get much money." Struggles regarding the relationship between work and rest times, the amount of food, the work load, conditions of labor, wages, and the definition of proper behavior were clearly central. The case of Mussongueia Samuel Mussana provides an African perspective of that challenge.

The Best-Laid Plans

The Experience of Mussongueia Samuel Mussana

In 1977 Mussongueia Samuel Mussana walked several miles into Maputo every day to cut grass for the municipality. He sat in a grassy area and cut the grass around him with a machete; then he got up, moved to the adjoining grassy area, sat down and began again until it was time to eat or go home. Everyone knew him as old Mussongueia, and everyone paused to greet him and visit. According to Mussongueia's documents, he was 103 in 1977, and many men claimed he must be older. Since he was hired during the colonial era as casual labor, he had no retirement benefits. So he just walked in and worked every day. He first walked to work in what was then Lourenço Marques around 1905.[7]

Mussongueia worked his first job in South Africa in the 1890s. He had walked from Gaza to the mining areas to market his labor, unencumbered by recruitment contract. He returned to his home after one contract, but by 1905 decided to return. He knew that if he asked the local administrator for a pass to work in South Africa, he would be refused and probably be seized for *shibalo* on the local roads. *Shibalo* road gangs were to be avoided, so he asked for a pass to seek work in Lourenço Marques.

Mussongueia's strategy was to seek a work pass for the city, and upon arrival try to sign on with Wenela and receive train transport to South Africa rather than risk another walk. That was a common strategy, a so-called stepping-stone strategy, among men who didn't have the money to hire their own passage, but wanted to avoid the long and dangerous walk to South Africa.[8] Men from Inhambane sometimes even let themselves be taken for *shibalo* in Lourenço Marques, hoping to take

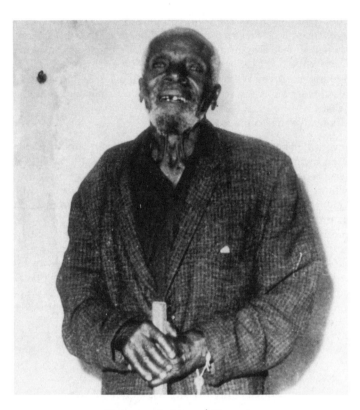

Mussongueia Samuel Mussana.

advantage of the ship passage to Lourenço Marques, and then to escape and arrange clandestine passage from there.[9]

Mussongueia received his pass for Lourenço Marques and then headed off on foot to the capital. He heard from people on the road that a new labor registration system had recently been implemented in the city. Workers could be harassed or arrested if they did not hold a municipal registration tag, a so-called *chapa*. On his approach to the city, he met a fellow countryman en route home from a stint of dock work in Lourenço Marques. As a precaution Mussongueia bought his comrade's *chapa*. He arrived in town with travel papers and *chapa* , thinking he was all set.

At Wenela's offices in the Malanga section of town, however, he was turned away because his travel papers were for employment in the city, not in South Africa. Foiled in his original plan, Mussongueia looked up a relative whom he knew worked in town as a domestic servant. He hoped the young man could tide him over while he revised his strategy. Coincidentally, Mussongueia's young relative had just secured a Wenela contract for himself. Mussongueia proposed that he take over his relative's job, and continue to pursue a mine contract or clandestine passage to South Africa. The young man arranged the deal with his employer and went off to South Africa. When Mussongueia showed up to take his place, however, the employer saw that Mussongueia was an adult, and refused to hire him as a domestic servant. Instead he had Mussongueia seized for *shibalo* on a public works job in which his firm had a part interest. Despite his well-laid plans and precautions, the next day Mussongueia was shoveling sand and hauling rocks with a *shibalo* gang on the city's enormous landfills.

Mussongueia's recollection provides a first-hand view of the most typical kind of *shibalo* gang labor at the turn of the century.[10] He was assigned to a road gang comprised of men from all over Sul do Save, and their monotonous unskilled labor was fairly closely monitored by overseers. Each day the overseer placed a stone in the distance and told the gang they would have to work until they reached the stone. If they reached the stone in daylight, the overseer usually moved the stone further and made them work until they reached its new position or until it was dark. It if got dark before they reached the place where the stone was put at the beginning of the day, they were punished.

Ten-hour days were normal, and thirteen-hour days were not unusual.[11] The overseer, armed with a wooden club, or *moca*, beat any workers who grumbled or walked away from the road. Under such conditions, people sensibly worked as slowly as they could while attempting to avoid punishment for foot dragging. There was no incentive to work hard, since that would only lead to raised expectations with no compensatory reward.

The worksong, "Wayiwona," or "You will see, my son," resonated with much of Mussongueia's testimony. One might as well accept shoveling sand with calm, survive, and escape the overseer's *moca*:

You will see, you are shoveling sand, you are here my son. . . .
You will see. . . .
I am shoveling sand here, my father. . . .
You will see, you are here shoveling sand, you are here. . . .
Get going! Get Going! . . . Devil snake Ndziwena!
You will see, you are shoveling sand, my son. . . . you will see.
Shovel sand, since you are here, my son.
You will see, shoveling sand, accept it my son . . . you will see.
You will see, you. . . . Work! Work! . . . Die! . . . Work to Death!
You will see, you are shoveling sand, be calm my son. . . . you will see.
Shovel sand, be calm my son.[12]

Shibalo walked to their work area daily. If the area was a long way from their housing sheds, their mid-day food and water would be delivered to the work area by donkey cart. They were allowed to eat and rest in the middle of the day, and walked back to the sheds at day's end. If the work area was within a mile or so from the sheds, however, they had to return in the mid-day heat for lunch. Because of the notoriously poor quality of *shibalo* food, families sometimes sent a young relative to accompany the conscript and arrange extra food to maintain his health and nutrition.[13]

Public works housing ranged from open hay wagons to barracks-type sheds, and it was generally of the worst possible quality. Mussongueia preferred sleeping in the open air. No doubt that was a wise decision, since in December 1907 the source of the plague epidemic that threatened the whole city turned out to be the public works *shibalo* housing.[14] Indeed, the worst sanitary conditions revealed in the city-wide investigation by the plague sanitation committee existed at the various public works housing sheds.[15]

When Mussongueia went to cut grass thatch for his sleeping shelter, however, he learned another lesson about life in the "white man's town." He was stopped by a concession holder's overseer and asked why he had not asked permission to cut the grass. Mussongueia responded that he had not asked permission to cut the grass because grass belonged to God; it did not belong to any man. "I did not ask you because I did not know you made this grass. I thought only God made the grass." Mussongueia had no intention of paying a man for grass he did not make, so he left the grass where he had cut it and went off in search of God's own grass.[16]

As early as 1905, some of the Mozambicans on Mussongueia's road gang lived in rural areas firmly under Portuguese control, and they chronically faced *shibalo* conscription. Men in such areas, who were not working in the mines or making enough money to buy themselves out of conscription, would be accused of vagrancy and repeatedly seized for *shibalo*. The inevitability of *shibalo* conscription sometimes encouraged depopulation of the area, and sometimes the development of accommodation strategies. Men eventually allowed themselves to be taken for *shibalo* when their enforced absence best coordinated with the demands of the agricultural calendar. They tried to make the best of it and avoid the most onerous work gangs.

Despite their accommodation, the men loathed their fate, the disruption of their agricultural production and resultant threat to their families' well-being. Their anger and lament was expressed in the familiar work song "*Shibalo muni magandana*." Virtually every informant knew this song, which bid the Portuguese (Magandana, the evil one) to go home, and leave them and their children alone. Its many verses ask:

> What kind of *shibalo* is this of magandana? . . . It catches everyone, even the women [mothers, grandparents, parents, brothers, sisters]. . . . [The Portuguese] don't even let us rest . . . We are killing ourselves. . . . Why don't you [Portuguese] go back to your country?[17]

Mozambicans who were chronically conscripted into *shibalo* eventually became familiar figures to city's public works overseers. That familiarity sometimes afforded them a measure of privilege. They were called *mwamu cholo*, or old-timers. The overseers knew these men were familiar with the system and would be less likely to challenge it because they would inevitably be back to work it again.

Mussongueia was not from such an area. He had landed in a *shibalo* gang through a stroke of bad luck, and was clearly contemptuous of his colleagues' accommodation strategies. *Mwamu cholo*, in his view, were not seen as privileged but despised. Mussongueia, who was as much an itinerant artist in 1977 as he was in 1905, found relief from the tedium of the work in performance, both on and off the work area. He occasionally sneaked away from the work area to nearby *cantinas* where he performed for money tossed by appreciative patrons.

Many of his songs and dances mocked the *mwamu cholo*. His songs told them to stop their noise, stop lamenting the Portuguese presence, and stop bidding the Portuguese to go home. The Portuguese didn't go home, Mussongueia taunted, because they were too busy bossing over fools like them. The Portuguese were always sick from lack of sleep, he sang. They couldn't sleep because they couldn't turn their backs on the stupid *mwamu cholo*—they had to keep them slaving away:

> Go away to your houses, get out of my sight,
> You witches' daughters

You are so tiresome with your stories of old times.
You say you are old-timers, call yourselves *mwamu cholo*,
As though that were a good thing. . . . It just means you are fools
Caught over and over again.
You make me tired, you witches' daughters.[18]

Even among the *shibalo* gang laborers, one could not expect solidarity! Mussongueia was caught in his performances sometimes, but he was let off easily by the overseers. He speculated that they too were grateful for some levity in the otherwise grim situation.

Mussongueia's experience suggests the vulnerability of casual labor to conscription, the varied response of men to their situation, depending upon their overall possibilities, and the tension that emerged between *shibalo* and the city's voluntary labor force. In this "white man's town," *shibalo* labor was increasingly manipulated by the government to undermine the interests of the majority labor force. But, as the next case study suggests, Africans were also capable of turning the tables and manipulating *shibalo* contracts to suit their own ends.

Tilling the Night Soil

The Case of the Chopi

Urban public works jobs were of two sorts. Infrastructure projects, such as the road and landfill project where Mussongueia worked, required hundreds of workers for short or irregular periods of time. The second sort was the city's basic sanitation, clean-up, and maintenance chores, which required a regular supply of workers for longer contracts. By the 1920s, middle-class European neighborhoods were tied into a sewerage system, but throughout the colonial era sewerage from African neighborhoods from Chamanculo, Mafalala, and the Alto Mahé to the peri-urban settlements was removed by sanitation brigades who worked the "night soil" wagons, or the *sumpango* as the wagons were called. The *sumpango* wagons, pulled by mules, went door to door throughout the city collecting, emptying, and replacing the buckets that served households as toilets. At the turn of the century, the sanitation bucket brigade work was done at night and in the early morning to take advantage of deserted streets. Except for the fact that mule-drawn carts were eventually replaced by broken down trucks, the *sumpango* system functioned throughout the 1950s quite like it had since its inception.[19]

There was a great deal of resistance to working on the *sumpango*. Around the turn of the century the work was done by prison laborers supplied to the public works contractors by the municipality. The task then passed to public works *shibalo* under the general direction of the railway.[20] Prison labor was unpaid, but the *shibalo* workers received the usual contract wage of between $180 and $380 per day. Unskilled casual labor in the city could earn between $350 to $800 over the same period, so *shibalo* earnings were generally about half those of voluntary workers. In 1908 the Portuguese firm of Carvalho and David, which had undertaken a large part of the landfill, contracted with the city to do sanitation. The contracts allowed Carvalho and David to conscript up to 100 laborers in the Military District of Gaza for each project.[21]

It is probably no coincidence that the private sanitation contract went into effect immediately after the plague episode of December 1907. The lack of toilet facilities, or poorly serviced facilities, for much of the population encouraged the use of any and all vacant lots as toilets.[22] During the boom period following the Witwatersrand gold strike, urban facilities were so inadequate that businesses threatened to relocate in Durban.[23] By 1908 of the more than 1,600 permanent structures registered in Lourenço Marques, only 850 rented slop buckets through the municipal sanitation system.[24] Carvalho and David took on a difficult task, but with the full support of the important foreign community and the highest level administrators.

The sanitation workers also realized that this was a strategic service, and used it to their advantage. By at least 1910, the Chopi people of Zavala circumscription became the preferred workers for sanitation.[25] Why did the Chopi became the exclusive labor force for sanitation *shibalo*? The literature on the Chopi is full of unhelpful clichés and half-truths.[26] It is clear, however, that the Chopi eventually became exclusively linked with municipal sanitation work, and that requires some explanation.

As we have seen, the hostile relations between Chopi areas and the Gaza state led some Chopi chiefs to ally with the Portuguese for arms and assistance in defending themselves. This alliance allowed the Portuguese to become better established in Chopi areas and thus enhanced their ability to make claims on Chopi labor. There were fewer places to hide in areas well penetrated by the Portuguese, and escape could bring strong retribution on the escapee's family. Furthermore, Chopi had extensive investments in agricultural and tree crops rather than cattle keeping. Cattle wealth could be moved with the group, but good lands and established tree crops were lost if the community dispersed to avoid labor demands. Finally, whereas a mine labor contract was remunerative, the twelve-month commitment it required ill accommodated the Chopi agricultural calendar. A sanitation contract in this era ranged between three and six months. By coordinating with their the chiefs, Chopi men could plan their absences around the agricultural calendar. In short, the specific situation of the Zavala Chopi made the cost of evasion high enough for men to seriously consider the possible benefits of accommodation.[27]

At the turn of the century, diverse groups of prison laborers and contract workers brought in from as far away as Quelimane worked the sanitation brigades. Little by little, however, requisitions were directed exclusively to Chopi areas.[28] Informants explained that only the Chopi didn't die or desert when working the *shibalo* sanitation brigades, but they were not sure why. Municipal records reveal an increasing number of communications about sanitation with Zavala circumscription, which would suggest a focus on Zavala-area Chopis. SNI records corroborate the pattern, at least by 1923, when thirty workers who had been sent from Massinga to work sanitation were repatriated with a note: "Your offices have already been informed that the only natives who will do for the cleaning of the city are those from Zavala. . . . kindly see to it that in the future only workers from Zavala be sent to [the sanitation firm] to avoid repatriations and complaints from the requisitioning firm."[29] The Chopi were no longer simply the preferred workers, they had an exclusive.

Under the municipal contract, Carvalho and David could be fined if the sanitation work of sweeping and collecting human waste and garbage was carelessly or improperly handled. It is possible that Chopi workers soon realized that they could create a costly mess for the contractor. Indeed, there were many complaints against Carvalho and David until about the end of 1913.[30] Around the First World War a

Chopi street cleaner.

compromise seems to have been reached, and then maintained, when Paulino Santos Gil's company took over the sanitation contract from Carvalho and David in 1918. Sanitation work became exclusively Chopi, and prison labor was dropped. The sanitation brigades may have brokered the contractor's need to have the work done carefully to avoid heavy fines, against their own desire to gain greater control over the work process and exploit it to their own ends. How was this done?

Informants indicated that sanitation brigades worked a task-oriented system. Each brigade cooperated to complete the work quickly, and thus maximize their leisure hours. They then used their leisure time for a variety of income generating activities to earn cash to spend in town or to add to their paycheck upon repatriation. They took on odd jobs as gardeners or cleaning men, made baskets and hand crafts to sell, and eventually began to sell items they had picked up in people's trash, and then cleaned and repaired. The sanitation brigades also developed a system of tipping. They took particular care with the slops and trash of homeowners who showed their appreciation with a weekly tip, and managed to overturn the buckets of those who didn't. By controlling the work process, Chopi sanitation workers gained access to marketable trash, and added income from tips, crafts sales, and opportunities for moonlighting—all of which considerably enhanced their *shibalo* wage packet.

The poor quality of room and board, which comprised an important component of the sanitation *shibalos'* wage packet, remained an issue of contention between the

Chopi workers and the municipal sanitation contractors from Carvalho and David to Paulino Santos Gil. In 1949 Lourenço Marques City Hall took over from Santos Gil when again the complaints by workers about living conditions and complaints by citizens about sanitation threatened scandal and fines.[31]

In Mussongueia's case, *shibalo* workers did not control task management, and their efficiency brought only negative rewards. The sanitation brigades struggled to gain control over their work situation and manipulate it to their advantage. Their strategy made being a *mwamu cholo* more advantageous. Exclusivity in this case had its reward.[32] In the Chopi case, their commitment to rural investments convinced them to make the best of regular periods of urban *shibalo*. Both of these case studies consider Africans working gang labor at a distance from European overseers or employers. Were conditions and strategies different in domestic service, where individual or small groups of African servants and their European "masters" worked in much more intimate contact? What patterns of domestic servant mobility, earnings, benefits, and skill levels emerged for Lourenço Marques in this period? Were the patterns similar to those in other sectors of the African wage labor force?

"Well Served"

Domestic Service in the Urban Context

Beginning in the late nineteenth century, domestic service was a growing, typically urban employment category. It was an important component in the making of a "white man's town," and since it was often a young Mozambican's first experience with "work for the white people," it was also a formative category. In a society that tied privilege to race and provided few channels for Africans to challenge white privilege, whim, and authority, the intimacy of domestic service placed young domestics within reach of white privilege but also dangerously close to whim and authority. The peculiar interdependency of domestic service, where work and living space were shared by employer and employee, produced a potent mix of possibilities. Some employers abused the trust and the persons of their domestics, and some domestics abused the trust and the persons of their employers. Africans and Europeans also found that domestic service allowed them to get beyond at least some of the social protocol that divided the races, and to form some kind of interpersonal relationships. It is difficult to evaluate the balance of positive and negative relationships in domestic service, but clearly both existed.

The number of domestic servants in the city increased rapidly from the turn of the century. As a group, domestics comprised an increasing portion of the urban labor force. The increase in domestic servants was most closely related to the growth of the city's European population. In 1891, the European population of Lourenço Marques was under a thousand. By 1900 it had more than doubled, and by 1904 it doubled again. Immigration then slowed, with the economic slump from 1907 to 1910. According to the census of 1912, over five thousand Europeans lived in the city. The 1927 census, the last for this period, put the white population at just over nine thousand.[33]

By 1904, when the majority labor force was employed in large construction projects at the port, domestic servants comprised about one-sixth of the urban labor force. By 1912 the number of domestic servants in town had increased ten-fold over

the estimates for 1899,[34] and by 1933 they comprised about one-third of the voluntary wage labor force in town.[35] As we shall see, the availability of domestic laborers was related to changing opportunities elsewhere in the urban economy. In order to prevent the movement of domestic servants to higher-wage casual labor, employers lobbied the government to tie domestics ever more firmly to their jobs.[36] Although domestic servants experienced increasing efforts to control their mobility and earning power, as long as demand for both unskilled casual labor and semi-skilled domestic workers was high, they remained among the most independent workers in the city.

Domestic labor, like port labor, included a full range of skills and work situations. By far the most common service position was a live-in general household worker, called a *criado* or *criada*.[37] Their tasks included home and yard sweeping, running errands, and basic housecleaning tasks accomplished under supervision. *Criados* were typically young, inexperienced boys. They received the lowest cash wages of any urban worker. Laundry workers, called *mainato* or *mainata*, could be either live-in or day workers. They washed and ironed clothing and earned slightly higher wages than the *criado*.[38] Domestic labor also included well-paid skilled jobs, such as chefs or children's nurse (*criada de criança*). Few African girls worked as general servants, and African women preferred to take in laundry rather than work as a *mainata* in an employer's home. Although women were often preferred as children's nurses, they remained a minority in that category.[39]

Throughout the city, servant wages varied by skill, household, and work situation. Servants in households, boarding houses, restaurants, and hotels could earn quite different salaries for similar work. First, the income and social standing of the employer had a direct impact on the employee's wages and benefits. Servants working in African or Asian households in the Ximpamanine area of town were not necessarily expected to know Portuguese or English. Their wages and room and board benefits were considerably less than those of servants hired by upper-class French or English households in the Polana or Ponta Vermelha neighborhoods. Second, the top wages paid to skilled domestic workers, such as the wage earned by an experienced cook or a trusted child's nurse in a wealthy household, were on par with the highest wages available to Africans in the city, such as those paid to stevedores at the port complex. Cash wages received by ordinary domestics were generally on the low end of the urban African wage scale. The cash wages typical for unskilled, newly arrived young boys and girls were usually the lowest paid to voluntary workers in the city, and could be even lower than wages received by *shibalo*.[40]

Domestic servants experienced both the relative disadvantage of low cash wages and the relative advantage of stable employment and generally better levels of room and board. In the first decade of the century, for example, 15$00 was a common monthly cash wage for an unskilled domestic. At that time, a hod carrier who worked a twenty-six-day month without overtime earned twice that cash wage, or about 30$00, but had no right to room and board.[41] The value of room and board figured into the wage packet of both *shibalo* laborers and domestics, but *shibalo* earned only about 9$00 cash per month. Volunteer hod carriers could choose to spend their cash wages on room and board to suit their budget and preference, whereas domestics

and *shibalo* had to accept whatever the employer provided. The advantage for the domestic was that the quality of room and board was unlikely to drop as sharply as the purchasing power of a casual laborer's cash wages in an inflationary cycle. The European population usually earned more inflation-resistant, gold-based currency, thus sheltering the household and food budgets that domestics depended upon for their meals. Finally, employment opportunities for casual laborers diminished rapidly in a declining economy from the late 1920s, but employers typically resisted firing their servants because of its immediate impact on their quality of life.[42]

The urban domestic service sector was characterized, nonetheless, by high turnover. Some patterns suggest the linkage of city-wide shortages of domestic labor with greater availability of unskilled casual labor opportunities. Shortages were noted in 1898-1899, 1903-1906, 1911, and 1915-1916. Except for 1915-1916, those dates coincided with expansion of port and rail construction or increased transit handling.[43] It is possible that at least some young men took advantage of such opportunities to leave domestic service for the higher cash wages of casual labor. The shortage of 1915-1916 was probably due to the threat of military conscription in the town and region just prior to Portugal's entry into World War I. Throughout the century, news of a military draft was enough to clear the town of any and all Africans who were not absolutely certain that their job would exempt them from conscription.[44] By the early 1920s, the jump from domestic service to casual labor lost some of its appeal as inflation cut into the value of cash wages.

"Well Served"

Relationships in Black and White

From 1921 to 1930 [age 11 to 20] I worked as a domestic servant for Sr. Lopes, who was a machinist at the railway. He was a bachelor, so I got his food from the restaurant at a boarding house every day and brought it to him at work. I did all the work around his house. The job didn't pay anything to speak of, but since he treated me well I stayed with him. He was like a father to me. In 1930, when Sr. Lopes left for a visit to his homeland, I was seized for *shibalo*.

Valente Pande Nhabanga[45]

What did European employers and African employees expect from domestic service relationships? What did employers mean when they claimed to have been "well served?" What did Africans mean when they recalled that their experience served them well? How did domestic service compare with other urban employment options with regard to labor demand, mobility, wages, skill levels, risks, and benefits? For this early period, the empirical evidence available to answer such questions is thin. Some answers suggest themselves between the lines, and they dovetail with empirical data from the later period.

In some ways Africans and Europeans wanted the same thing from a domestic service relationship, but from different perspectives. Skill, trust, and loyalty were high on each list. Young domestic servants typically hoped to gain experience with the language, protocol, and geography of urban life, and to acquire marketable skills. Servants had to trust that their employer would not find an excuse on the twenty-ninth day of their first thirty-day pay period to fire them and deprive them of a month's wages. They also had to hope that, should their employer move or be transferred, she or he would provide the references or networks necessary to find a new placement in the best areas.

Employers also hoped that employees would quickly acquire the skills to complete the tasks at hand in the manner agreed to and the time allotted. Employers had to trust that an employee would not take advantage of access to the household, receive a month's pay, take what she or he wanted without warning or authorization, and disappear. Finally, should their employee decide to seek more remunerative work elsewhere, employers hoped that she or he could help find an appropriate replacement. From both the employer and employee's perspectives, a domestic service work relationship had equal potential for success or disaster. An employer's perspective was provided by a woman in late nineteenth-century Lourenço Marques who felt herself, on the whole, "well served" by African domestics.

Rose Monteiro was a woman quite out of her time. She lived alone in what was still open countryside in the Polana bluffs of Lourenço Marques in the 1880s and 1890s, and went about her business collecting and cataloging butterflies and other flora and fauna. She much preferred her scientific work to household chores, and could not do both successfully. The daily reproduction of a household in Lourenço Marques was a time-consuming task. Someone had to draw fresh water daily, collect firewood, plant, tend, gather, or purchase food crops, process foods, and gather fodder for domestic small stock. Monteiro hired a whole range of local people to do such tasks.[46]

Monteiro hired women to take out her laundry, and quite approved of their technique of smashing the linen on stones "until thoroughly clean." Unfortunately the women were also passionate pipe smokers so the laundry sometimes came back "with holes burnt through many folds by tobacco falling from pipes."[47] She hired young boys to get her water, but again they sometimes spent half the morning visiting around the fountain only to return with a broken water jug. Throughout the colonial era, domestic service was predominantly a male occupation. Monteiro explained, "The small boys and girls soon learn to wait at table very nicely, but the girls will not keep in service when they are beginning to grow to womanhood—they think it derogatory to their dignity, and prefer the regular woman's work of tilling the fields."[48]

Although Monteiro judged herself generally "well served," her attitudes toward domestic servants reflected the arrogance of the era. She considered them hopelessly slow and unreliable, and alleged that "many" were "habitual thieves and liars."[49] She paid her servants between three and thirty shillings per thirty-day month, according to their age, experience, and her estimate of the value of their service. However, she claimed, "at the end of perhaps 25 days the boy will show you a piece of string with 30 knots or a piece of wood with thirty notches cut in and declare his month is finished."[50] Her counter-strategy was a ticket system similar to that used in the mines–she gave her servant a ticket at the end of every day's service and upon accumulation of thirty tickets, he or she was paid.[51] She also found it odd that servants formed no attachment to their "masters," showed no gratitude, and would leave without warning for reasons she never quite understood.[52]

Although Monteiro's personal situation was unusual for the era, her anecdotes about domestic labor reflected attitudes and issues commonly expressed in European sources of the early twentieth century.[53] Servants should be skilled, willing, omnipresent, and "seen but not heard." Young servants were not to play, older servants were not to drink or be sexually active, unless "the master" wanted to play with the young servant or enter into a sexual relationship.[54] The principal concerns of employing classes, and the special situation of youthful employees emerged concisely in Junod's classic dialogues:

When I ring the bell, come to me. . . . Take away the plates and clean them well. . . . If you break the plates, you will have to pay. . . . Wash your hands. Clean my boots. . . . Don't waste time looking at your self in the looking glass. . . . Put on a clean cloth and come and play with the child. If you play with the boys, your companions, I shall beat you. . . . Put the child to bed and quiet it. You can love him in your heart, but don't kiss him.[55]

A lead editorial in a city newspaper in 1911, entitled "The Rights of Monsieur Houseboy in View of the Needs of White People," echoed the typical mix of vulnerability, anger, and arrogance employers expressed toward domestic servants. The classic complaint was always that one could not live with servants, and one could not live without them:

For a long time the local press has advocated that steps be taken against the despotism of the Messieurs, the Negro servants, who in this city enjoy the enviable prerogative of doing exactly as they please without any regard to discipline by the inhabitants who, unhappily, depend upon them. In Lourenço Marques they gather in obvious vagrancy under the complacent eyes of Monsieur Police person and other authorities. Mornings in the market one often sees large groups of Africans rubbing elbows with whites . . . but if any head of household asks an African if he would like a job, the immediate response is either negative or he demands a wage of *"cume quinhenta"* which in the White man's language means $500 *reis* per day. But what does this houseboy know how to do [for $500 *reis* per day]? Nothing![56]

Employers may have felt that domestics were overpaid, underskilled, arrogant tyrants who, whenever they felt themselves mistreated, simply quit to live at large in the municipality as thieves; servants obviously saw their situation in a different light. They worked long hours, and their cash wages, when computed on an hourly basis, were much lower than those earned by casual labor at the port. Domestics performed exacting or tiresome chores under relatively tight supervision, and were vulnerable to fraudulent allegations by employers seeking to avoid paying their wages. With no viable channels to challenge a totally unfounded allegation by an employer, innocent domestic laborers could suffer a talking-down, a beating, a prison term, or even deportation.[57] They clearly saw the relationship from a different perspective, and took appropriate steps to protect and advance their interests.

Africans commonly referred to domestic labor as working "back yards." *Quintal* (pl. *quintais*) is the Portuguese word for back yard. Domestics usually lived in small quarters in the household's *quintal*, and many of their cleaning, gathering, and processing tasks were carried out there. Domestic servants lived and worked in their employer's back yard, but despite their employer's best efforts, they were not isolated. Time spent in daily lines at the public fountains, local bakeries, and urban markets in pursuit of the household's daily bread, food, and water provided servants extensive opportunities to make contacts and exchange information on jobs, wage rates, and the like. Junod's and Monteiro's complaints about domestics "playing" with companions, gathering at the market, or "visiting" at the fountain were common, and employers realized that such communication was not idle. Conditions of employment, wage rates, and job mobility were delicate issues for domestics, and every bit of market intelligence a servant gathered helped him or her navigate in dangerous waters.

Recruitment relied upon patron-client networks because of the intimacy of the workplace. Although some people got their jobs simply through the "anda procura" method (walking door to door asking if anyone needed a domestic), most informants got their jobs in this period through friends, previous employers, or families.[58] Virtually all the best jobs were tapped through extensive personal networks. Patron relationships developed while in domestic service frequently served workers for future mobility. Domestic servants especially depended upon employer networks to find a new job if their employer was transferred or returned to Europe. João Ndoconga Machanga, for example, began work for a middle-class English-speaking family in Beira in 1906 when he was fifteen. Machanga got on well with the family, but in 1910 his employer was reassigned to South Africa. Before the employer left, he helped Machanga get a job as a *mainato* for the head of Shell Company, who lived in Lourenço Marques. Employment in the household of English-speaking business executives was an enviable situation, possible only through personal connections.[59]

The essential fact of domestic service from an African perspective was its potential as an entry-level occupation, or bridging occupation. It enabled a very young person to enter the urban economy with a place to live and something to eat. It provided an opportunity to bridge the gap from rural to urban, to familiarize oneself with city ways, different languages, different sections of town, and the range of alternative jobs available. It could be an opportunity to prepare oneself for another job that required more skills and perhaps better connections. Indeed, domestic servants often put up with the long hours and demanding chores for just such reasons. If everything worked to their advantage, they could exploit domestic service as an education.

Domestics learned *Português do quintal* (backyard or kitchen Portuguese), which served as the city's vehicular language. The more ambitious servants attended night school, seeking to complete the fourth-class certificate that was the prerequisite qualification for the entry-level good jobs in civil service. Just as important for entry and promotion in good jobs were the patron networks cultivated among employers and colleague networks developed by servants as they chatted in the daily lines at the bakery and water fountain. Domestic service was a kind of internship in the ways of life and making a living in Lourenço Marques. In that context, domestics might consider the difference in cash wages between their work and volunteer labor in the city as a kind of tuition. At some point, however, servants either had made maximum use of the internship and were ready to move on, or had arrived at an age where higher cash wages had more value than the potential network or education contacts.

Valente Pande Nhabanga was one of many informants who recalled his employer had been "like a father" to him.[60] Nhabanga and Sr. Lopes had many years together, and despite his low pay, Nhabanga gained familiarity with the city and skill in an important vehicular language. The protection domestic service afforded healthy young African males was apparent to Nhabanga when he was seized for *shibalo* soon after his employer left.

Manuel dos Santos Tembe worked as a domestic for a childless Portuguese couple at about the same time (1920–1934). Like Nhabanga, he began as a young boy, and developed a close relationship with his employers. In Tembe's case, the couple also treated him "like a son."[61] When the couple prepared to take home leave for a year in Portugal, they proposed to Tembe's parents that he accompany them for the year to take advantage of the better schools available in Lisbon. Neither Tembe nor his parents doubted that he would be well treated and that the opportunity would serve him well. Tembe's parents eventually agreed that he should go, but as the time came to leave the young Tembe was overcome with fear of homesickness. He finally asked to be left behind, and the couple left without him.[62] Both Nhabanga and Tembe had positive experiences from domestic service. Both ended their service when their employers returned to the metropole. The other typical closure in a satisfactory domestic service relationship was for the employee to seek the employer's assistance finding higher-wage employment when they began to assume adult responsibilities or aspired to marriage.

About the time Mussongueia first came to the "white man's town," the Portuguese were experimenting with urban labor controls. Over the next two decades, the major components of the *indigenato* were articulated in law, and the administrative and police systems necessary to implement them were put in place. The process did not go forward uncontested. By 1933, in the most discouraging period of the depression, however, it seemed that the process had broken the urban African spirit.

4

The Components and Costs of Inequality

> It is no longer by one's merits that a person's worth is judged, it is by one's color. What one needs in order to compete for a position today is to be white.... If you are colored, live on a few crumbs of bread—the land is for the whiteman.
>
> *O Africano*, 7 April 1909

Throughout the colonial era, the Portuguese colonial administration and the African population of Lourenço Marques clashed around the definition, organization, and control of labor. Between the late nineteenth century and the depths of the Depression, both the colonial administration's strategies toward African labor and African strategies toward employment changed markedly. This chapter presents an overview of the articulation of the *indigenato*, the implications for Africans, and the struggles that erupted around the process of articulation during the Republican era. It considers the intellectual and political struggles the *indigenato* raised in Lourenço Marques and beyond. Chapters 5 details the issues raised here in a case study of the key port and railway sector.

Prelude to the *Indigenato*

In the late nineteenth century, private employers in Lourenço Marques relied on professional recruiters for their labor supplies. Recruiters invariably fared far better than the laborers. In 1889 private recruiters typically received 11$700 *reis* per worker contracted, while the workers, if they were paid at all, received only $225 *reis* per day (rpd). In short, recruiters' fees were equivalent to nearly two month's wages.[1] Once the recruiter had received the fee, the worker became the employer's concern. One of the employers' chief concerns in this period was to keep the recruit at work long enough to recoup the value of the recruitment fee.

That was apparently no easy task. High recruitment fees and equally high levels of worker escape were the major complaints among all employers. The key complaint among the labor force was nonpayment. By the first decade of the twentieth century, Mozambique's Governor Freire de Andrade claimed that recruitment speculation, frauds and labor brokerage were "a regular business undertaken by many individuals who profit from it at the expense of Africans whom they frequently do not pay."[2] Workers could become mere pawns in a contest among labor speculators and employers. Their principal recourse in such situations was to escape, thus sacrificing the chance that they might actually be paid wages for the days they had worked prior to escape.[3]

The colonial government employed more direct and forceful means, but they did not always succeed. In 1882, for example, Governor Aguiar hoped to gather sufficient labor for his pressing public works agenda by ordering the summary arrest of all seemingly idle Africans in town on drunkenness or other charges. Within hours of his order, most of the urban labor force, employed or otherwise, had fled into the countryside.[4] Between the 1870s and 1910 the government periodically resorted to surprise round-ups, but often with similar results.[5]

In 1892 the British consul in Lourenço Marques, Mr. Smith-Delacour, suggested the developing system had changed somewhat:

> When the Public Works Department has work for two or three hundred men . . . they are detained here without food. . . . but with the promise of the ordinary wage of one to four shillings a day. After two or three months the men are sent back to their country with a few shillings each. . . . I have known of cases where the men received nothing at all.[6]

A decade later an official in Lourenço Marques described state and municipal labor recruitment as the "usual practice" of commandeering and summarily sentencing Africans to prison labor on public works for ill-defined offenses such as disobedience, drunkenness, vagrancy, "morals," disorder, and petty theft.[7] He found no legal justification for the "usual practice," nor any legal definition of criminal vagrancy. He wanted such arrests continued, of course, "for were it to be abandoned the safety of the city would be gravely prejudiced, and if each offender had the privilege of a lawyer, evidence, testimony, witnesses, etc., the state would have insufficient personnel to prosecute, and these criminals would go free."[8] He felt summary judgment without recourse to defense was appropriate treatment for African residents of Lourenço Marques, but he wanted it sanctioned with a "proper law."

By the turn of the century, Portuguese settlers pressured the state to take over the labor recruitment system to diminish their expenses from high recruitment fees and labor speculation, and to coordinate a registration and control system that would curb escapes. The colonial state undertook to satisfy settlers and bureaucrats through the regulation of recruitment and the transformation of "usual practice" into "proper law." The vehicle for that transformation was the *indigenato*. Articulation of the *indigenato*, however, inspired a hornet's nest of resistance and conflict.

Sorting out the "Natives"—Differentiation and Solidarity

The first initiative to promulgate a "proper law" to legitimate the "usual practice," was the *Regulamento de Serviçais e Trabalhadores Indígenas* (RSTI) of September 1904.[9] As we have seen in Mussongueia's case, the regulation targeted domestic servants and day laborers at the port, requiring them to purchase a *chapa* for five hundred *reis*. The *chapa* fee was the equivalent of a usual day's pay. Workers had to wear the *chapa* to confirm that they worked only one job and worked that one regularly. The goal was to ensure that these critical workers stayed on the job so that port traffic and European households could carry on without interruption.

The law turned sensible strategies among hod carriers into criminal offenses punishable by forced labor. Hod carriers typically investigated the whole range of waterfront jobs for the day, and then tried to sign on for the best-paid or least dangerous job. Others developed flexible day plans, such as working the coal lines in the cool morning, running rickshaws at the noonday rush, and weaving baskets for sale in the heat of the afternoon. Under the new laws, such strategies could all be construed as vagrancy. The law was framed in an already familiar ideology: "all *indígenas* of the Portuguese overseas provinces are subject to the moral and legal obligation to seek to acquire thorough work, the means that they lack to live and to improve their social condition."[10] The moral and legal obligation to work was defined to suit the European-dominated government and employing classes, not the *indígenas* who wanted to live and prosper.

There were other problems. At the turn of the century, the "usual practice" of arbitrary arrests and round-ups worked because conquest was still fresh in everyone's mind, the town was still fairly small, and it was obvious to the police which Africans they could harass and which they couldn't. By the Republican era, however, that was less the case. The ideological focus of civilizing Africans to their moral obligation to work collided head-on with the inconvenient reality in Lourenço Marques. By Portuguese middle-class standards, there were a large number of Negroes who were clearly civilized, hardworking, and moral, and there were an equally large number of Portuguese who were uncouth, immoral, and unemployed.

Since middle-class people did not work as domestics or hod carriers at the turn of the century, the first law did not effect them directly. By the end of the decade, however, efforts to subordinate African labor as a whole met sharp resistance from the city's black middle class. African office workers, merchants, proprietors, and the like were exempted from legal subordination on class criteria, but they had to confirm that exemption. The state soon dropped the class-based exemption tactic, opting for articulation of a new category of citizenship it hoped would accomplish the same ends. Africans defined as *indígenas* were subject to the full burden of colonial labor and civic controls that defined them as subordinate. Africans who acquired the newly articulated status of *assimilado*, however, were supposed to be full citizens of African heritage. The fact that their race qualified them for the privilege of buying and wearing a document to demonstrate their citizenship suggests only the most obvious irony in the assimilation morass.[11]

The Assimilation Morass

The piecemeal development of *indigenato* components and the struggles they tripped off illustrate the differential consequences for urban Africans, and the internal divisions those encouraged. *Assimilados* and indígenas struggled with their subordinate status, but they often fought distinct battles and sometimes at cross-purposes. Although the main focus here is on the majority labor force who were *indígenas*, it must be clear from the outset that *assimilados* and *indígenas* were but two halves of a whole. The subordination of the majority population on the basis of race and its justification in terms of Portugal's "civilizing" mission required both categories. Although the status of *assimilado* was proffered as a confirmation of the black middle class, the hollowness of the claim that such status conferred unfettered citizenship on the black middle class was obvious from the outset. The battle lines were drawn, and the issue of citizenship became central to the differential engineering of inequality for all people of African heritage.

Local people tended to be wealthier and better educated than most immigrants. Of the first ninety-three people to pay 3$75 for an assimilation certificate between 1917 and 1920, fifty-one were born in Lourenço Marques and four hailed from across the bay in Catembe. In short, just under 60 percent of the original *assimilados* were locals.[12] But the assimilation process also set the local black middle class apart from others of their social class by the fact of their race. Indeed the *indigenato* ensured that the black middle class was disadvantaged in relation to ordinary Portuguese immigrants.

The attitude among local middle-class Africans toward the promulgation of assimilation was best captured by João (dos Santos) Albasini (Nwandzengele) one of Mozambique's leading twentieth-century intellectuals.[13] Albasini's grandfather was an important Portuguese trader in the area, a colleague of Diocleciano Fernando das Neves. His mother was from a leading family of one of the city's most important African clans. Beginning in 1908, João Albasini and his brother José Albasini (Bandana) collaborated, editing and directing publication of *O Africano* and its successor paper, *O Brado Africano*. Until his death in 1922, João Albasini was the principal editor and writer. Although José Albasini also contributed articles and editorials, most of his attention went to keeping the endeavor financially solvent. The paper, the organ of the Grêmio Africano, reflected the interests of predominantly middle class, Catholic, Portuguese-speaking Africans and Afro-Europeans living in Lourenço Marques.[14]

João Albasini criticized the formulation of the *indigenato* through a companion series of editorials that highlighted the dual purpose of the legislation. His column "Vozes de Burro" (The Braying of an Ass) addressed the *indígena* component and "A Tal Portaria" (That Law!) the assimilation legislation. His approach in "Vozes de Burro" was that the legal concept of *indígena* was racist as articulated, and that it was hopelessly flawed as a labor regulation. With regard to the assimilation component, Albasini demanded: "Portugal deports her unclean, illiterate *kubvanas* [rabble] here to live off rural African women, must we assimilate to be their equal?"[15] Furthermore, he argued, "If Africans have to pay [for an assimilation document] to prove they are civilized and fit to mix with whites, why not tax whites who are uncivilized and live in common law arrangements with Africans?"[16]

In some ways, the *indigenato* diminished divisions within the urban African community by incorporating all persons of African heritage into subordinate status, regardless of class, age, gender, or language. In other ways, it deepened the existing divisions. The *indigenato* forged a closer alignment of privilege and vulnerability with citizen status. It did so by linking benefits and privileges to citizen status as part of the strategy to deny them to *indígenas*. In a piecemeal fashion, beginning in the first decade of the century, the whole range of worker benefits were related to citizen status: the right to be paid in inflation-resistant currency, family bonuses, access to apprentices, the right to organize, and the like. Although *assimilados* certainly did not enjoy the same benefits and privileges as European citizens, their status protected

João dos Santos Albasini.

José Francisco Albasini.

Estácio Dias.

Grêmio Africano leadership, 1935.

them from the heaviest burdens of *indígena* status. None of the middle-class Africans in Lourenço Marques aspired to demonstrate equality through assimilation. They found the concept repulsive and humiliating, but it was eventually regarded by *assimilados* and *indígenas* alike as the best of a bad deal.[17] The changed perspective reflected the increasing burden of *indígena status*.

The currency crisis around the First World War was the catalyst that made assimilation almost irresistible for Africans who were in the position to qualify for it. The strong economic links between South Africa and Lourenço Marques had encouraged widespread use of the pound sterling as well as local currency. Until 1914 exchange rates between the pound sterling and gold-based Portuguese currency remained fairly stable, but the situation then changed dramatically. With the declaration of the Republic, Portuguese bank notes, *reis* (royals), were replaced with *escudo* (shields). The *escudo* got off to an inauspicious start. Between 1914 and 1919 the value of the pound against the *escudo* nearly doubled, and by 1920 it had quadrupled. By 1924 the pound was twenty-four times its 1914 *escudo* value![18]

Commodities not commonly exchanged directly for pounds were also effected by the crisis, and the cost of living in Lourenço Marques increased sharply. Wartime disruption of food and consumer supplies exacerbated the situation. Between 1918 and 1920 prices for staples such as rice, beans, potatoes, soap, and charcoal more than doubled. Corn flour and cooking oil prices increased 70 to 80 percent by 1917.[19] The problem was even more severe among workers and the aspiring petty bourgeoisie, whose normal expenditures also included shoes and Western-style clothing.[20]

Commodity Prices in Lourenço Marques in the Postwar Era[21]

Commodity	1918 Price	1920 Price
Rice (kilo)	$41	1$00
Beans (kilo)	$21	$50
Potatoes (kilo)	$09	$34
Soap (bar)	$50	1$20
Charcoal (bunch)	$07	$16

In this context, the state tied payment of salaries in the more stable gold-based currency to civil status. Paper-based currency was not acceptable for most expenditures in Lourenço Marques, including payment of one's taxes. Workers who received paper-currency wages, therefore, had to sell them to buy gold-based currency, clearly a costly disadvantage. Portaria Provincial 1507 of May 1920 finally reserved payment of gold-based currency to "*não-indígenas*" (non-natives or citizens).[22]

Privilege is a relative phenomenon. Although the linkage of important economic criteria to citizenship status increasingly set *assimilados* apart from *indígenas*, a further set of equally important economic and social criteria continued to set *assimilados* apart from Portuguese. Although people's appreciation of the gradation of privilege was usually closely related to their position in the pecking order, the profound racism and cultural arrogance at the base of the *indigenato* was apparent to everyone.

Both categories of the *indigenato* were shackles. People resented shackles, but aspired to the limited privileges that were increasingly firmly tied to the assimilation shackle. Raul Bernardo Honwana explained his decision to assimilate in 1931 in those terms. "People assimilated more to avoid *shibalo*, native military service . . . in short, to escape the complete absence of minimum civil rights."[23] When Manuel João dos Santos Tembe assimilated just before the statute was abolished in 1960, he did so "not to become white or to be like the whites. Look at the color of my skin! I'm black. No, I assimilated to get a little ahead, to earn a bit better for my family."[24]

When the assimilation statutes were first implemented, mulattos with powerful friends or relatives still living in the city were sometimes able to have their situation "fixed" without filing for assimilation status, whereas most Africans could not. Mulattos were undeniably in a better position to ignore the law quietly, whereas Africans had to suffer the humiliation of petitioning for assimilation if they wanted to salvage their jobs and salaries. João Albasini persevered in his rejection of what he called "the collar of assimilation." He was too closely connected to important political figures to be denied hard-currency wages or to be harassed socially, but even he paid a price for sticking to his principles in exclusion from the considerable privileges of tenured state employment.[25]

Lingering family patronage links are suggested by the fact that almost all the people who took out assimilation status between 1917 and 1919 were African or Afro-Asian.[26] The first important split among middle-class Africans dates from this period, and closely reflects African and mulatto lines.[27] Although most direct evidence suggests that social tensions around race triggered the split, it is probable that economic tension and mutual recriminations stemming from the assimilation controversy exacerbated the problem.[28]

Subsequent legislation reinforced the divisions: apprenticeships, union membership, wage ceilings, and employment in certain job categories were all eventually tied to non-native status.[29] Such laws not only firmly excluded the majority population from upward mobility in the labor force, they encouraged middle-class leaders to distance themselves as much as necessary to gain a "little better treatment." *Assimilados* and some mulattos received only "a little better" treatment, and neither group enjoyed unfettered mobility within the labor force. Depending upon one's color, one received more or fewer "crumbs of bread," but increasingly the land was indeed "for the whiteman."[30]

The Indigenato—Getting Nothing for Something

It was one thing to legislate urban African males into economic disadvantage, but it was another to implement such laws. For about the first decade (1904–1914), the application of the RSTI was halting and uneven because the town's police force was inadequate to the task. Employers and the black press complained, albeit from different perspectives, that the police were more concerned with collecting the five hundred *reis* registration fees or the fines for failure to register than with seeing to it that workers went to and stayed at work.[31]

The police could only really see that workers worked when there were sufficient police and administrative cadres to cover the town. The collection of fees and fines, what the African press called the "*caça de quinhenta*," or the hunt for the five hundred *reis* (*quinhenta*) fee, eventually financed extension of the necessary police and administrative cadres. In 1908 the RSTI cost the town as much to implement as it brought in, but two years later it generated a regular surplus that was applied to expanding and strengthening the labor control bureaucracy. The oppressed paid their oppressor's salary and contributed to the development of a more effective system of labor coercion.[32] As we've seen, a companion process of funding the extension of labor coercion was already underway with drunkenness fines and labor sentences, and the two combined in interesting ways.

As it became increasingly clear that the battle against registration of African workers was being lost, the Grêmio press urged that a portion of the funds generated from labor registration, vagrancy, and drunkenness fines be diverted from investment in police and labor control systems to the development of housing, health care, and social services for urban Africans. If Africans were to subsidize the municipal budget through such fees and fines, they should expect at least some benefit from those revenues. Urban Africans fought hard to secure municipal funds for clean water, paved streets, and public transportation for their neighborhoods, but often only to see their minimal, hard-won gains outstripped by the pace of labor migration.[33] As it was, they argued, the African community received nothing for their money.

In 1912–1913 the municipality tried to crack down on the most common worker resistance strategy—the evasion of labor registration. They staged a series of raids into African neighborhoods to check that workers had all purchased their *chapa*.[34] The timing could not have been worse: the devastating drought of 1911–1912 had driven desperate rural people into the already overextended urban neighborhoods to escape certain death in the countryside. The influx further strained relations between migrants and the African middle class due to competition for water and over-taxation of neighborhood services.

The upshot of the raids was that the municipality faced as much resistance from the African middle class, who were not required to buy a *chapa*, as from the workers who were. Although many urban workers had been paying their annual *chapa* fee since 1905, and the middle-class Africans also contributed taxes, fees, and fines, the urban African community felt they had precious little to show for these payments. The drought refugees made the marginal improvements in African neighborhoods appear insignificant. The generalized anger and fear sparked by the shock of the drought and the threat of *chapa* raids was captured in an extraordinary editorial published in O *Africano* under the pseudonym Nhlomulo, meaning pain or affliction. Nhlomulo made it clear that African tax moneys and "public labors" paid for white comforts, yet did not provide Africans with so much as a hole in which to rest when the state finally squeezed the last from their bodies. Despite friction within the urban African population, these *indigenato* raids promoted a sense of solidarity.

"Hunger," by Nhlomulo[35]
There is hunger, thirst, and death in the bush, and no work and no money, and the government turns the other way.

Perhaps the Africans won't just die without wondering where the people are who took their tax money and the sweat of their labor and gave them what in return? At least water to mitigate the thirst that these days the north wind turns monstrous and fatal?

Whites, nationals and foreigners, remember that you live in this city full of comforts, with water in abundance, with all kinds of foods, with electric light, good hard-surfaced roads, luxurious buildings, and convenient means of transportation! Remember, Europeans, that everything you enjoy today, everything that surrounds you originated in black sweat. The sweat of those blacks who are hungry and thirsty and are dying after having contributed to all these benefits which only you are able to enjoy—they paid for it with their hut tax.

Yet you do not give them jobs, you do not distribute food to them, you do not furnish them water, you do not even provide a hole in which to bury them. Because the whites flee from blacks as soon as the black has no money to pay you who exploit him in all ways and for all he has, since he has no voice with which to cry out and demand those things to which he has a right. . . . Without blacks there is no gold in the mines, there is no labor for you whites, and there is no money with which to support you either.

In response to such anger, the RSTI was amended to earmark 80 percent of revenues from *chapa* fees to the construction of urban worker housing. The housing concession won through community solidarity, however, was developed in a manner that contributed to further differentiation among urban Africans. *Bairros*, planned family neighborhoods, were envisioned for local families, while barracks-style compounds were promoted as appropriate to house the male migrant population. Furthermore, local people would have some say in the investments designed for their benefit, but migrants would have none. Given their experience with conditions in the existing public works and railway compounds, migrant workers understandably had little enthusiasm for such housing.[36]

Although the principle that worker-generated funds should be reserved in part to build housing for working people had been conceded, Africans still had to face the problem of forcing the city to spend the allocated funds on African urban housing. By 1914 the *chapas* had generated over 14,000$00 *escudos*, but no plans had been set forth to invest it in worker housing or services. By January 1916, over 23,000$00 was in the till and still nothing had been done.[37] Wartime inflation rapidly diminished the value of the accumulated savings, and patience wore thin.

Albasini complained that the state always found it hard to spend money on projects that benefited Africans. He suggested that since the state was reluctant to invest in African workers, worker non-compliance with registration was a reasonable protest.[38] It is uncertain whether Albasini initiated the move toward non-compliance or whether he simply supported worker action once it was underway. Whatever the case, during 1915–1916 many workers refused to buy the chapa and were arrested. Although comparable statistics are not available for the period before 1915–1916, some 2,271 *indígenas* were arrested for infractions of the labor registration law that year. The chief of police claimed those arrests reflected a sharp rise in the level of non-compliance, and he blamed Albasini: "the number of infractions [of the RSTI] has increased greatly due to the campaign against the regulation taken up by the newspaper *O Africano*, with intentions known and supported by an official authority [Albasini] well known to Your Excellency.[39]"

Without comparable numbers for previous years, it is difficult to put the incident in proper perspective. By 1916 arrests dropped to 1,892, but that was still high for an urban African population of perhaps 10,000.[40] Although the police blamed Albasini and the Grêmio editors, they were not directly prosecuted. Workers who refused to register, however, made their statement and paid for it with *shibalo* or prison labor.

With the pressure of wartime inflation, *O Africano* shifted its attention from construction of worker housing and urban facilities to bread-and-butter issues. The paper published extensive and supportive coverage of worker salary grievances, strikes, resistance to tax increases, and demands for disability insurance, training, and promotion.[41] In the midst of the currency crisis in 1918, *shibalo* workers fled their jobs in record numbers. When some employers seemed puzzled by the exodus, since there had been "few complaints" regarding food, housing and work, Albasini dryly suggested the "inexplicable" shortage of labor might have something to do with the fact that the *shibalo* received their "ridiculous" wages in "useless" paper currency.[42] *O Africano* celebrated the New Year with the observation that "the government only cares if Africans work, not whether they get paid."[43] Albasini's exact role in this period remains unclear, but his paper expressed solidarity with the workers and voiced their substantial grievances.

Political and labor tension in Lourenço Marques was exacerbated by war, local revolts, and strikes. The colonial government responded to the combined crises with a declaration of martial law in early June 1917. Upon the arrival of Governor Álvaro de Castro on 20 June, *O Africano* began to display prominent blank spaces carved by the censor. To that extent, at least, the African middle class also paid a price for resistance.[44]

The incentives for caution were always much greater for those considered *indígenas*. That became especially clear between 1918 and 1924. Receipt of paper-currency wages was a heavy burden, but that burden was greatly exacerbated by the explosive demand for *shibalo* labor in the immediate postwar period. Postwar opportunities for settler agriculture greatly stimulated requisitions for agricultural *shibalo* in the most arduous and ill-paid conditions. Sul do Save census and labor conscription tallies for the early 1920s revealed that between one-sixth and one-third of the adult male population in most circumscriptions was taken for *shibalo*, and most of the other men were off working in South Africa. In 1923 a staggering 75 percent of the adult male population of the circumscription of Sabié was taken for *shibalo*.[45] The most secure strategy for avoiding *shibalo* was to engage in regular wage labor. Lourenço Marques was the only place where steady wage labor was available, and if one had a steady job in this period, it was a good idea to keep it, despite falling real wages.

By this period the principal dynamic that drove Mozambicans into wage labor and encouraged them to invest in their future as workers was the sustained threat and physical danger of *shibalo* conscription in their home area. Most Mozambicans did not become wage workers because they were proletarianized or could no longer sustain themselves given the quality of their lands—although that was undoubtedly the case for some. Rather, they worked for wages and strove to protect and enhance their position at the workplace because such an investment provided protection from *shibalo* conscription.[46]

By the early 1920s, the government was wary of the development of a common stand within the African urban population. Worker commitment to bread-and-butter issues and broad middle-class sympathy for those goals were threatening. The municipality may have tried to eclipse middle-class interest in workers' issues, at least in part, by undertaking construction of the first long-awaited *bairro*. The city built a relatively small housing and market complex at Ximpamanine, but the Bairro Ximpamanine was clearly not designed to accommodate the housing needs of *indígenas* who had paid the registration fees. The municipality set rents so high that the tidy new houses were only affordable to middle-class locals.[47]

By the early 1920s, the key components of the *indigenato* were in place and the most direct challenges by both *indígenas* and *assimilados* in Lourenço Marques had been blunted. The African middle class was divided over its own issues, and the death of João Albasini in 1922 further weakened elite leadership on labor issues. Although the Grêmio group managed to rally several initiatives in support of urban workers in the 1920s, they never regained the momentum they had under Albasini's leadership a decade earlier. The Depression-inspired policies of the late 1920s and early 1930s dealt the African middle class a blow from which its mature leadership never recovered.[48]

The Discourse of Inequality

The Ross Report

Throughout the century the contrast between Portugal's labor practice and law was periodically thrust into the international limelight by English-speaking "detractors," some of whom (British Consul Smith-Delacour and Marvin Harris) have already been introduced. When the English-speakers made a scene, Portuguese diplomats rallied to articulate an appropriate response. Portugal's usual response to an international challenge was multi-faceted. The public posture was typically a flurry of formal denials and rebuttals, followed by the publication of liberal labor legislation to emphasize the benefits Portugal's civilizing mission had brought to Africans through the discipline of paid, productive labor.

The legislation was frequently dismissed by Africans as meaningless window-dressing designed to mollify the English-speaking "detractors." In their view, the laws and denials were written "Para o Inglês Ver," for the English to see.[49] After the English saw them, the reports would be put to "sleep in a drawer" with all the other such reports. At a second level, however, the colonial administration often worked confidentially to correct some of the worst abuses and to camouflage those remaining. The development of the these public and confidential strategies enhanced the visibility of labor policy and practice in the written records. The periodic scandals, therefore, provide convenient chronological windows into the relationship between policy and practice. This period contained several such scandals, the most important of which was that caused by the Ross Report.

Thirty years after British Consul Smith-Delacour's complaint about Mozambique's slave-like labor system caused a minor scandal, the issue was rekindled by another foreigner. In 1925 Wisconsin sociologist Edward Alsworth Ross visited Angola and Mozambique. On the basis of the data gathered during that visit, Ross concluded that labor relations for Africans in the Portuguese colonies amounted to nothing less than a system of "state serfdom."[50] When Ross's *Report on Employment of Native Labor in Portuguese Africa* was submitted to the Temporary Slaving Commission of the League of Nations, it touched off a major scandal and evoked a flood of Portuguese rebuttals.[51] The Grêmio press always found such episodes amusing and fair game for ridicule. Its tongue-in-cheek editorial from an earlier scandal was typical of its attitude:

> Every now and then our English friends . . . accuse us of being slavers and other nasty things. We must truthfully say that slavery as such does not exist, at least in the Province of Mozambique. The police unconstitutionally seize peaceful citizens on the pretext of not having a *chapa*, and then rent us out to anyone needing labor. This isn't slavery. We don't really know what it is, but . . . it isn't slavery. Local administrators order citizens to be seized and rented to white planters. . . . Clearly this isn't slavery, just as it isn't slavery to imprison women on the pretext that their husbands owe their hut tax . . . etc. etc. But when foreigners . . . who are not familiar with our administrative processes see such things, . . . they think of it as slavery.[52]

Ross spent two weeks in Mozambique, traveling from Lourenço Marques to Inhambane and on to Beira.[53] Like Smith-Delacour, Ross concluded that Mozambicans worked in slave-like conditions, were subject to arbitrary conscription for unknown periods of time and uncertain remuneration, and could be posted to work in unstated locations. Although Ross's allegations were flatly and emphatically refuted by the Portuguese, virtually every one had been openly raised in the Grêmio press between 1909 and the mid-1920s: rural women were seized for roadwork and often sexually abused by police while working; *shibalo* discouraged the development of a skilled, settled labor force by conscripting rather than hiring skills and muscle; *shibalo* wages were sometimes paid, sometimes not paid, depending upon the local administrator, and *shibalo* pay (when received) was inadequate; the recruitment and distribution of labor provided opportunities for embezzlement and bribery by bureaucrats; African workers paid for bureaucratic corruption through lost wages; and finally, "sheer terrorism" was a fundamental tool for labor control.[54] Ross's findings may have been revelations at the international level, but they were hardly surprising to anyone who read the local newspaper.

Ross blamed some of these problems on the Portuguese Republican govern-ment. He alleged that the civil service was fairly stable and disciplined under the monarchy, but that high turnover and lack of long-term development strategies dur-ing the Republican era allowed incompetent, corrupt, and undisciplined administra-tors to develop profiteering schemes at the expense of the local population.[55] Labor abuse and bureaucratic corruption were clearly not introduced during the Republic.[56] Although some of the sweetheart deals of the turn-of-the-century build-ing boom survived the Republic, many of the large-scale development plans did not.[57] With less contract money available to support corrupt officials, some turned to opportunities in the bureaucratic niches, and the bureaucratization of labor supplies through *shibalo* provided a veritable Swiss cheese of niches.

The accumulated wages of workers who escaped or died before they received their pay and the deferred payment for *shibalo* labor amounted to a great deal of money in the hands of generally ill-paid bureaucrats. Payment seems to have stuck on their fingers en route to the pockets of the workforce. The *shibalo* system curbed recruiter competition, but the bureaucratic distribution of labor had generated its own costs in graft and bribery. Ross observed that "in the circumscriptions about Lourenço Marques perhaps nine-tenths of the boys get their stipulated pay. But off at a distance it is possible that nine-tenths of the boys get only a part of what is due them or nothing at all."[58]

A Portuguese official, J. A. Lopes Galvão, published a report reflecting the administration's view on African labor the same year the Ross report was published.[59] The contrast was stark. Lopes Galvão admitted the existence of forced labor only in the "recently occupied" interior. He concluded that the system that Ross deemed "state serfdom" actually contributed greatly to the "'natives'" quality of life because such jobs guaranteed clothing, food, minimum wages, hospital care, and the freedom to work. Settler opinion throughout Sul do Save denied forced labor and nonpayment, while emphasizing the moral benefits of laboring for the Portuguese. The area's most outspoken settler, the lawyer and newspaper editor Eduardo d'Almeida Saldanha, commonly argued that the *shibalo* labor system was progressive in comparison with indigenous labor practices, which he invariably characterized as the enslavement of African women by their menfolk.[60]

Settlers and colonial government officials publicly postured about the outra-geous allegations hurled by foreign detractors. At the same time, they generally ignored virtually identical allegations published in the African press. The colonial labor archives of the era, however, contained much more complete and damning evidence of labor abuse than anything uncovered by foreigners or published in the African press. The archives richly illustrated that *shibalo* were beaten, sexually assaulted, starved, sublet, exposed to the elements, underpaid, and swindled by pri-vate employers and government officials throughout this entire period.[61]

Moreover, the archival record revealed key spokesmen for Portugal's civilizing mission, like Saldanha, to be insufferable hypocrites. While Saldanha decried the enslavement of Mozambican women, he treated his own *shibalo* worse than slaves. From 1912 through 1928, workers chronically fled Saldanha's farms and urban build-ing projects. All Saldanha's properties enjoyed a reputation for unreasonable work hours, unfair pay deductions, bad food, mistreatment, and late payment of wages. Saldanha exploited every avenue to evade even the minimal legal protection due his labor force. He regularly requisitioned workers for the lower agricultural wage, but then employed them on his urban industrial projects to avoid paying workers the higher industrial *shibalo* wage.[62]

Saldanha was notorious for discounting *shibalo* contract days on the basis of rain breaks, lost tools, or incomplete tasks. By 1915 a SNI official complained: "Only Saldanha's workers always take seven months to complete a 180-day contract." He revealed his disgust with Saldanha's pettiness: "While Saldanha has done a great deal to develop agriculture, the SNI owes him nothing, . . . especially not forced labor!"[63] During the high inflation period of the early 1920s, Saldanha steadfastly refused to comply with the SNI's recommended higher minimum wage.[64] Conditions at Saldanha's Umbeluzi sugar plantation were so bad by the late 1920s that Africans from all over Sul do Save referred to it as the *matadouro*, the slaughterhouse.[65]

Local SNI officials resented Saldanha's abuses because they heightened resistance to all recruitment. But the SNI continued to supply him with *shibalo*, and turned a blind eye to his abuses because they were instructed to do so by higher authorities. Saldanha's political star seemed to rise when João Belo was appointed minister of the colonies after the military coup in 1926. Belo was Saldanha's principal patron and a similarly strong advocate of the "benefits" of labor for Portuguese settlers rather than in South Africa's mines. But Saldanha's star fell just s quickly as it rose. Belo died suddenly in January 1928. By April 1928, all further supplies of *shibalo* to Saldanha were cut off.[66] The last straw for the SNI officials was his failure to repatriate seventy-six *shibalo* conscripts from Mozambique district until six months after their contract was completed.[67]

Saldanha was only one of hundreds of settlers who regularly requisitioned conscript labor from the state throughout the first third of the twentieth century, despite the series of laws that both denied and legally prohibited the process. His case is highlighted because it revealed the sheer bankruptcy of Portuguese discourse on the *indigenato*.[68] It also illustrates the essential role of patronage in linking metropolitan policy and "administrative processes" in Mozambique. Patron ties were the glue that linked settlers with men in the corridors of power in Lisbon, and embezzlement opportunities in bureaucratic labor distribution were the glue that held corrupt colonial administrators to labor hungry settlers. At times metropolitan reforms struggled with colonial practice, but at other times one hand washed the other. "Administrative processes" and hypocritical discourse were designed to camouflage the relationships.

The annual report of the SNI director for the year Belo died fully documented the generalized use of *shibalo*. The director expressed exasperation with continuing forced labor requisitions and the resultant abuse of Mozambican labor in rural and urban areas. Despite Galvão's claim that forced labor existed only in "recently occupied" territories, the report revealed that just under twenty-nine thousand *shibalos* were supplied in Sul do Save in 1928, although "no law exists that openly permits that [the requisition of forced labor]."[69]

The 1928 report provided a useful benchmark—overview of the impact of the *indigenato* on this region during the last year of fairly normal economic activity before the great Depression settled over the area. The report revealed regional and hinterland patterns that directly affected urban labor strategies. It clearly supports the argument that men in Sul do Save turned increasingly to voluntary wage labor to escape arbitrary conscription in rural areas. Although the report itself questioned the validity of its census figures, it calculated the number of healthy adult males by subdistrict, the number of male emigrants to South Africa by sub-district, and the total

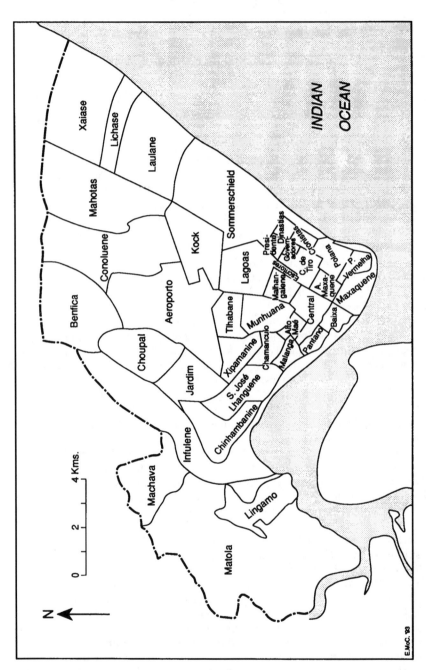

Sul do Save (showing Guijá, Magude, Inhambane, Chibuto, Xinavane and Manhica).

number of *shibalo* conscripts for agriculture and industry by district. Those figures corroborated the general sense of the archival and oral data. For example, they confirmed that emigration to South Africa was much more important in some subdistricts than others. Marrracuene, right next door to Lourenço Marques, had a relatively low proportion of its male population in South Africa, whereas the great majority of men from Maputo worked in South Africa.

Male Emigrants as a Percentage of the Healthy Adult Male Population by Circunscrição in 1928[70]

Marracuene	7	Manhica	58	Sabié	41
Maputo	85	Magude	52	Bilene	67
Mchope	26	Chibuto	64	Guijá	58
Vila João Belo	71				

The report also places the threat of *shibalo* conscription in a more relevant context. Whereas *shibalo* conscripts in 1928 comprised just over 4 percent of the total population of men, women, and children in Sul do Save, the more detailed figures for the District of Lourenço Marques in 1928 revealed that 46 percent of all the healthy males who did not work in South Africa were conscripted for *shibalo*.[71] If a man chose to remain in rural agriculture, he risked a fifty-fifty chance of being seized for *shibalo*.

Ross's report had brought the grim harvest of the *indigenato* to international attention. The official commission that composed Portugal's public response to Ross's charges also encouraged a confidential review and revision of labor legislation in Mozambique.[72] The formal response to the scandal was the promulgation of further legislation—Decree 12,533 of October 1926 was reformulated in a similar decree, 16,199 of 6 December 1928.[73] This legislation predictably reiterated that *shibalo* was only to be employed for urgent public works, never to private employers, and it must always be fully paid. It also perpetuated the contradiction of lauding *shibalo* as a civic duty while simultaneously confirming that it was fit punishment for crimes or tax default.[74] The U.S. consul dutifully passed along a full translation of the legislation with the comment that such labor legislation was more often ignored than enforced.[75] The *Brado Africano* corroborated the consul's cynicism, proclaiming the new decree yet another piece of paper "Para o Inglês Ver."[76] The 1928 SNI report corroborated the cynicism—it was business as usual, despite the spruced-up window dressing.

The *indigenato* was formulated and extended in a piecemeal manner. It bound all Africans and mulattos of Mozambique together in subordinate citizenship. Whether in the top category of *assimilado* or the bottom category of *indígena*, people of African heritage were forced to carry documentation of their inferior status. The laws and their implementation encouraged a mutual sense of indignity within the African community, but the specific statutes and an individual's capacity to evade them also fueled divisions within that community. The legal system was engineered to constrain the workers of Lourenço Marques to regular contract labor, inferior pay and work conditions, and unequal competition with whites. Despite sustained resistance, the system was successfully implemented and expanded over this period. Chapter 5 details the capacity and creativity of workers' struggles for dignity and security through a case study of the port and railway complex until 1933.

5

Port Complex Struggles through to the End of an Era 1900-1933

Loku vaku lanja, lanja ka wena—lanja!
Maputukezi i male mi Ntxontxaku leyi—lanja!
When they say heave that shovel, shovel—heave!
The Portuguese live by stealing our wages—heave![1]

This chapter focuses on the experience of African workers in the city's core port and railway zone. It reveals a process of worker experience with various labor strategies and relates the latter to the changing economic and political context. The overview parallels Chapter 4, in that it opens with the fluid situation at the turn of the century, follows the crescendo of labor action in the 1910s and early 1920s and closes in 1933. Port and railway workers had carried on much of their struggle during that period with the support and sympathy of the urban intelligentsia. By 1933, the atmosphere of economic crisis, Portuguese protectionism, and harsh labor repression threatened middle and working class alike. It was probably sufficient to dampen even the liveliest spirits. As it happened, this period of economic crisis also marked the end of an era of African leadership.

The Extension of State Control at the Port Complex

African workers, private employers, and the colonial state struggled to assert their interests in the fast-expanding port zone in the first third of the twentieth century. Junod's port collage suggested the main lines of those struggles. Shipping and handling firms wanted to get employees to work for low wages as long as necessary to turn a ship around, while workers competed for the best-paid jobs at port, seeking to balance rest and work time and to protect themselves from the most dangerous working conditions.

Virtually the entire labor force in the port and railway complex was male, with one exception. From the turn of the century to the early 1930s, women occupied a particularly unattractive niche at the waterfront—loading timber on lighters in the wood lots just upriver from the central port zone. Private firms hired women at about half to two-thirds the wages paid to volunteer males to handle rough timber, working the lighters in and out of the water. Men only challenged women's employment in this ill-paid, unpopular sector when urban unemployment increased sharply.[2]

From the inauguration of the city's port and rail complex until 1933, several important processes and transformations got underway. The state significantly extended its control over both the physical plant and the labor force of the port complex. The centralization of port and rail functions under state control was accompanied by a tendency toward specialization and hierarchical organization, with increasingly rigid racial categorization. Finally, the port labor force was transformed from one comprised largely of casual volunteers to one with large contingents of *shibalo* labor strategically placed throughout the complex. This section considers these important changes.

By the turn of the century, as we have seen, the port and railway complex was the economic heart of Lourenço Marques and its service economy, and Portugal quickly extended her hold over the complex. With the formation of the Concelho de Administração do Porto e Caminho de Ferro de Lourenço Marques (PCFLM) in 1907, private (mostly foreign) companies were excluded from formal decision-making.[3] Upon its creation in 1907, the authority assumed responsibility for all port and railway transportation, although handling remained divided between private firms and the state. In 1899 the state assumed full control over railyard handling, and in 1929 it took over waterfront handling, except for stevedoring and some special handling sectors.

Goods Handled at Lourenço Marques 1897–1933
(*Source: Delagoa Directory*)

Year	Metric Ton	Year	Metric Ton
1897	170,934	1915	775,852
1898	141,126	1916	1,071,993
1899	174,834	1917	1,142,931
1900	63,941	1918	1,444,952
1901	134,654	1920	1,463,054
1902	250,334	1921	1,455,054
1903	454,120	1922	930,392
1904	469,179	1923	1,168,973
1905	499,968	1924	1,145,128
1908	471,122	1925	1,302,518
1909	641,502	1926	1,276,761
1910	786,320	1927	1,067,519
1911	601,729	1928	1,246,819
1912	864,394	1929	1,233,692
1913	1,055,278	1930	1,112,730
1914	922,973	1931	1,001,502
		1932	847,997
		1933	1,002,476

Bringing ships and trains together in a port zone; loading, unloading, and servicing the carriers; cleaning and maintaining basic facilities; taxing, tallying, sorting, guarding, and distributing the cargoes; and managing, feeding, housing, and paying the necessary labor force clearly required a great, yet fluctuating number of workers with a variety of specialized talents.[4] The progressive incorporation of formerly private-sector workers under the umbrella of the port and rail authority reinforced shared experience within the workforce. The tendency to centralize, however, was counterbalanced by the development of subzones (such as cold storage, caustic substances, and coaling) and special upriver facilities (such as petroleum storage and woodlots at Matola), which tended to pigeonhole workers by work processes and workplaces. The port authority also instituted the enormously complex Portuguese schedule for pay, promotion, and benefits, which encouraged further fragmentation of the workforce.[5]

Legislation and control mechanisms were extended parallel with state authority. As we have seen, with the RSTI of 1905, port workers had to register and wear an armband (*chapa*) confirming their registration to be admitted to the port zone. Registered port workers were guaranteed uniform wages throughout the port zone regardless of their employer, but they were also required to work whenever and wherever employers needed their services.[6] The RSTI was clearly designed to direct African labor to the dirty, dangerous, and heavy jobs that volunteer laborers always resisted.

Two more shifts occurred parallel with the extension of state control. First, race and nationality became more rigidly correlated with employment category—upward mobility was sharply curtailed for all but white Portuguese. In 1900 there were still some white hod carriers working the waterfront, and in the early 1920s there were still two Africans working as head checkers. By 1933, however, hod carriers were black and head checkers were not.[7] Pressure to hire Portuguese immigrants posed the clearest threat to educated, skilled Portuguese-speaking Africans holding better jobs.[8] By 1929, even the English firms that had typically employed Mauricians and locally educated Africans as assistant and head checkers were pressured to replace them with more expensive white Portuguese workers. The Depression crisis hastened the pace of racist exclusion, particularly in the better positions.[9] By 1933 tally clerk was the top position commonly held by Africans.[10]

The second shift was away from dependence on a largely volunteer casual labor force recruited competitively by private firms. By the early 1930s, the labor force included large contingents of *shibalo* labor. The *shibalo* lived and worked apart from volunteer labor. They had their own headmen, and they were tied to contracts paying about half the cash wages earned by casual labor. Part of their cash wage and all of their overtime income was paid at the work site, but most of their earnings were paid upon repatriation at the end of the contract. There certainly were conscripted workers in the port zone in the 1890s, but most of those worked on construction rather than handling. And there was still some private competition for labor into the 1930s, but the overall transformation from a predominantly competitive market to a predominantly bureaucratic distribution of labor accurately describes the transition between 1900 and the early 1930s.

Throughout Africa, colonial port authorities used coerced labor to undermine worker action.[11] That was also the case in Lourenço Marques, but the introduction and extension of *shibalo* labor went beyond disciplining the majority labor force. Large contingents of conscript labor were first employed as construction workers at

The coal carrier.

the port between 1900 and 1902. In 1906 conscripts were introduced for the first time as hod carriers, supposedly as a stop-gap measure to handle the dramatic increase in coal traffic. In 1909, however, the composition, function, and management of *shibalo* labor at the waterfront changed. The state introduced hundreds of *shibalo* on three- to six-month contracts specifically to regularize labor supplies and to undermine the strong position of casual labor in the portside rail yards:

> It is absolutely necessary to house at least 1500 to 2000 natives at the port to carry out port handling. The recent resolution that 1,000 of these natives be contracted by the government and housed within the railway yards at Lourenço Marques will have the effect, among other advantages, of cheapening native labor, which in Lourenço Marques is very expensive.[12]

The move had dramatic implications for casual labor because it was implemented in conjunction with confidential orders from the Governor General that any African in town without work be prosecuted as a vagrant and "put at the disposal of those who can use them."[13]

Between 1910 and 1929 regular use of *shibalo* gangs in port handling was restricted to the rail yard and the coaling zones. With the state's takeover of wharf-side handling in 1929, however, a core group of *shibalo* labor was introduced at dockside.[14] The move could not have come at a worse time for casual labor. With the drop in transit traffic due to the global recession, casual labor at the port was reduced by 15 percent in 1928–1929. A fifth of that cut was among dockside hod carriers.[15] The following year, wharf labor was cut an additional 23 percent, but the number of *shibalo* employed in their stead was up between 4 and 5 percent annually between 1929 and 1933.[16] The Grêmio Africano charged that the conscripts jeopardized the livelihood of over 4,000 local people who had spent much of their adult lives in casual labor at the wharf:

> The native, who also has some common sense will say, and rightly so, that the state obliges him to seek work, but when he does so, [the state] turns him down, but then comes around later, seizing him in his own home to do the same job [as *shibalo*] which he had already volunteered to do.[17]

While the state's role as manipulator was not entirely lost, by the 1930s, workers eager to keep their jobs became most concerned with the specific group that threatened their security. Thus between the late nineteenth century and 1933, skilled Mozambicans holding good jobs at the port were increasingly threatened by unemployed white Portuguese, particularly the so-called *afilhados*, men who enjoyed strong patronage support.[18] The majority labor force, on the other hand, faced the growing threat of displacement by "a battalion of *shibalos*."[19]

Labor Organization in Black and White

The Portuguese labor force was both a model and a threat to African workers. Despite their racial chauvinism, Portuguese unions provided tangible examples of the utility and effectiveness of worker organization and working class action. Africans quickly learned, however, that their imitation of Portuguese labor action would not necessarily evoke a similar response from employers or the state. The *indigenato* placed African and Portuguese workers in markedly different categories.

Between 1910 and 1925, the number of Portuguese employed at the port and rail complex tripled. Over the same period the Port and Railway Personnel Association (Associação do Pessoal do Porto e dos Caminhos de Ferro de Moçambique), better known as the União Ferroviário, constructed an impressive package of wages and benefits for its membership.[20] The União Ferroviário's newspaper, *O Emancipador*, strongly advocated socialist principles and solidarity within the labor force.[21] Although João Albasini was a member of the Associação do Pessoal because of his position as head of African labor at the port and rail complex, the group included almost no Negroes or mulattos. Indeed, the African press periodically pointed out to the União Ferroviário that it could increase its membership manyfold if it accepted African members.[22] Portuguese labor unions avoided alliances with the majority African labor force and were ambivalent toward mulattos and *assimilados*.[23] The African press wondered aloud: "What the devil kind of solidarity does *O Emancipador* promote—solidarity that discriminates by race?"[24]

The first documented initiative for African unionization occurred the same year the port and railway association was formed, in 1911. A small group of mission-educated African workers tried to take advantage of Republican rhetoric about liberty, fraternity, and equality to form a union representing all African workers in the city. Very little is known about the general union called the União Africana.[25] The organizers included Luis Augusto Guimarães and Francisco Domingos Campos. Both were familiar with the advantages of unions from their own membership in the Associação de Artes Gráficas (Graphic Arts or Printers Union, AAG), which formed around the national press.[26]

The AAG was unique in the colonial era; it was the single labor union with a significant African membership. The national press had been founded a half-century before conquest, and the earliest industrial arts schools included apprenticeships for Africans in graphic arts. By 1904 a quarter of the AAG membership was African. A half-century later, when skilled African labor had become just a tiny minority in virtually every other sector of the urban economy, the AAG had about the same percentage of African members. Mulattos comprised an additional 19 percent of the membership. In 1954 over 40 percent of the AAG membership was not white, whereas all the other unions were nearly 100 percent white. Indeed, statistics for that period acknowledged only sixty-seven Africans among the entire membership of Mozambique's registered trade unions. The AAG members comprised nearly half the total.[27]

The fact that the leadership of the fledgling União Africana was not representative of the majority urban labor force may have contributed to their failure to generate support among the majority labor force to subscribe to and claim the union as their own. The leadership was also unable to convince the government to accept their credentials.[28] In short, despite the strong example of unionism within the Portuguese community, African workers were excluded from those unions and were unable to promote unionization for their own purposes. The AAG was the single example of incorporation. Although African port and railway workers were not members, they learned early and difficult lessons from the Ferroviário experience.

Rise and Fall of Labor Action at the Port Complex

Although semi-skilled and skilled positions for Africans were less competitive at the port than elsewhere in the city, informants generally agreed that unskilled port labor was considered a good job.[29] Even port authority *shibalo* earned almost double the contract wage paid to agricultural *shibalo*, and when the potential for overtime employment is included, port *shibalo* were in a position to earn much more than their counterparts elsewhere. In the overall context, of course, Africans occupied positions with the fewest benefits, lowest pay, hardest physical work, and least security.

Despite their relatively favored stand among African wage earners in the city, port workers were directly and seriously hurt by the surge in inflation beginning around 1914. With few exceptions they were considered casual labor (*pessoal eventual*), and as such received their wages in paper currency. Port workers at first tried to accommodate the inflationary spiral with overtime income, but soon the loss was too great to be compensated.[30] Workers then demanded payment in gold-based currency or failing that, wage increases and a fixed rate of exchange for tax purposes.[31]

During the first sharp drop in real wages in the late 1910s and early 1920s, tension around wages, overtime, taxes, and currency exchange erupted into a flurry of strikes. In the three-year period of peak inflation, seven strikes occurred among African port workers over wage grievances. African and Portuguese waterfront workers tried to force wage gains in 1917, 1918, twice in 1919, three times in 1920, twice in 1921 and again in 1925.[32] Details of much of the strike activity at the port remain fuzzy, but it is clear that strikes involving the largest numbers of workers occurred between 1918 and 1925.

The strikes of that period were also qualitatively different from earlier activity. At the turn of the twentieth century, waterfront labor struck individual firms, and then only when their wages were cut. The state's takeover of port and rail labor from various private concerns increased the likelihood that any strike would include more workers..[33] Between 1918 and 1925, nine strikes were called to force wage hikes, and only one was called when an employer reneged on a promised hike.[34] The developing momentum was pro-active rather than reactive.

Inflation impinged unevenly on the port labor force. Most of the basic privileges and benefits were tied to permanent employment in the "scheduled" (quadro) rank. Only a tiny group of Africans ever qualified as permanent scheduled employees in the colonial era. Virtually all whites were paid in more inflation-resistant gold-based currency, whether they were permanent employees or not, but Portaria Provincial 1507 of May 1920 specifically extended that privilege to all "não-indígenas," non-natives. That law was designed to protect those Africans who qualified as assimilados, whether or not they were permanent employees. The vast majority of port workers, however, were considered "native personnel" or "native laborers." The racial breakdown of the port labor force is difficult to quantify until 1929, when employment by race was stipulated clearly. At that time only 2 percent of the entire African labor force worked in positions above that of simple laborer—a total of fifty-four men. Those fifty-four men began work at the port between 1906 and 1916. They were therefore not only a tiny elite, they were a diminishing rather than an expanding group.[35]

Despite their privileged position relative to African labor, Europeans were the first to undertake direct labor action in the face of falling real wages. The União Ferroviário led its first important strike in May 1917, during World War I.[36] The grievance was the abolition of Sunday wages. Portuguese Catholics had not normally worked on Sunday, but permanent workers had long received Sunday wages. Workers seized upon the abolition of Sunday wages to try to force an overall improvement in benefits and wage rates for the lowest level (white) civil service workers, the so-called pequeno funcionário (petty bureaucrat). They formed the largest single employment category of Portuguese in the city.

The state met the strike with a two-pronged strategy. All press coverage of the strike was censored, workers were arrested, and the port was eventually placed under martial law. At the same time, the state tried to implement a settlement. It publicly called on strikers to demonstrate their patriotism in a war period and return to work. It also quietly put out the word that pending wage increases would make up for the loss of Sunday wages. The overtures were met with a firm challenge from union members: "Down with Charity, Up with Solidarity!"[37]

After twenty-two days, however, the union members returned to work. They accepted a compromise settlement after the state threatened to militarize the entire port and draft all the men between seventeen and forty-five into the army.[38] Workers familiar with the Portugal's casualty toll for sickness, famine, and accidents in the Africa campaign read that as a virtual death sentence. The final settlement included wage hikes for all permanent staff, "regardless of race." The race stipulation, a familiar component to Portuguese legislation and proclamations, was a window-dressing concession since the number of Africans who qualified as permanent staff could probably be counted on the fingers of one hand. Raises varied from 10$00 to 24$00 *escudos* per month; the largest increases went to those who earned between 45$00 and 75$00 per month and the smallest to those earning below 45$00 or above 110$00 per month. *Pequeno funcionários* did not emerge the winners.

African workers supported the Ferroviário's call for solidarity in the strike of 1917, but quickly found their support was expendable. When the government excluded native labor from the settlement package for the 1917 strike, the union made no protest.[39] The tiny group of Africans in the *quadro* made some gains through this strike, but overall the strike action by the white union had a mixed impact on African workers. It set a positive example of what strike action could accomplish, while not hiding the risks involved. It also reinforced the divisions between skilled and unskilled, black and white, permanent and casual workers. Africans learned that white unions expected solidarity, but then easily set aside the fate of the majority. The majority labor force also soon learned that the risks and consequences for African labor action were quite different than for whites.

The first significant African labor action at the port took place in May of 1919. African volunteer labor on the waterfront walked quietly off the job at mid-day demanding a wage increase of $20 *centavos* per shift, bringing overall wage levels to between $80 and 1$00 per shift depending upon skill category.[40] They refused to return to work pending the state's acceptance of their wage demand. The increase demanded was similar to that recently granted to the whites who organized waterfront handling.

Once word of the strike managed to muddle its way up the somewhat unclear chain of command from the port police to the Governor General, the state's action was swift and firm.[41] All of the more than four hundred strikers who refused to return to work unconditionally were arrested, and of that group approximately three hundred were then immediately imprisoned. By late the same afternoon, a special train was sent to fetch a gang of 280 *shibalo* workers who were building an airstrip in nearby Matola. The airstrip gang completed port handling for that day. Faced with blanket arrests and displacement by *shibalo* gangs, most strikers returned to work the following day, and the *shibalo* train returned to Matola.

Although the strike was quickly and firmly broken, the state subsequently concurred with the Chamber of Commerce's recommendation to raise wharf wages by $10 per shift.[42] The following January the state raised salaries for *serventes*, entry-level civil servants, to a standard minimum, thus the two largest groups of African port workers, hod carriers and *serventes*, received raises in this period.[43] Overall wage levels for the majority increased, but the pace at which the majority fell behind the privileged minority receiving inflation-buffered currency, increased more sharply. The chart on the next page indicates falling real wages (*escudo* to sterling) and the extent of wage differentiation within the African labor force.

The more important figure (sterling) dropped in some cases by about half, despite the *escudo* increase. Ironically the discrepancy tended to minimize the range between the lowest- and highest-paid African workers, since the highest-paid lost ground faster than the lowest-paid. The state encouraged potential leaders among educated, skilled African labor to identify with the Portuguese by offering them access to strong currency if they became *assimilados*. Africans who identified with and led the majority labor force, however, were punished and humiliated. The 1919 strike leaders were sentenced to three months of *shibalo* labor. Foreign shipping interests,

African Port Labor Wages, 1914 and 1920[44]
(Escudos and Sterling)

Category	1914		1920	
Hod carrier	$60	2 sh. 6 p.	1$50	1 sh. 3 p.
Load arranger	$75	3 sh.	1$50	1 sh. 3 p.
Crane operator	1$20	5 sh.	2$50	2 sh. 3 p.
Tally clerk	1$20	5 sh.	2$50	2 sh. 3 p.

which directed much waterfront work on contract, applauded the sentences as a clear lesson to discourage workers from "inciting their comrades to leave work without warning." Although the foreign firms decried such labor action, they nonetheless advocated much higher wage increases than the state was willing to concede.[45] The African press strongly protested the treatment of the strike leadership. If forced labor was fitting punishment for labor leadership, *Brado Africano* complained, Portuguese strikers should be similarly condemned.[46]

Testimony subsequently collected by the Chamber of Commerce among shipping and forwarding managers confirmed their view that only wage hikes through currency reform would curb mounting labor unrest. When the state failed to take meaningful measures to correct the currency situation, foreign firms became conspicuously casual about identifying strike leadership. That may suggest their underlying sympathy with the workers' grievances. In any case, they explicitly recognized that a breakdown in worker discipline was inevitable if men were pushed to work for increasingly inadequate wages.[47]

Port labor confrontation in this era took place in the larger context of inflation-aggravated worker action. By 1920–1921 strikes exploded throughout the city. Workers at the wharves and the woodlots, sanitation workers, and trolley car personnel all stopped work and demanded higher wages. Most strikes in this period resulted in some wage gains.[48] Even *shibalo* wages were increased by 50 percent, but most workers still did not manage to recover the level of real wages they had enjoyed in 1914.[49]

By the early 1920s, the combination of sharply falling real wages and increasing demands for *shibalo* labor under the worst possible conditions had generated a crisis in the city and hinterland. Some Native Affairs officials warned of a general breakdown in worker discipline, or a widespread exodus of the African population to South Africa. In one exceptional case, the administrator of Chibuto circumscription flatly refused to honor further labor requisitions for the port, rail, or plantation labor as long as the state continued to pay what he alleged was a "disgraceful" wage. He argued that Africans risked their health, particularly working six months of dawn-to-dusk farm labor, but at the end the wage packet did not even meet the annual tax obligation. In such circumstances desertion was a sensible response, and the official refused to persecute his constituency for doing what was reasonable.[50]

Despite the clear justice of worker claims, labor unrest was increasingly met with force. The government's response to the 1925–1926 strike by the União Ferroviário was the watershed. The strike, which began over a personnel dispute in autumn of 1925, ended after about four months with an unconditional return to work. In the meantime, the state had closed down the workingmen's lodge and posted African soldiers as guards at its doors. Striking workers were arrested, and the railway service was militarized. When several trains were sabotaged, the government responded by evicting workers' families from railway housing, and forcing strikers to ride, again under guard by African soldiers, in an open box car in advance of trains traveling to and from the Transvaal. Francisco Guilherme de Brito, whose father had been an important railway director, vividly recalled his family's shock on the Sunday morning when mounted Portuguese soldiers charged the railway strikers and their families as they demonstrated in the major thoroughfare of the city.[51] Most of the community had not anticipated such a forceful state effort to smash striker activity.

Ultimately hundreds of workers were fired, some were relocated in other colonies, and a small group of militant leaders was sent into penal exile in northern Mozambique. Railway labor was transformed from civil service status to a daily wage labor at a slightly higher rate. The loss of civil service status meant the sacrifice of retirement and auxiliary benefits. Strikers with more than ten years' service were ultimately allowed to receive their pensions with a 20 percent discount, but the only other concession was that those not deported or relocated could apply for rehire as daily wage laborers.[52] The state basically dismantled the wage and benefit structure the union had build over the past quarter-century.[53] It was a shocking example for the entire urban labor force, and it took the edge off any strike plans for about seven years.

The state's response to the União Ferroviário strike was a bellwether of policies that would be fully developed under the New State. The implantation of New State policies coincided with the region's slide into economic depression. The state's response to the growing economic crisis in Mozambique was to further consolidate their control.[54] The first important decision was the incorporation of waterfront cargo handling under the umbrella of state control on January 1, 1929. The decision received a mixed response in Lourenço Marques.

For twenty years private firms had handled Lourenço Marques's wharf cargo efficiently through competitive bidding. The contract agreement between the companies and the state paid the state six pence per short ton handled. That amounted to a quarter of the companies' handling revenues.[55] Not surprisingly, the companies were opposed to the takeover. Given the example of the South African Railway takeover of wharf handling in Durban, the private companies feared a drop in efficiency and increase in handling costs. Indeed, six months after the takeover, the shopkeepers association complained that handling fees had been increased from 50 to 500 percent on some items.[56]

The African press and the top African wage earners at the port originally supported the state takeover, because they anticipated that the accompanying emphasis on Portuguese language skills would give educated Mozambicans an edge over the English-speaking Mauricians who held top jobs at the private shipping and forwarding companies. Their assumption that a state takeover would benefit any category of African labor seems naive in view of the prior experience.

When the state took over rail yard handling in 1911, for example, *O Africano* charged that casual labor was turned away from work at six in the morning only to be rounded up for rail yard *shibalo* by early afternoon.[57] By 1914 *shibalo* outnumbered casual labor in the rail yards by four to one.[58] African leadership clearly failed to anticipate an analogous situation, even when the state proposed in October 1927 to replace over 300 casual laborers, employed by private companies at wharf side, with a 150-man unit of *shibalo* which would work in around-the-clock shifts, and thus lower wages and eliminate overtime costs.[59]

Less than two weeks after the takeover, the state plan to replace casual labor with *shibalo* was evident to all, and the African press changed its editorial tune from enthusiastic support to firm opposition.[60] Dick Khosa, a gentlemanly Mozambican disciple of South Africa's Industrial and Commercial Workers' Union (ICU) leader Clements Kadalie, argued emphatically against the extension of forced labor to the wharf, particularly in light of the encroaching economic depression. Khosa stressed the hypocrisy of defending *shibalo* as a way of enforcing the "moral obligation to work," when:

> our skilled [black] workers are on the verge of famine! . . .
> There ought to be no unemployment if the standards of native life were raised by education to increase purchasing power concomitant with [a worker's] increased productivity.[61]

The extension of *shibalo*, he claimed, undermined both skill acquisition and the potential development of the black consumer market by restricting employment opportunities for blacks to unskilled, ill-paid jobs.[62]

Three months after the state assumed wharf handling, over three hundred *shibalos* were brought in from Inhambane, threatening the jobs of over four thousand suburban Africans who depended upon wharf labor for their living.[63] The Grêmio elite protested that for years their newspaper had urged rural Africans to sell their labor in the city, but the state's use of *shibalo* in a period of high urban unemployment undermined all such previous effort. Furthermore, the tiny and marginal African petite bourgeoisie that depended upon the urban African consumer market would also be badly hurt if the state continued to undermine the urban labor force with *shibalo* gangs.[64]

The port authority responded that the number of *shibalo* alleged to be working at the port and railway was exaggerated, and argued that those who were installed at the port would regularize the supply of labor rather than replace volunteers. Volunteers, the port authority charged, worked the morning shift, but after lunch only cared to lie around drinking in *cantinas* or at the market. If the authority needed half a dozen men to do a small job in mid-afternoon it was nearly impossible to marshal the labor. Furthermore, during the annual cashew harvest and brewing season, people returned to their home areas for social renewal and feasting, and consequently labor at the port was scarce. State and private firms alike turned to *shibalo* during that period every year. Finally, they concluded, if any individual had been turned down for work at the port, it was because he was too old or "unfit for service."[65]

The case of Wilson C. Matola illustrates the problem regarding allegations of being "unfit for service" in a system where state, police, and employer authority over Africans was both arbitrary and without appeal.[66] Matola was a Swiss mission graduate and school teacher. Since 1925 he had worked as a cashier in a British Indian shop. When the shop closed in 1928, Matola became unemployed. Matola's wages had supported a family that included his father's two widows and their six children as well as his own wife and son. In February 1929 he petitioned the SNI to sponsor him for a suitable job with the state. Africans who did not have a personal patron, a *cunha* or a *padrinho*, within the civil service to sponsor and "protect" them in the patronage-ridden system commonly petitioned the SNI to intervene on their behalf— presumably as part of the SNI's mandate to protect and promote African affairs.

A Swiss mission graduate and teacher, Matola was obviously literate, and having worked as a cashier for three years, he was also clearly competent with numbers and accounts. The SNI sent him to the port and railway authority for job placement. He was sent back to the SNI two days later with a note from the authority simply saying that Matola was "unfit for service." In Matola's case that probably meant he was too black to be hired for well-paid office work, too educated to be hired to sweep floors, and too "unprotected" in this bastion of patronage to be hired at all. Matola was left to stand in line at the wharf with hundreds of others in the predawn hours hoping he would be selected to shovel, tote, or haul to support his eleven-person household.[67]

Finally, Africans in the top positions as tally clerks and head checkers, who originally had met the state's proposal with some enthusiasm, soon experienced a change of heart.[68] English-speaking Africans were not displaced by Portuguese-speaking Africans, but by Portuguese *afilhados*. Workloads were redistributed, but not as workers had anticipated. Personnel were cut and pay schedules altered so that overtime income was diminished. In 1928, for example, private firms paid overtime on the basis of one twenty-four hour stint equal to four full shifts. With the state takeover, a round-the-clock job counted only two and a half shifts.[69] Workers who wanted to keep their jobs had to work harder for less pay. Work accidents declined, but that was attributed to the overall drop in transit handling rather than a more generous distribution of labor.

The Depression and the End of an Era

The extension of state control over both rail and waterfront handling by 1929 had led to the expanded use of *shibalo* labor to undercut volunteer opportunities at one end of the spectrum. At the other end of the spectrum, racism and patronage were fine-tuned to undermine upward mobility for the most qualified Africans. It was in this strained context that African port workers took their last important labor action prior to the Second World War. The *quinhenta* strike of August 28, 1933, was more important than its short-lived existence suggests.

The Depression encouraged personnel layoffs in all labor categories at the port and rail complex. By 1933 the state decided to put through an across-the-board wage cut of between 10 and 30 percent to minimize further layoffs.[70] For most African workers, the cutback amounted to fifty *centavos*, a *quinhenta*, per shift.[71] The "cutting of the *quinhenta*," as the workers described it, was a severe blow to workers who were already struggling with short work weeks and inflation. The reduction amounted to five times the increase African workers had won through the 1919 strike. Many men were lucky to work five to ten days a month—thus every *quinhenta* counted.

News of the wage cutback arrived at the port on a Friday just prior to lunch. Hod carriers refused to return to work after lunch, but gathered on the green near the city market, several blocks from the port zone. The chief of police from the wharf zone addressed the workers, promising that if they returned to work on Monday he would see that the *quinhenta* was restored. The men returned to work on Monday, but they were met with a double surprise. The promise to restore the *quinhenta* had been a trick. Instead of being allowed to leave the port zone as usual to buy or eat their lunches in the nearby *cantinas*, they found themselves locked in the zone. They were forced to turn around all the ships in port under police guard, and only then were they allowed to leave, eat, or rest.[72]

Brado Africano described the situation: "Workers with empty bellies faced the boss, who with his full belly, answered them with empty promises."[73] The *Brado* charged that the authority was cutting corners at the expense of those who most needed the money. Both *Brado* and *O Emancipador* commented on the discipline of the strikers, and concluded that they had little choice but to return to work.[74] In contrast, the *Lourenço Marques Guardian*, which reflected private shipping and handling firms, and *Notícias*, the principal Portuguese paper, tried to discredit and play down strike grievances. Both papers alleged the strikers had been foolishly drunk, and that the police had simply rounded up those not too drunk to work and set them back to their jobs without resistance.[75] Hod carriers felt themselves deceived and defeated.

By 1933, African workers throughout the city felt humiliated and cheated. In the desperate economy of the 1930s they also felt frustrated and fairly helpless. Their direct and appropriate protests against serious wage grievances had been dismissed by the port authority, and they had been ridiculed in the process. The climate of workplace despair fed a more diffuse form of protest. On the New Year's night following the *quinhenta* strike, hundreds of Africans ran through the city's white residential areas, attacking people and property as they went.[76] The attack was an expression of African hostility and frustration. It was more spontaneous than planned, but both informants and the contemporary African press felt it was a predictable turn of events, given the provocation Africans faced. Whites responded with shock and alarm.[77] The attack vented African anger and frustration, introduced a note of caution into the white community, and fueled the tendency already underway since the 1926 coup toward government curfews and stronger controls over African social activity and mobility.

Although the port and railway complex was the scene of a good deal of labor action since the turn of the century, by 1933 African workers had little to show for their efforts. At all levels they were worse off than they had been in 1910. The depressed economy turned anger into despair. Informants typically asked, "What were we going to do then?" and frequently answered their own question, "There was nothing we could do about it!"[78] Certainly by 1933 port workers had lost much of the advantage they had enjoyed when labor demand was high and controls over labor mobility were still weak. They also had gained over a third of a century of experience as wage laborers in Lourenço Marques. When the economy began to recover in the postwar era, port workers once again tried to exploit more buoyant labor demand to recoup some of their losses. That is the topic of Chapter 8.

6

The New State—"For the Good of the Nation" 1926–1962

The Portuguese New State regime consolidated itself as a political reality in Lourenço Marques between the coup of 1926 and 1933, although it did not develop and extend the rudiments of a corporativist structure in Moçambique until the late 1930s.[1] The period of consolidation coincided with economic, social, and ecological crises. The global Depression was reflected in the principal economic engines of the entire region, mining, port and railway traffic, and agriculture. All began a sharp decline in 1927, reaching their lowest levels around 1932–1933.

The early 1930s was also a low point for the elite African leadership in Lourenço Marques. The economic crisis and social retrenchment detailed below took a devastating toll on the aspirations of the mature generation. They witnessed the disappearance of many of the hopes they held for their children's future, and eventually succumbed to internal divisions and apathy. Despite the economic revival, elite attempts to consolidate and revitalize urban leadership were frustrated by press censorship and the barriers to upward mobility posed by increased white settlement.

In the late 1930s Portugal began to implement economic policies to forge a new relationship between her colonial and metropolitan economies.[2] The political, economic, and social vision that inspired such policies was captured in the slogan used in all official correspondence, "A Bem da Nação" meaning "For the Good of the Nation." In Mozambique's case, the crucial shifts were the development of cotton supplies for the metropole's textile industry and an enhanced commitment to develop transport and communications with South Africa, the Rhodesias, and Nyasaland. By the mid-1940s Portugal reshaped fiscal, trade, and industrial development policy toward the colonies. Although Portuguese capital was strongly favored, those sectors of foreign investment in Mozambique that generated foreign exchange revenues were tolerated and quietly supported.[3]

By the late 1950s conditions in the colonies, metropole, and international markets had changed sufficiently to put great pressure on the earlier configuration. The dynamics of the developing colonial and metropolitan economies combined to highlight the need for basic reforms. Portugal's decision to join the European Free Trade Agreement in 1957 and to sign the International Labor Organization's basic statutes signaled the shift that led to the labor and social reform package of the early 1960s. The abolition of the *indigenato* was its centerpiece.[4] Economic contradictions began to challenge Portugal's system of colonial rule just as a new generation of African leadership began to consolidate a political challenge.

This chapter considers the watershed crisis of the early 1930s and the subsequent pace of economic change that encouraged the late 1950s shifts and early 1960s reforms. It begins with the foundering of African urban leadership and its frustrated and camouflaged efforts toward revitalization between 1926 and 1962. It then develops the context of the economic and demographic changes that shaped labor policy through to 1962. Chapter 7 explores those labor controls and African strategies to evade, manipulate, and mediate them.

Crisis in African Urban Leadership

From the turn of the century, the process of white ascent had been vigorously and openly contested by the Mozambican elite. The contest had to some extent been a losing battle, and the Depression extinguished much of their remaining vigor. The worst years of the economic crisis coincided with the passing of the generation of Portuguese, Afro-Portuguese, and African individuals who had both spearheaded resistance to government abuses and sustained social contact among locals, metropolitans, blacks, browns, and whites in their lives.[5] The result was a crisis of leadership and a growing chasm between the increasingly metropolitan-dominated white community and everyone else. The centers of power were increasingly inaccessible to African voices.

The transition in the local white community was marked by the deaths of Rufino de Oliveira and Francisco Roque de Aguiar in 1932. Both were recognized as "pioneers," a term reserved for whites only. Oliveira had come to Mozambique with the police force in 1888. He served in many civil service posts and remained in Lourenço Marques after his retirement. Oliveira was a frequent contributor to *Brado Africano* and a welcome guest at Grêmio social functions. After he retired from the civil service, he inaugurated and administered the Fund to Aid the Native Poor, which provided some support for indigent Africans in Lourenço Marques.[6]

When one of the earliest pieces of New State legislation, the so-called João Belo press law, threatened to end publication of the *Brado Africano*, Oliveira stepped in and saved the paper. The law prohibited civil servants from acting as newspaper directors and required newspaper directors to hold a post-secondary degree. The law was obviously designed to quiet the city's lively opposition press, and in particular those papers directed by workers and local people. The law reduced the number of newspapers published in the city by about one-fourth, but Oliveira, who held a degree and had retired from the civil service, stepped in as titular director of *Brado Africano*.[7]

Roque de Aguiar, whom local people called "Nwa Dambu" ("the friend," or "the just"), arrived in Mozambique just in time to become an unwitting hero in the Luso-

Gaza wars of the 1890s.[8] During the first third of the twentieth century, he was a civil servant and ran a small farm in Catembe, across the bay from Lourenço Marques. He had several children with local women and, like Oliveira, he was part of the Grêmio Africano's social circle. Aguiar used his status as a Portuguese citizen of standing to intercede on behalf of Africans, socially or legally.[9] The Portuguese community counted him among the city's honored pioneers and the African middle class remembered him as an ally and a kind old settler.[10]

Aguiar and Oliveira had worked and lived in colleague and patron relationships with Africans of many social backgrounds, but particularly with the Grêmio Africano leadership. Although many Portuguese were cultivated as patrons and served as godparents for dozens of African children, Aguiar and Oliveira were among the last of their generation who were explicitly identified as so-called "friends of the natives".[11] Neither challenged the dominance of Portuguese colonialism, but both mediated the nature of colonial oppression in their daily lives because they related to Africans as social beings. Because of such relationships, they sometimes found themselves courted for the awkward position of "native representative," faced with the dilemma of assuming the right to speak for people whom they knew could speak perfectly well for themselves, or allowing those people to continue with no voice. Both embodied a kind of social spirit that became largely a footnote of the past in the 1930s.[12]

The Grêmio Africano also experienced a changing of the guard in this era. Despite the prominence of Negro leaders, such as Estácio Dias, the Grêmio's overall makeup had slowly changed from one that included as many Negroes as mulattos to one that was predominantly mulatto.[13] The Grêmio had long counted the dominant mulatto families among its members, including Albasini, Fornasini, de Haan, Loforte, Bruheim, and Pott. With the death of João dos Santos Albasini in 1922, the Grêmio and its press lost a good deal of its passion.[14] The 1930s marked the passing of the generation that had founded the Grêmio and its press, and had confidently, if ultimately unsuccessfully, struggled against implantation of the *indigenato* in all its components. José Francisco Albasini (Bandana), ceased active participation in the newspaper in 1933 and died in 1935. Estácio Dias died two years later.[15]

Frustrated in their efforts to revitalize political struggle in the grim context of the 1930s, Grêmio members turned to a kind of hagiography around the memory of Dias and the Albasinis. The three became revered by the younger members as "the trinity of distinguished sons of the colony."[16] Poet Rui António de Noronha captured the frustration and pessimism of the era in his homage to João Albasini on the anniversary of his death, observing simply, "We have wrought no changes."[17] With the passing of Dias, the Grêmio's director pondered, "Who remains? Who is left on this coast to take his place—this man of the native race [who was] intelligent, idealistic, capable, willing, and a persistent servant of the African cause?"[18]

The man who assumed the helm of the Grêmio Africano in 1932 was Karel Pott. By the mid-1930s, the Grêmio leadership was dominated by mulattos.[19] Unlike Dias and the Albasini brothers, Pott was a very light-skinned mulatto. (The mid-1930s Grêmio leadership is shown in the photograph on page 67.) He was more than a generation younger than the founders, and his experience and training were vastly different.[20] Pott completed his secondary education in Portugal, where he distinguished himself as a scholar and world-class athlete. He took his law degree from Portugal's prestigious University of Coimbra. When he returned to the city to establish a practice in

May 1931, he was not only the second man born in Lourenço Marques to have earned a higher degree, he one of the best-educated people in either the colony or the metropole. The torch at the Grêmio had been passed to a man who had spent much of his youth in Portugal, but when Pott returned to Lourenço Marques, according to Raul Honwana, he confirmed that his past and future lay in Africa:

> Karel Pott returned by boat from Portugal, and at the dock, before greeting any of the other people waiting for him, he turned first to embrace his mother, an African woman in traditional dress and with whom he had never lived. The point is that by that time Karel was already politically mature.[21]

Even a man of Pott's education, complexion, and intellect would find himself too black for the whitening town.

The high point of Pott's tenure at *Brado Africano* came in 1932. With famine in the interior, worsening unemployment in the city, and mine recruitment at it's lowest point in the century, Pott was so angered by the contrast between what the government demanded from the African population and what it was prepared to provide for it, that he revived the paper's tradition of a protest editorial. "Basta!" (Enough!) framed and inspired a whole series of protest editorials in the African press from the premier issue of *O Africano* throughout the Republican era. Pott's editorial, published in both Portuguese and Tsonga, echoed themes from Nhlomulo's 1912 essay, "Hunger." While productive, taxpaying, and laboring rural communities suffered famine and drought, he charged, the government provided no relief. Yet unproductive Portuguese cronies and bureaucrats were well taken care of because the bureaucracy's "exclusive function is to suck up public moneys, generated virtually in full by the product of our labor, by our blood!"[22] As we shall see below, Pott's analysis was correct. As was the case with the Ross report of the 1920s, the archival record revealed an even more shocking situation than that asserted by the editors of the African press.

Almost a half-century after Pott's editorial was published, Roberto Tembe and Joaquim da Costa beamed when they discussed it. Although Pott was distrusted by many in the white community because of his African heritage, his education and profession endowed him with undeniable public prestige and some protection from censorship. "Everybody [in the black community] liked Karel Pott," Tembe recalled, "because he could openly complain about the Portuguese, particularly about the lower class Portuguese *kubvana*."[23] João Albasini's similar critiques of the hypocrisy of Portugal's "civilizing" mission was ridiculed by some whites who charged that Albasini himself was not really "civilized" because he was largely self-educated.[24] They could not dismiss Pott on those grounds. The mature generation that survived the 1930s emerged profoundly sobered and discouraged.[25] They were shocked by the petty and systematically racist statutes passed in the crisis atmosphere.[26] The narrowed horizons for the African elite obviously shaped expectations for those who aspired to join their ranks. If the African elite had become so vulnerable, what was the message for ordinary working people? Unlike the situation in the late 1920s, the deterioration of conditions for all urban Africans did not bring the community together. Instead, the crisis fueled schisms along ethnic, racial, generational, and class lines. Government censorship exacerbated the situation. Apathy, infighting, and a proclivity to honor the successes of past leadership characterized the era, rather than attempts to develop contemporary leadership.[27] By the late 1930s, both the Grêmio and the Instituto Negrófilo had become markedly insular, a posture they basically sustained to the end of the colonial era.[28]

In the 1940s and 1950s Mozambican-born Portuguese, mulatto, and *assimilado* intellectuals tentatively rekindled a challenge of the colonial definition of Africans as lesser beings. Intellectual and cultural discourse among poets, writers, and artists in Lourenço Marques moved away from the state-promoted celebration of Portuguese culture to focus on the African heritage and the dilemma of Mozambicans who consciously struggled between the images and culture of both. Some of these writers focused on the very groups their education and assimilation was designed to draw them away from, in works such as José Craveirinha's classic celebration of defiance in the anger of mine workers and Noémia de Sousa's daring poetic embrace of life among the prostitutes and hod carriers at the waterfront.[29] João Bernardo Dias, the talented son of *Brado Africano*'s first-generation leader Estácio Dias, struggled with his African manhood in elegant and sensitive essays while a law student at the University of Coimbra in the late 1940s.[30] The challenge suggested by these well-educated urban writers emerged more fully in the 1960s. These intellectuals generated an important cultural and literary challenge, but prior to the 1960s, they failed to intersect with or promote working-class challenges, as had been the case in the first decades of the century. That linkage was generated later under Frelimo's patronage.[31]

Despite scattered initiatives, no united front emerged in the urban African community. In 1949, letters in *Brado Africano* denounced the petty infighting among Africans, mulattos, and *assimilados*, and divisions between "cultured" locals and less-educated immigrants. Community solidarity and effective leadership was impossible, they claimed, if "everyone arranged the charcoal to grill his [own particular] sardine."[32] Despite the uneven and schismatic nature of African opposition, the late 1940s and 1950s cultural initiatives of urban intellectuals and the work they published in the Grêmio press had at least broken the mold of defeatism formed in the early 1930s.[33]

Layered Crises—The Region, The Hinterland, and The City

The New State's response to the crises it confronted in its first years was to retrench and to offer increasing protection to Portuguese employers, entrepreneurs, planters, laborers, and bureaucrats in the colonies. Its policies to shelter the Portuguese community from the worst effects of the Depression were implemented at great cost to Mozambican lives and livelihoods. Although the New State took quite different forms in the metropole and the colony, it was clear to Mozambicans that the slogan "For the Good of the Nation," referred only to the metropole. In no era was that more true than during the Depression.

Crisis seemingly pervaded every aspect of life in Sul do Save during the sharp downswing of the pendulum from 1927 to 1933. Everywhere the economy was in crisis: in the mines at the regional level, the farms of the hinterland, and the port and railway complex in Lourenço Marques. The economic crises were exacerbated by the weather. In February 1932, prolonged drought combined with economic displacement to trigger famine in Guijá, Chokwé, Chibuto, and Inhambane.[34] At least 255 Africans starved in Guijá, and farmers were forced to sell off their plow oxen to buy water and corn from suppliers along the rail line. The following February drought struck further west in Sabié and Magude. Locust invasions throughout much of Sul do Save in 1934 and 1935 diminished the gains people had made from the 1934 rains. Rains failed again in October and November 1935, pushing areas of Magude, Guijá, and Chibuto into famine. When the first rains of the season finally fell in late January 1936, they were torrential. Flooding in February and March 1936 severely damaged banana and maize plantations all along the Incomati, Umbelúsi, and Limpopo river valleys.

At the regional level, the opportunity to contract with Wenela for mine labor diminished sharply. The decline began precipitously with a 50 percent drop in recruitment between 1927 and 1932. Recruitment figures suggest that 1932 was the bottoming-out year for the mineral Depression. The number of emigrants from the district of Lourenço Marques who were issued passes to work in the Transvaal in any capacity also dropped by half between 1927 and 1932.[35]

Southern Mozambicans Contracted for Mine Labor in South Africa 1927–1946[36]

Year	Recruits	Year	Recruits
1927	75,866	1938	73,617
1928	66,094	1939	73,921
1929	60,831	1940	71,129
1930	56,258	1941	78,880
1931	54,077	1942	74,507
1932	39,129	1943	84,479
1933	41,398	1944	78,950
1934	50,665	1945	78,806
1935	58,923	1946	74,117
1936	70,092	1947	78,308
1937	64,365		

Conditions also changed drastically in the agricultural hinterland. European farmers could not produce enough to sell at current prices and cover their debt, let alone show a profit. Sugar prices, for example, had plummeted from their peak level of up to £100 in 1919, to £8/3 by 1929 and £4/10 by 1936.[37] By 1930 European capitalist farmers comprised the single largest category of registered unemployed persons in Lourenço Marques, and their number doubled over the next three years.[38] Many abandoned their bankrupt holdings and sought government relief in the city.[39]

Despite the bankruptcy of much of its membership, the Association for Agricultural Development in the Province of Mozambique (Associação do Fomento de Agricultura da Província de Moçambique, or the AFA) remained a politically powerful lobby with important patron links to New State leadership.[40] The AFA urged Sul do Save farmers who managed to stay on their lands to increase production and cut their costs by employing *shibalo* labor without regard for legal minimum conditions. In 1932 an AFA spokesman defended that strategy, arguing that the Depression created an "urgent" situation, and that the survival of settler agriculture was in the "public" interest—thus conscription was in accord with existing legislation.[41] The spokesman argued that "for the good of the nation," the government should increase conscription for private agriculture, raise taxes to force more Africans into wage labor, drop all minimum welfare and wage regulations, and implement strong market protection for cash crops produced by Europeans.[42]

The AFA had its way. New State legislation prohibiting conscription except for urgent public projects was conveniently reinterpreted. Despite the fact that "no law exists that openly permits [requisitions of forced labor for private employment]," the state increasingly participated in a "clandestine" system of *shibalo* recruitment for Sul do Save planters.[43] The "clandestine" system survived because it was in theinterests of the settlers and petty bureaucrats.[44] The interests of the colonial bureaucratic cadres were not to be underestimated. The American consul observed that *shibalo* would continue: "It will be a question of how much the estate manager and farmer are willing to pay . . . the official in question to . . . resort to government recruitment as before."[45] One disgruntled bureaucrat even complained that too many Africans from his area worked in South Africa: "How can I get rich like the other administrators if there is no *shibalo* to recruit here?"[46]

The "clandestine" recruitment system was finally challenged in 1948 because, in combination with forced cotton and rice cultivation, it produced such disruption in rural society that women and children were fleeing in record numbers.[47] The official who investigated the exodus concluded that, despite the AFA's argument that "The Good of the Nation" justified dawn-to-dusk, no-minimum-standards *shibalo*, "the regime of 'tolerance' of the past eighteen years [1930–1948] has gone on too long to the marked *detriment of the common good.*"[48] "Clandestine" *shibalo* may have provided the lifeline to carry marginal settler farmers through the Depression, but its tacit tolerance of the most appalling labor and living conditions jeopardized the lives of thousands of Mozambicans. Alfeu Cumbe explained:

> I was caught and made to work *shibalo* in Makuagimba's plantation in Marracuene. . . . The only food we had was a kind of porridge and pumpkin stew, but the pumpkin was often poorly cooked—many people died from eating that food. Others became incapacitated. . . .[49]

As detailed in Chapter 5, port and railway traffic also dropped steadily from 1926 through 1933, reflecting the loss of transit traffic as the Transvaal mines and farms closed down.[50] Jobs in the port and rail complex, the second most important employment sector for Africans after the mines, dried up as a result. The average number of Africans to find work daily in either waterfront or rail car handling dropped from 766 in 1929 to 537 in 1931.[51] Although registered unemployment was a more reliable indicator for European than for African workers, it is nonetheless significant that it reached its peak in Lourenço Marques in 1934.[52]

Economy, Immigration, and Entrenched White Advantage

The single benefit African workers enjoyed in this crisis was the stabilization of commodity prices and currency. The runaway inflation of the late 1910s and 1920s was finally brought under control by the New State. Retail price indices and available commodity prices reveal a significant price pause in the early 1930s in an otherwise upward incline. The retail price index base of 100 at the beginning of World War I had increased to 2,108 by 1934, with wartime inflation and the immediate postwar currency crisis accounting for the sharpest increases.[53] Between 1931 and 1935 staple prices held, and even dropped slightly in 1932. War shortages boosted prices for items not subject to state control.[54] As indicated in the chart below, inflation only reemerged as a serious problem in Lourenço Marques again due to wartime conditions.

Retail Price Index for Lourenço Marques 1914-1946[55]

1914 (base)	100	1942	131.08
1934	2,108	1943	140.92
1935	2,074	1944	144.92
1939 (base)	100	1945	169.43
1940	119.95	1946	180.77

Price stabilization made it somewhat easier to contend with unemployment.[56] Registered unemployment increased steadily after 1927, reached its peak in 1934, and by 1937-1938, the British Consul observed, "Mozambique [was] clearly reviving from the Depression."[57] One of the key factors in improving the urban unemployment situation was the state curb on Portuguese immigration.

Average Registered Unemployment [ARU] in Lourenço Marques, 1927-1938[58]

Year	ARU	Year	ARU
1927	198	1934	642
1928	366	1935	481
1932	354	1936	229
1933	570	1938	102

The New State's goals for white settlement barely survived the Depression. In 1931 the government abolished state-assisted passages for settlers, and by 1933 even those settlers who had sufficient capital to pay their own way were turned back. Local whites strongly lobbied the government to keep immigration very low.[59] In 1933, for example, 407 Portuguese were hired in compliance with the Depression-inspired quota laws discussed below, but the same year 422 immigrants were refused entry into Mozambique because they could not prove they had secure employment there.[60] Had the state not curbed immigration, it would have offset any benefits wrought by the quota legislation.

Between 1931 and 1938, only about 275 settlers arrived annually to settle in the district of Lourenço Marques, and the majority were women.[61] Immigrant women did not threaten male jobs; indeed the Depression revived pressure to exclude most women from wage labor.[62] Although Portuguese women were allowed in throughout the Depression, they were nonetheless among the chief beneficiaries of government assistance to the indigent.[63] Settlement of Portuguese women was perhaps sustained despite the grim economy to curb casual and legal liaisons between Portuguese men and African women, which clearly threatened the New State's social vision.

Portuguese Settlers Entering at Lourenço Marques, 1931–1946[64]

Year	Total	Male/Female	Year	Total	Male/Female
1931	199	78/121	1937	264	127/137
1932	230	84/146	1938	196	89/107
1933	282	122/160	1942	39	15/24
1934	329	144/190	1945	99	34/65
1935	329	163/186	1946	343	198/145
1936	352	192/160			

The restraint on Portuguese immigration was temporary, however, and was lifted at the first opportunity.[65]

The protectionist lobby of unemployed Portuguese workers promoted and eventually won hiring quotas in three key sectors of the urban economy: waterfront, construction, and commercial employment. The quotas were based on ethnic, language, and racial criteria.[66] The Republican government had passed a general preferential hiring law in 1925, but it was not buttressed by fines or quotas.[67] Although Portuguese artisans and laborers had already protected themselves from African competition through licensing and registration, they successfully exploited high levels of unemployment to entrench that protection. Every procedure that further constrained African labor mobility at the upper levels resonated among workers at all levels. Again, if skilled, qualified labor experienced exclusion and harassment, what could semi-skilled or unskilled labor expect?

New taxes were also introduced to accommodate declining government revenues and to support the increasing costs of social welfare benefits paid to unemployed or indigent Portuguese. On the whole, taxes were levied lightly and expended heavily on Portuguese whites. The costs were shifted piecemeal to the African population. At the beginning of the crisis, the Portuguese community was assessed a so-called "emergency tax." It was imposed on the salaries of all Portuguese civil servants, and was specifically designed to cover social support services to unemployed whites. New taxes were also levied on the African community, but they were not tied to provision of benefits.

In 1934, for example, wharf duties were extended to cover all transport operators, even if they did not use the port authority's cranes to unload their cargo. Catembe fishermen and upriver charcoal dealers who unloaded their rafts and boats in the small craft harbor were the target of this new tax. For men and women living through tough times on a tiny profit margin, the new tax was a heavy burden.[68] African tobacco growers who sold small packets of rolled tobacco in the suburbs and women who sold surplus produce also faced a new tax.[69] Neither of these taxes was likely to generate significant sums of money, but both reinforced the tendency to impose claims on African labor and capital without providing any services in return—the very tendency that provoked Karel Pott's "Enough!" editorial.

In 1937 the state instituted a major tax revision in Lourenço Marques; a head tax was instituted to replace the existing hut tax. The hut tax had become confusing in urban areas where Africans owned or rented wood and zinc housing. Sometimes the city charged a building tax (*contribuição predial*) and sometimes a hut tax–many confused and frustrated African proprietors were assessed both and the municipality was swamped with claims.[70] The new head tax, or *mudende* as it was called, was payable by all resident African men and women over the age of sixteen. It was the first time the colonial government had directly required African women to pay a tax in cash. The tax was 100$00 per year for women and 150$00 for men. It could be reduced by 50$00 if a person could prove that he or she had already paid a hut tax outside the municipal area that tax year.[71] The year the *mudende* was imposed, the emergency tax on Portuguese civil servants was lifted. The British consul observed that the estimated four million *escudos* the emergency tax would have generated from white taxpayers would now come into the treasury from African pockets.[72] In 1942 the *mudende* was extended from Lourenço Marques to the entire province.[73]

In sum, the key components of New State policy were articulated in the crisis atmosphere obtaining between 1926 and 1933. Those components cemented the systematic advantages of Portuguese throughout the economy and did so to the marked disadvantage of Mozambicans. Mozambicans who lived through that period never forgot the trauma of the experience, and subsequent generations were never able to reclaim most of the lost advantages.

Postwar Expansion and Contradictions

Portugal's neutrality in World War II allowed her to move into the postwar era with a strong currency and with her limited national and colonial infrastructures intact. Those advantages encouraged the New State to lift some constraints on investment and colonial settlement. The result in Lourenço Marques was state investment in basic infrastructure, increased and diversified private investment in construction, manufacturing, and industry, renewed state support for Portuguese settlement, and greater demand for semi-skilled and service labor. Rapid economic growth and revived labor demand promised new opportunities for the urban African labor force, but that promise was compromised by a combination of renewed Portuguese immigration and the state's continuing commitment to tight control over urban labor.

Despite the rapid growth of the private sector in the postwar era, the colonial state, its civil service pay scales, and its policies toward both Portuguese and African workers continued to shape labor relations throughout Lourenço Marques. The bottom and top wage brackets available to Africans in the city were set by state legislation. Although these regulations may not have been observed to the letter, they nonetheless set the parameters and, on the whole, functioned to keep African wages low. Mozambicans could only legally benefit from the higher pay and benefit schedules if they were *assimilados*.[74] The state actively discouraged private sector wage increases throughout the economy in order to minimize competition between state and private sector wages.[75] The specifics of state, municipal, and private labor relations are explored through the case studies in the following chapters.

Portuguese workers found that the state's commitment to development through white settlement could also be a disadvantage. The preamble to New State immigration legislation confirmed Portugal's commitment to development through white settlement as a means to ensure its political hold on Mozambique.[76] The development of Mozambique would be achieved through the state-subsidized placement of Portuguese immigrants, "to whom work must be guaranteed."[77] As early as 1944, Portugal began to encourage soldiers to settle in Mozambique, but legislation from 1951 promoted settlement on a grand scale.[78] Between 1940 and 1950, the European population of Mozambique increased 67 percent and continued to grow at just under 5 percent per year during the following half-decade.[79] Despite the state's commitment to planned agricultural settlement, most of the settlers remained in Lourenço Marques.[80]

City of Lourenço Marques White Population, 1928–1960[81]

Year	Total	Male/Female
1928	9,001	5,486/3,515
1935	12,162	6,937/5,225
1940	14,316	8,022/6,294
1945	16,149	8,968/7,181
1950	23,439	12,843/10,596
1960	41,165	21,751/19,414

Many new immigrants were so "uneasily received" in the Lourenço Marques job market that they pursued clandestine networks to employment in Southern Rhodesia or South Africa.[82] Indeed, rapid immigration soon fostered growing urban unemployment. The Bureau of Civil Administrative Services [DPAC], which was charged with settler placement, continued to encourage immigrants even when it was clear they would not find employment upon arrival.[83] High unemployment encouraged some employers to exploit Portuguese vulnerability through unpaid probationary employment and dead-end apprenticeships.[84] By 1962 over 200 Portuguese unemployed marched on City Hall to protest continuing immigration in the face of high unemployment.[85] Registered unemployment in Lourenço Marques increased from about 350 in 1955 to just over 1,000 in 1962. During those five years immigration averaged 1,600 per year.[86] Despite the expanding postwar economy, the policy of sponsored immigration curbed the ability of Mozambicans to move into better urban jobs. As was the case throughout the century, unemployed whites formed a strong barrier to the mobility of African workers.[87]

Until the policy shifts of the late 1950s, local industries were only encouraged if they did not compete with metropolitan industrial interests.[88] On the whole, industries that served the internal market and contributed to the strategy of accumulating foreign exchange earnings were established on a monopoly or limited competition basis. Some were exceptionally profitable, as was the case with the soap, oilseeds, tobacco processing, cement, and beer industries.[89] Beer production increased by an impressive 275 percent between 1937 and 1946, and then doubled between 1947 and

1954.[90] Cement production expanded a bit later, but even more dramatically, buoyed by postwar urban residential and business construction and the construction of a series of hydroelectric dams, the most important of which was the Cahora Bassa dam on the Zambezi.[91]

Industrialization to serve the developing domestic market got a jump start with a 60.7 percent increase from 1947 to 1950; the decade of the 1950s was ever more important for Lourenço Marques, as urban industry grew 62.2 percent.[92] In 1947 Lourenço Marques had a total of 150 industrial establishments with a capital value of 796,000 *contos* (a *conto* was worth 1,000 *escudos*). By 1961 there were 1,025 establishments with capital value of 4,610,000 *contos*.[93] By 1961 the industrial production base index of 100 set in 1955 had more than doubled to 223.5.[94] The New State held a tight reign on foreign capital investment until the mid-1960s. Foreign investors provided capital for the new production facilities during the late 1940s and 1950s, but the Portuguese "managed to retain control of production itself."[95]

Service sector growth was largely linked to tourism. The natural beauty and sweeping beaches of Lourenço Marques had long been touted for their tourist potential. South African and British investment in and promotion of hotels, beach resorts, deep sea fishing ventures, and excursions date from the first decade of the century, but tourism became a major source for foreign exchange in the 1950s.[96] The tourist population in Lourenço Marques increased more than fourfold in the 1950s as Rhodesians, South Africans, and metropolitan Portuguese flocked to the city's beaches, cafes, and resort clubs. In 1950 about 30,000 foreign tourists visited Moçambique, but in the peak year 1962 their number increased to almost 180,000.[97]

Employment in Selected Sectors of the Economy[98]
District of Lourenço Marques, 1950–1970
"Non Qualified" (African) Male/Female

Year	Processing Industries	Construction Public Works	Transport & Communications	Personal Services
1950	8,200/210	2,050/-	3,260/-	13,000/1,000
1960	15,180/2,420	3,500/-	4,370/-	20,000/6,000
1962	13,843/4,050	3,750/-	4,931/-	24,000/6,600
1970	19,397/9,874	4,800/-	6,951/-	34,840/11,360

Each of these developments was reflected in the African labor force. Although the above figures are for the district, rather than the city of Lourenço Marques, three of the four economic sectors were strongly concentrated in the city and its suburbs. Only the transport and communications labor force extended much beyond the city. The changing size, distribution, and nature of the urban African labor force presented important challenges to New State labor control tactics. That is the topic of Chapter 7.

7

Tailoring Labor Control in the Postwar Economy Contrasting Perspectives

The increasing affluence of Africans who come to look for work in the cities has created social discipline problems that must be resolved if we are to maintain rigorous control of the African urban population; not only to avoid vagrancy and its companion, criminality, but also to discipline domestic servants and other workers.[1]

Preamble to Labor Control Legislation, 1944

Ach! At the municipal labor office? The police there would only listen to your employer, they would nod, "Yes, Madame! Yes, Madame! Yes, Madame!"—they would look like pigeons nodding—"Yes, Madame!" And then they would beat you with the *palmatória*, Dha! Dha! Dha! Six times on each hand. That's the way it always was, it was no use to complain.

Silvestre José Zuana[2]

The pace of economic and population growth in Lourenço Marques from 1945 to 1962 seriously taxed the colonial government's ability to maintain a tight reign on urban labor. The postwar political climate also challenged the Portuguese to refurbish the window-dressing regarding "native" policy: was *assimilation* an avenue to full citizenship or not? Indeed, many SNI officials complained into the late 1950s that Mozambique had no "native" policy. They could not and did not develop a vision or plan for the future because they were too overwhelmed by the daily bureaucratic nightmares inherent in the existing labor control system to contemplate seriously policy beyond the moment.[3] It is at least reassuring to know that Mozambican workers were not the only ones to feel oppressed by the weight of Portugal's labor control bureaucracy.

This chapter addresses New State strategies to tailor urban labor controls to the postwar situation and African strategies to thwart those controls and exploit the more promising economic situation to their own ends. It is divided into two parts. The first surveys three key components of the urban labor control system and suggests how they changed between the end of the war and the abolition of the *indigenato* in 1962. First, the urban registration system was designed to constrain the mobility and earning power of the great majority of urban Africans, thus entrenching their subordinate position. Second, the systematic use of corporal punishment was designed to break the resistance of the inexperienced, the recalcitrant, and the foolhardy. Finally, the New State developed a network of fences to blunt the upward mobility of educated, skilled, ambitious African men and women whose very competence threatened the paternalistic base of the entire *indigenato*.

The second part of the chapter focuses on the experience of two Mozambican individuals with the New State's labor control system in this era. They were selected because their experience captured many of the central elements of labor relationships in Lourenço Marques that emerged strongly from the overall interview program, and because they cut across and linked the specific economic sectors selected for main case studies.

The *Indigenato*, Carrots, Sticks, and Fences

Mozambicans, whether *indígenas* or *assimilados*, were disciplined by the carrots, sticks, and fences incorporated in the *indigenato*. The city was a minefield for the unsuspecting newcomer. Although inexperienced urban migrants were the most likely to fall unwittingly into a sentence of *shibalo*, and educated or skilled local people were most likely to struggle with the fences the system erected to prevent them from competing openly with whites, the whole range of sanctions could be applied to any African. An African earning the impressive salary of 1,200$00 per month could find himself summarily sentenced to twenty months of *shibalo* at 180$00 per month for "abuse of confidence."[4] The urban labor registration system left workers little room to maneuver, and additional legislation promulgated between 1944 and 1949 further narrowed those spaces, even while the economy expanded.

The labor control system incorporated many fences and sticks and only a few carrots. We begin with the carrots because they can be despatched fairly rapidly; sticks and fences follow. The lure of the tiny handful of carrots suggests the grimness of the overall situation. Access to housing in municipal-owned "native neighborhoods" and consideration for employment in civil service "native classified jobs" were the principal carrots proffered to urban Africans through the municipal labor control system. Housing in the "native" Bairro Ximpamanine, completed in the 1920s, had no individual access to electricity or running water, although the *bairro* had its own fountain. Houses in the Bairro de Munhuana, completed in the 1940s, had plumbing and electricity, but the neighborhood was always unhealthy due to flooding in the rainy season.

The major advantages to state "native" office jobs were security and an escape from hard manual labor under the sun. They paid little more than manual labor and demanded diligence, competence, and deference.[5] In 1953, the government planted a big stick amidst this rather pathetic bunch of carrots. The government always found it difficult to draw educated Africans into the military, as trainers and officers for "native" troops. It therefore offered a carrot to men to complete military service. They would receive priority placement for "native" housing and for state and municipal "native" jobs.[6] Mozambique's horrific experience with conscription in World War I had cemented the military's already terrible reputation. Military service was considered "the worst luck you could have, even worse than *shibalo*."[7]

Registration—Curbing the Majority Labor Force

The *indigenato*, built as it was from the nineteenth-century criminal codes, embraced many and varied sticks: fines, beatings, deportation, forced labor, imprisonment, repatriation, wage reductions, and wage caps. The *Regulamento de Serviçais e Trabalhadores Indígenas* (RSTI) structured implementation of the *indigenato* in Lourenço Marques through the registration system. For most urban Africans the RSTI was the linchpin. More than any other single challenge, workers had to cope with the registration system monitored by the ubiquitous and often hungry bureaucracy. They had to get to the front of registration lines to initiate, change or renew annual labor contracts, to pay taxes and fines, to make any change in their status and to answer any charge. Men and women who ignored their obligations to the registration lines were commonly sentenced to *shibalo*. At particularly busy times, workers found they could only get to the front of the line if they demonstrated their gratitude to the attending bureaucrat or police assistant.

The registration system served to compromise African workers almost across the board. Registration held down wage increases by tying workers to annual contracts, by normally permitting wage increases only at the end of the yearly contract, and by monitoring the size of wage increases. It held workers to poor contracts or difficult work conditions. It allowed the labor control bureaucracy to monitor workplace conduct and, in the case of casual port and railway labor, to monitor absenteeism. The case studies below illustrate how these constraints worked in practice.

Although the urban RSTI was technically a control system for volunteer labor, it also provided many avenues into *shibalo*. *Shibalo* was the central stick of the *indigenato* in both rural and urban areas. It was wielded in a changing manner during this period. The *shibalo* system, like the RSTI, also served several purposes in the state's strategy to control labor. In the immediate postwar period when state and settler labor demand was high, *shibalo* was developed to generate labor in minimum wage contract conditions. As the labor supply situation began to improve in the 1950s and 1960s, *shibalo* was more commonly used to supply labor to the least attractive jobs and to discipline workers.

In the half-decade following the end of the war, *shibalo* requisitions were condoned and sharply expanded in both rural and urban areas. The basic legal concept was sustained: Africans who were willing to work were free to chose their employer, but "lazy" Africans could be conscripted for "urgent" public employment. The SNI was divided over the use and abuse of *shibalo*, in particular the validity of the concept of "laziness." One contingent asserted that were no "lazy" Africans; all Africans were willing to work and worked well if they were paid a wage that justified their effort. A second contingent found "laziness" a convenient concept that legitimated state intervention to generate requisite labor supplies without having to offer just wages.[8]

The urgency of the state's extensive postwar transportation and communication projects, in combination with increased labor demand from Portuguese settlers hoping to cash in on buoyant postwar prices for agricultural exports, encouraged the contingent willing to play the "lazy" card. In October 1946 rural administrators throughout the south were told to "give all legal help to recruiters for state service."[9] A month later they were reminded.[10] By 1947 the secretary general added his encouragement to conscript all and any "lazy" Africans, and went a step further, confirming that *shibalo* could be provided to private employers once state requisitions were filled. In 1950 confidential circulars opened the floodgates for the supply of *shibalo* to private firms.[11] Once again "bush officials" enjoyed the opportunity to "get rich in one assignment."[12]

Not since the late 1910s and early 1920s were rural areas squeezed so hard for *shibalo* labor. Subterfuge and outright abuse rendered the distinction between legal and illegal recruitment academic. Again, rural conscription directly shaped urban labor strategies. In the period immediately following both World Wars, when the market favored workers' chances to bid up wages, a coalition of settlers and bureaucrats blocked that possibility. They resorted to conscription to fill both urban and rural jobs, thus undercutting the strength of volunteer labor. Efforts by Mozambicans to press for improved wages and employment conditions were consistently compromised by *shibalo*.

Although raids (*rusgas*) for *shibalo* spilled into urban suburbs in the late 1940s, urban *shibalo* was more commonly generated by the registration system itself, through violations. Registration violations were punishable by fines or forced labor, usually depending upon the municipality's labor needs at the time. According to the new registration system inaugurated in 1949, all of the following were considered violations and therefore punishable by fines or forced labor: failure to register with the authorities within three days of arrival in town, failure to report to the registration office if one did not find employment within two weeks from original registration, failure to declare oneself self-employed, quitting without signed authorization, unregistered casual labor, working an unregistered second job or selling handicrafts on the side, any form of "moonlighting," absence from the municipal area without permission, and inciting co-workers to quit.[13]

Upon arrival in Lourenço Marques or at the end of an existing contract, Africans had two weeks within which to find a job and register the new contract according to law. Employers were well aware of the pressure this put on the work seeker. Informants explained that if they did not find work in the city within the requisite time period and return to the registration office, they would be "sold" into *shibalo*. The municipal labor officers "sold" such people to employers who did not attract volunteer workers because the wages and conditions they offered were intolerable.[14] Indeed, registration cards for this period record such incidents simply as "vai para *shibalo*," sent off to forced labor. Much evidence demonstrates that rural administrators were well paid for the labor they made available to employers. Informants were certain that the urban registration bureaucrat received something for contracting unemployed workers to particularly bad employers. They considered that something to be the worker's "sale price."[15]

Unemployment was a violation of the RSTI and *shibalo* was the most common punishment for unemployment.[16] Informant's perception of the unemployed being "sold" into *shibalo* was graphically corroborated by the cover of a municipal logbook used to register unemployed urban workers between 1960 and 1961. The unemployed were indeed all assigned to *shibalo* under various state, municipal, and private employers. The book was first titled *Shibalo*, but the word *Desempregos* (unemployed) was later superimposed.[17]

Arrests for Violation of RSTI—Lourenço Marques, 1926–1963[18]

Year	Arrests for RSTI Violations	Arrests as a Percentage of African Urban Population
1926	4,691	
1927	4,306	20
1928	5,852	
1931	4,934	17
1932	6,070	
1933–1945	no comparable statistics available	
1946	3,494	
1948	8,117	
1949	7,323	
1950	7,307	13
1956	7,239	
1959	8,462	
1960	6,620	5
1961	1,525	

Despite the fact that between thirty-five hundred and seven thousand Africans were arrested in Lourenço Marques for RSTI infractions every year in Lourenço Marques, those arrested comprised a diminishing percentage of the total urban labor force. When the New State first came to power, 20 percent of the urban labor force was sanctioned for registration violations. But by 1950 that percentage had dropped to 13, and by 1960 to 5. What changed?

Several explanations are possible, and we shall return to the question. Deteriorating conditions in rural areas due to agricultural *shibalo*, forced rice and cotton cultivation, and alienation of some of the South's most productive farm land for agricultural settlement schemes contributed to urbanization and eventually to the development of a surplus of unskilled labor in Lourenço Marques. The same phenomenon tended to diminish the strength of rural production and support networks enjoyed by urban workers and thus made them increasingly dependent upon urban income and networks. Some evidence at least suggests that as workers became more dependent upon waged labor, they were more careful to comply with registration regulations.

The municipal official charged with implementing RSTI in the city in 1950 explicitly linked increasing proletarianization with worker compliance, but also confirmed sustained forms of resistance. He claimed that Africans native to Lourenço Marques were by and large "educated hard workers" who rarely broke the law.

Nearly all court cases in the city involved migrants, not locals. Locals purchased virtually all their food and worked to sustain their family whose "sole resource was the salary of the head of household."[19] He allowed, however, that urban taxes were always collected "with difficulty."[20] By the early 1960s many migrant families living in Lourenço Marques were in a similar position—living with difficulty from the wages of one man.[21] The U.S. consul remarked in the early 1950s that there were "no outward signs of resistance" among the urban African population in Lourenço Marques. Africans dutifully carried their registration papers and went about their business—or at least that's what it looked like to Europeans.[22]

Palmatória—Breaking the Recalcitrant

Self-surveillance was not simply a product of increased proletarianization. In Lourenço Marques it was directly related to worker experience with the battery of sanctions regularly employed by the SNI. Perhaps the most important factor in the development of worker self-surveillance was both figuratively and literally a stick. It was a flat paddle called a *palmatória,* which had five or six holes in it that sucked in flesh so that each blow caused swelling and bleeding. The *palmatória* was used to terrorize, humiliate, and discipline Africans into self-surveillance. It was such an ubiquitous instrument of domination that it was featured in songs, stories, and art that captured images of colonial rule.[23]

According to government documents of the 1940s, all of the following were offenses legally punishable by a *palmatória* beating: insubordination, indiscipline, provoking revolt or grave misbehavior, offenses to public morality, violence against European women and children, quitting one's job, and disrespect, threats, or violence toward Europeans.[24] African women, children, and men apparently did not require protection from violence or threat. Beatings for indiscipline, insubordination, misbehavior, and disrespect toward Europeans clearly returns us to Sianai Chichongo's assertion that the Portuguese did not think Africans had "two legs like they did."[25] The U.S. consul in Lourenço Marques in the mid-1950s made the same point: "It might be said that native labor in Mozambique . . . is first considered by the Portuguese as being NATIVE and only secondarily if at all as being LABOR."[26] Racist subordination, discipline, and respectful behavior were essential for the reproduction of a dominated and devalued population that could be forced to work for wages and under conditions that would otherwise not draw or hold labor—any labor. Physical violence enforced subordination and encouraged self-surveillance. As Daniel Nhangumbe said, "Europeans could order you to do anything, if you refused you would be beaten. This [pointing to his mouth] was your beak, not your mouth! It was not a black person's place to say anything. The only thing a black person was permitted to say was 'Yes, Sir' or 'Yes, Madame'."[27] People with two legs did not have beaks.

The same system of domination which ensured that Africans were beaten for disrespect, threats, or violence toward Europeans, and explicitly European women and children, prevented African men from protecting African women and children from European threats, violence, or disrespect. Alfeu Cumbe and many others bristled, recalling that: "any Portuguese who looked at your wife and saw she was beautiful could to go right into the house after her. If they wanted your wife they could see that she was taken away by the police, and they would have her there—it was bad, a lot of bad things went on."[28] African men, even young boys, who were accused of looking indiscreetly at a European woman were beaten and deported.[29] Yet Europeans and Africans backed up by European authority commonly used sexual violence to assert their authority over African women. Finally, the prominence of explicit sexual references in African performance and songs about colonial relationships clearly reveals that sexuality, violence, and social domination were closely related.[30]

Whites could take advantage of the entire spectrum of sanctions against Africans at any time, and blacks always had to keep them all in mind. Part of the power of the *palmatória* was its arbitrary and often unjust use. Silvestre José Zuana's description was typical of informant testimony and broadly documented in municipal records for the 1950s and 1960s: "If any little thing went wrong on the job, my employer [Madame] would beat me, a good solid beating—and often for nothing."[31] An old man working as a day laborer on the docks was beaten for trying to sneak a nap.[32] A cook, who knew the authorities would not allow him to receive the high wage he had been offered by a prospective employer, was beaten for trying to secure that wage by evading registration.[33] The simplest forms of resistance, or the least lapse in respectful demeanor toward whites, could earn one a beating.

Fences—Blocking the Upwardly Mobile

Discipline and control of African labor took on a slightly different cast as one moved up the economic ladder in Lourenço Marques. Workers at these loftier heights were less likely to be beaten or sent off to *shibalo*, but more likely to confront the system's fences. There were two kinds of fences, an explicit legal fence and an implicit social fence. The implicit social fence was designed to ensure that the legal equality technically enjoyed by *assimilados* did not permit people "of the Negro race or descendent therefrom" to hold positions above or enjoy lifestyles superior to those of Europeans. As we shall see, if that situation threatened to materialize, legal technicalities were sometimes invoked to head it off. Informants usually described the social fence as a reflection of Portuguese petty jealousy.[34]

The explicit legal fence created a special space between ordinary *indígenas* and *assimilados*. It enclosed a group best described as "native" professionals. This second fence was designed to do at least two things. It ensured that trained Africans supplied essential goods and services to the weaker African market, but were not allowed to compete with Europeans in the more lucrative white market. It also ensured that African communities received the basic health and educational services necessary to reproduce the labor force at minimum standards, at the lowest possible cost. Teachers, nurses, artisans, and merchants could be required to work in the least attractive situations at low wages if that was all that was available to "natives." The "native" prefix to "professional" status confirmed their subordination: "native" teachers, "native" nurses, "native" office workers, "native" carpenters and merchants, and so on.

The contradictions inherent in the fenced-off area of "native" professionals emerge in the story of "native" nurse Lídia Felizmina Tembe, who was in fact an *assimilada*.[35] Of all the subordinate professions, nursing was the most attractive because it offered the highest wages. The prerequisites for applicants were the same basic qualifications required for assimilation applicants, a fourth-grade primary certificate and a state-registered birth certificate. Each was a costly social investment requiring fees and a host of expensive supporting documents, and they were only the beginning. When Lídia Tembe applied to train as a nurse midwife in Lourenço Marques in the late 1940s, the requisite fees and certificates cost a total of 500$00 to 600$00—the equivalent of two months' labor for women in fairly good jobs. Since Lídia was an unemployed single mother of two when she applied for school, she was only able to pay the fees and attend classes with the help of her mother and grandmother. They helped care for Lídia's children and loaned her the money they earned illegally brewing millet beer.

Lídia paid the same fees as Europeans, but unlike them, she did not receive room and board. After graduation, her European colleagues began work at more than twice her wage, and most soon earned ten times more.[36] Lídia's first post (1952–1959) was at Monte Pois in Porto Amélia, so she could no longer live with her mother and grandmother or depend upon them to help care for her children. In order to have her daughters nearby, she had to place them in a boarding school. Despite her "professional" status, Lídia did not earn enough to pay her daughters' tuition without resorting to delivering babies at peoples' homes instead of the hospital—a practice that was technically illegal. In short, despite her "professional" status, Lídia had to resort to "illegal" income to make ends meet, much like her uneducated mother and grandmother.

The contradictions of the implicit social fence were particularly well illustrated by a series of municipal investigations undertaken in the late 1940s in connection with the revision of assimilation legislation in 1944.[37] According to the law, *assimilados*, once granted their *álvara de assimilação*, became full citizens whose situation was no longer shaped by the *indigenato*. The first contradiction was that government inquiries or questions involving *assimilados* were usually channeled through the SNI.[38] The second contradiction was that although the central dynamic of the so-called civilizing mission and assimilation process was to encourage *indígenas* to live and behave like Europeans, the closer Africans came to accomplishing those ends, the more uncomfortable Portuguese were with them.

The 1944 law stated that only *assimilados* who "lived like Europeans" qualified to receive European wage levels; all others would be subject to a wage cap of 1,000$00. Obviously, living like a European was one of the core qualifications of assimilation, so one begins with something of a contradiction. Furthermore, such laws clearly took the lifestyle of the European lower middle class as their benchmark, conveniently ignoring the fact that hundreds of Portuguese lived in Lourenço Marques in poverty and could not meet either the economic or literacy minimums required of *assimilados*. In response to the new law, the SNI undertook investigations to be sure *assimilados* met the new qualifications. If they did they could continue to receive their present salary; if not, their wages would be reduced to a maximum of 1,000$00 per month—still quite high in terms of 1949 African wage rates.

Jeremias Dick Nhaca was investigated in 1949. Nhaca was educated in the Wesleyan mission schools, and since the early 1930s he had been a prominent member of the Instituto Negrófilo. He applied for assimilation in 1938, along with many other educated Africans, to avoid conscription into the military as an *indígena*.[39] His position as a tally clerk at Lourenço Marques Forwarding Company paid 1,200$00 per month, about the highest salary any African earned in the city. His job required him to speak and write both English and Portuguese.[40] Nhaca was clearly an educated, well paid, and respected member of the urban African community, yet the inspection report found him only marginally qualified for the privileges his status accorded him:

> [Nhaca lived] . . . without a shadow of the comforts indispensable to Europeans.
>
> Only his children benefit from [his] assimilation, since he sends them to school:
>
> one is a nurse, one a printer, one daughter with a fourth class primary education and two minor sons—one who attends the fourth class [primary] and the other who is preparing for the exam to enter the Technical School.[41]

The inspector concluded that Nhaca's notion of comfort was "a house of four partitions, and a nook of a back yard destined to be a bathroom."[42] Nhaca was temporarily living in such conditions, because he had been forced to sell his best land to Radio Marconi, and in 1949 he was paying off a piece of land where he planned to build "a big house."[43] That an educated man who had managed to see his children through to the highest positions available to Africans at the time could be subjected to such a silly ritual spoke to the depths to which the New State stooped to humiliate Africans.

David Thomé Magaia was also among those investigated. His case clearly revealed the tensions between assimilation and racist domination. Magaia earned 800$00 per month in cash wages, but his salary packet also included room and board for himself and his family. He met the new legal standard for education and lifestyle, but the administration's investigator nevertheless lobbied against allowing him to receive further salary increments, noting that "many Europeans, indeed the majority, don't have an income equal to that of the *assimilado* in question."[44] Another case drew the comment, "How many Europeans aspire to a position such as this black man has, but are unable to find one?"[45] Similar comments throughout the investigation clearly documented the administration's commitment to promote and sustain social distance with race fences, and confirmed informant testimony on the extent and nature of Portuguese petty jealousy.

Negotiating the *Indigenato*

Gabriel Mabunda—Learning to Lie

One informant's story so clearly reveals many features of the New State's efforts to dominate workers (and workers' strategies to get around that domination) that it is worth an extended telling. It is the story of Gabriel Mabunda, yet Mabunda's experience echoed testimony by dozens of informants and reflected the general patterns that emerged from the sample overview.[46] When Gabriel Mabunda left mission school in Chibuto to seek his first job in Lourenço Marques, he did so with a good deal of pride in himself and his accomplishments. He arrived in the city hopeful of a bright future. He was sixteen. Happily, he never lost his pride or his hope, but he quickly learned not to wear it on his sleeve. He had been taught to value honest and forthright discourse, but he quickly learned to be a skilled liar.

The transformation of Gabriel Mabunda was part of his education with the Portuguese labor system. His first job was as a general cleaning person and helper at a Portuguese boarding house:

Since I was new the boarders wanted to know about me, my training, and all. I told them I had passed the fourth class. They began to ask me about history, geography, and I answered their questions. They were pleased, and the Senhora of the boarding house was pleased too, because her daughter was in the fourth class, and she asked if I could help her with science. But the Senhor of the house wasn't pleased. He wasn't pleased because he didn't know how to write.

When I washed up the dining room . . . I used soap, and he began to say that I put on too much soap, and he beat me. Then when I put on a little soap, he would say I had put on too little, and he beat me again. He would say that I knew how to read and write, but I didn't know how to wash the floor, so he beat me again.

It did not take many beatings for Mabunda to decide that he had registered for the wrong job, with the wrong boss, but changing the situation entailed struggle with the registration system. When he tried to cancel the contract, the clerk told him he had to complete it, despite the alleged beatings.

Mabunda returned from the registration office to find the boss waiting for him with a knife. With the help of some of the staff he escaped uninjured, but he was still stuck with the incomplete contract. He cautiously returned to the boarding house in search of the sympathetic Senhora. She signed off the contract, but when Mabunda took it to the registration office for confirmation, the clerk recognized him and accused him of having signed off the contract himself—a common strategy among domestics hoping to extricate themselves from similarly bad situations. But then Mabunda blundered badly, saying that he didn't sign the contract, and he could prove it because his handwriting was much better, and he offered a demonstration. Africans were not supposed to be, have, or do anything better than whites, and if they did they were certainly not supposed to flaunt it. Mabunda quickly found himself in trouble. The clerk snapped, "You see those people over there? Those people over there are going to São Tomé . . . now if you are lying about this you might be going right along with them. Why did you sign this off yourself?"

Mabunda quickly replied that he would go back to the boarding house and straighten it out. But he did not go back; he just hung out of sight until that clerk left and another took his place. Mabunda then returned to the line and worked his way to the front to cancel the contract. When the clerk asked why he hadn't finished the contract, Mabunda told him his boss said he was not a good worker. When the clerk then asked who had signed the contract, this time Mabunda knew better than to say that the Senhora signed it because the Senhor did not know how to write. Instead he lied again, saying that the Senhor was ill, so the Senhora signed him off. The clerk then dismissed him with, "OK you have five days to get a job" and "Bang!" he stamped the contract. Having nearly gotten himself deported by telling the truth, Mabunda saved himself by lying. He had learned his first major lesson about maneuvering on the margins. But he was also lucky. If the first clerk had unexpectedly returned, Mabunda would certainly have faced a beating and might have ended up in São Tomé after all.

His next venture was more successful, in part because he was becoming accomplished in deception. He got a job at a grocery store. The job paid 125$00 per month, an increase from the 75$00 he had earned at the boarding house. When he went to register his new job, the clerk refused to allow him that increase with so little experience. That is a classic example of how the registration system functioned to keep wages down despite market forces.[47] Mabunda cleverly responded that his job entailed delivering goods by bicycle, and were he to drop and break anything he would have to pay for it. How was he going to pay for his bungling if he only earned 75$00 per month? The ploy of incompetence worked and he was signed for 125$00.

In truth, Mabunda was not at all worried about breaking his deliveries. He was ambitious and wanted money to pay for typing lessons. He wanted to earn a typist's certificate to improve his chances for an office job. He soon found a woman who offered lessons, but at 150$00 per month. When he showed her his registration, corroborating that he only earned 125$00 per month, she agreed to teach him for that amount. Mabunda then tackled the problem of taking typing lessons while he worked. He developed a scheme to collect his deliveries for the day and ride slowly away from the store. As soon as he was out of sight, he rode as fast as he could to complete the deliveries and get to his class. He then hid the store bicycle in the bushes, took his one hour class, and returned to the store as though he had been on the road the whole time. Despite the sacrifice, he managed the scheme for six months and became a certified typist.

After a few false starts, Mabunda finally got a break and cracked a job as "native" office assistant at the port complex. There he typed, composed, and computed for European colleagues who took the credit and earned three to four times his salary. But Mabunda's education, skill, and youth put him in a good position to take advantage of the 1960s promotions designed to give upwardly mobile and ambitious Africans a stake in the system. Mabunda's time as a "native" office worker was therefore shorter. When we met in 1977, he was a top official in the port and rail complex. Mabunda's strategy of playing to Portuguese stereotypes of Africans as bad workers, bunglers, and dimwits worked to his advantage. Fear, luck, and a timely appreciation of the danger involved in risk-taking informed the transformation of the proud, youthful Mabunda. He sustained his self-confidence and drive. As a young, educated, unmarried male he had more space to maneuver and less to risk than many others, but there were doubtless others who played a similar game and also won.

Samuel Chipoco Miuanga

Risks at the Margins

Although fear clearly sharpened Mabunda's wits and beatings convinced him to put distance between him and his unpredictable employer, Mabunda was in some ways more challenged by the situation than he was cowed. But the Portuguese definitions of disrespect and insubordination were so arbitrary and biased and the penalties so draconian that some workers actually accepted unjust punishment rather than risk a confrontation that would almost certainly lead to even greater punishment. Even Mabunda walked away from two months' back pay at his first job that required typing rather than challenge a false allegation of theft by an employer, explaining, "Was I going to risk my hide for 690$00?[48]" Some informants were beaten or imprisoned on false charges, but put the incidents behind them, considering themselves fortunate that their treatment had not been worse.[49] Others, like Saul Tembe, would not risk working in Mozambique at all. They preferred the clear racist barriers in South Africa to the arbitrary minefield of sanctions in Lourenço Marques. According to Tembe, "Here everyone walked with fear!"[50]

One informant, however, took a lot of risks before he learned fear. His case illustrates some of the links between risk, fear, subordination, and brutality.[51] If Mabunda's experience was in some ways a best case scenario, Samuel Chipoco Miuanga's falls toward the other end of the spectrum, and provides special insight into the phenomenon of self-surveillance. Samuel Chipoco Miuanga became discouraged working for low wages in Lourenço Marques, and in 1950 decided to join his cousin and others to seek work in South Africa. Instead of applying to Wenela and being tied to a twelve-month contract at an unknown mine, Miuanga and the others attempted to evade the border guards and seek employment as free agents. By the 1950s clandestine emigration was a regular business, involving as many as two hundred thousand people each year.[52]

Unbeknownst to Miuanga, however, the municipality had set up a special police sting unit to target clandestine emigration networks barely six months earlier. Miuanga and his group were apprehended by the border police. For several days he was intermittently beaten and sent to work in the fields of a nearby Portuguese planter. Eventually he and others who had been caught in the same sweep were marched back to Lourenço Marques where they were set to work on road gang *shibalo* labor for the Geological Survey team.

Miuanga soon noticed that some members of the gang returned to eat and sleep at their own homes after each work day instead of returning to the barracks, jails, or compounds where *shibalo* gangs were fed and housed. Some agreement had apparently been made with the overseer to enable the workers to eat and sleep at home as long as they appeared at the work place daily and did their work. The arrangement also saved the state the expense of feeding and housing the men and again speaks to the issue of the cost of *shibalo* and who paid it.

Once again Miuanga decided to take a risk and try spending the night with a friend. When he returned the next day he was sent to administrative headquarters where he was beaten with a *palmatória* until his hands and feet bled and swelled to half again their normal size. The police then made him lie on the floor with arms outstretched while they stood on his painfully swollen hands. He was then sent back in that condition to finish the day's work on the road gang. He was to be an example to others who might assume unconfirmed privileges. Surveillance and discipline on the job remained casual as before, but Miuanga did not risk further incident. From that point on, he succumbed to self-surveillance.

Tailoring Labor Control to the Postwar Economy

The combination of interviews and a 5 percent systematic sample of the labor registration records for the city from 1950 to 1962 provided a good overview of the labor control system in the postwar era. The source bases proved complementary. The systematic sample provided a quantitative measure of the validity of informant recollections. Together, they confirmed that right up to the end of the *indigenato*, Lourenço Marques Africans worked in a highly coercive system where racist and arbitrary sanctions promoted a level of self-surveillance. The written record corroborates the extent of force, apprehension, and punishment, whereas the oral record reveals a whole range of successful strategies to evade labor limitations, which did not appear in the written record because they passed unapprehended.

Forced labor and beatings were not exceptional, nor were they merely the pre-dictable part newly independent Mozambicans chose to recall about their colonial past. They were clearly an integral part of the overall control system. *Shibalo* was a more common problem for rural workers than for urban workers. Indeed, as we have seen, men moved to Lourenço Marques and committed themselves to a life of wage labor in order to escape brutal and dangerous cycles of *shibalo*. The urban sample nevertheless revealed that fully 12 percent of registered workers had served at least one term of *shibalo* for violation of the RSTI.[53] That strongly corroborated informant testimony that *shibalo* was an important sanction routinely faced by urban workers—it was indeed statistically significant. It also confirmed that the state and municipal-ity routinely had sufficient *shibalo* workers at their disposal to continue to organize transit handling, sanitation, and a whole range of public works projects around con-scripted gang labor. That allowed two large employers in the city to conscript an important component of their labor force, contributing to the overall depression of African wages. Furthermore, those two large employers could simply replace striking volunteer labor with *shibalo*, also obviously undermining the ability of city workers to exercise a strike weapon.

The sample also revealed that nearly 5 percent of the registered African labor force received at least one *palmatória* beating at the labor offices—one in twenty workers. Other common beatings, such as those received by Mabunda, Miuanga, and dozens of other informants, were not revealed in such records. The extent of corpo-ral punishment was if anything much higher.[54] As we shall see, *palmatória* beatings were most frequently administered to young domestic servants, and *shibalo* sen-tences were most often served by recent migrants and unskilled workers. *Shibalo* sen-tences for RSTI violations and urban labor roundups peaked in the early 1950s, fueled by the strong labor demand from urban construction in the public and private sector. RSTI arrests dropped off sharply in the mid- to late 1950s when a surplus of unskilled labor combined with labor reforms to render them both unnecessary and politically unacceptable. Forced labor sentences and *palmatória* beatings also peaked with the labor shortage in the early 1950s, and declined rapidly after 1957.[55] After Portugal signed the International Labor Organization statutes and moved toward further integration with Europe, fines became the most common punishment for all offenders, with the exception of youthful domestic servants, who continued to be disciplined by *palmatória* beatings.[56]

To what extent was this record of labor violations and punishment an overall indication of serious worker resistance? First, the high incidence of beatings was less a measure of worker resistance than a reflection of very young domestics being se-verely disciplined for "any little thing," and of a state policy to foster cheaper self-surveillance through an arbitrary atmosphere of terror.[57] Second, urban workers who posed any serious challenge to employers or the state in this period were few. Their punishment was commonly deportation, either to São Tomé or northern Mozam-bique. Workers who had a long history of arrests for petty offenses, frequently alco-holics, were similarly deported.[58] The majority of arrests for labor regulation violations fell into two broad categories: working casual labor without authorization and failure to report to authorities when not legally employed.[59] Both reflected the efforts of individuals to market their labor to maximize income and protect themselves from long-term, low-wage contracts.[60]

Risks of being apprehended as an unregistered casual worker were somewhat diminished by the fact that thousands were hired on a daily basis, and it was impossible for the authorities to do much more than spot check without greatly slow-ing production.[61] Sentences for working unregistered casual labor ranged from three to twelve months' *shibalo*, three for first offenders, and more for workers with a history of evasion.[62] In short, while the incidence of arrests for violation of labor regulations was high—about one in ten arrested at least once between 1950 and 1962—the nature of the violations revealed a pattern of workers cautiously evading the system in an attempt to gain time to find a satisfactory legal niche for themselves, rather than any persistent on-the-job confrontation between labor and capital. Employment records revealed very little turnover and little *apprehended* resistance among workers in ac-knowledged good jobs.[63] The case studies in Chapters 8 and 9 demonstrate that when men decided to seek work in Lourenço Marques, they also usually decided to make their way carefully.[64] Many case studies, such as Mabunda's, revealed resistance pat-terns that did not show up in the statistics because they were unapprehended.

The abolition of the *indigenato* registration system cleared much of the Lourenço Marques minefield. For the first time since 1904, most Africans could legally quit their job. For the first time since the Depression they could work as many jobs as they could arrange, in whatever order they liked. Whereas petty service and commodity production were still subject to licensing constraints, the abolition of registration also facilitated entry into these areas. Finally, and crucially, the state was no longer able to intervene directly to depress wages in the private sector. Although state-mandated minimum wages continued to play a role in an urban economy where the state sec-tor was so large, it became much easier for most Africans to bid up their wages. The changing situation was best described by an anonymous informant speaking to Mar-vin Harris in the early 1960s, "Formerly the faucet was completely shut. . . . Now it is open and the water is flowing . . . drip . . . drip . . . drip."[65]

At the practical level, the abolition of registration and a range of *indigenato* con-straints was crucial to enhanced labor mobility, but it surely did not remove the weight of racist domination. This chapter closes with an incident that occurred in 1959 between a Mozambican man, named Major Choque, and a Portuguese child, named Henrique de Sousa.[66] The incident illustrates the charged chemistry of Afri-can anger and Portuguese insecurity. It suggests African awareness of a threshold of change in the early 1960s, but also confirms the fact that, despite the abolition of the *indigenato*, the threat of Portuguese sanctions was not to be taken lightly.

Choque was supposed to pick up a prescription for his employer at a pharmacy, but when he arrived, the pharmacy door was closed. Choque began knocking at the door. Henrique de Sousa, who was playing on the balcony of the upstairs apartment, saw Choque knocking and called down to the pharmacy employee to open the door and attend to "o preto," the blackman. Choque called up to the child, "Look here lit-tle boy, I am not 'o preto,' I am an African. I know very well, little boy, that this is 1959, but in 1960 you will no longer call me 'o preto.'" Choque's insistence that he be politely addressed by a child seems quite innocent in comparison with João Albasini's irreverent lampoons of Portuguese *kubvanas* and Karel Pott's angry editorial "Enough!" It is indicative of the tension of this transition that Choque's rebuke was deemed subversive. He was arrested and deported to a labor colony in northern Mozambique for two years. To some extent he was lucky; the local authorities had recommended a four-year sentence.

8

A Hierarchy of Struggles in the Port Sector 1933–1962

On the Waterfront
by Rui de Noronha[1]

The clashing metal throws sparks out
Into the calm waters of the bay.
White seagulls come and go, spearing up
Little fish and making their insane racket.

Gradually darkness comes and they begin to arrive,
The old women loaded down with fishing gear,
The buoys sending out to the sea their gentle refrain
Of lights all in a row.
And meanwhile, on the wharves, the drudgery begins.
Floodlights suddenly awaken,
Illuminating even the most distant objects.

And then one hears, stronger and more vibrant,
The blacks at their song, all the night long
Among the clatter and dust of the coaling machines. . . .

When Rui de Noronha wrote this poem in the early 1930s, the clatter, dust, and night work at the port was slow compared to the pace that accompanied the postwar expansion of waterfront facilities and the extension of the rail line to Rhodesia. The transit trade recovery began slowly in the late 1930s, but between 1940 and 1954 port traffic doubled and domestic railway traffic tripled.[2] Port earnings at Lourenço Marques nearly doubled between 1945 and 1947, and between 1950 to 1952 port receipts were double the level of expenditures.[3]

Portugal's investment in transportation and communications focusing on the port capital's transit traffic and revenues in foreign exchange enhanced that sector's strategic position in the postwar era. Port construction and upgrading promoted

Port photograph.

increased mechanization of handling, but Lourenço Marques remained fundamentally dependent upon unskilled African labor. African port and railway workers had lost virtually all their earlier gains during the economic depression from 1929 to 1933. To what extent were they able to exploit the economic revival, construction, and the strategic nature of transit handling to claim some of the increased prosperity for themselves and their families?

This chapter considers a range of workers' strategies to regain some of what they had lost in the earlier crisis, to hold their ground, and in some cases merely to mediate the extent of their exploitation. After a brief survey of the extent of port and railway development, the chapter is divided into two sections. The first section contrasts the strategies developed by a range of manual laborers, from stevedores in the best-paid and most critical jobs, to casual laborers who comprised the majority, to *shibalo* gangs who worked in the tightest margins. The second section concerns the separate struggles waged by those few Africans who worked office or management jobs. The chapter confirms that different strategies developed, depending upon workers' location within the port labor hierarchy. Manual labor tended to develop group strategies and confronted African police, overseers, and managers in their struggles, whereas office workers depended upon intensely personal, individual strategies that bridged the tense racial divide between black, brown, and white. It concludes that the state's coercive and authoritarian labor relations strongly tempered worker initiatives at every level.

Moving More for Less: The Burgeoning Waterfront

As part of the port and rail complex reorganization, the timber yards were moved upriver to Matola. The wharf was extended another 300 meters, adding two more berths, coaling capacity was expanded, cold storage was increased to accommodate 180,000 tons, a second rail line was laid to Manhica to ease congestion on the main line, and in September 1952 the Limpopo rail line to the Rhodesias was begun. With the completion of the rail line to Rhodesia in 1955, the port gained a second international hinterland. The Matola upriver depot for petroleum, mineral products, and lumber was also significantly extended after 1955. Finally, the port's sugar handling and cold storage facilities were expanded to accommodate sugar and fruit exports from South Africa and local producers. By the late 1950s, Lourenço Marques was one of the busiest, most modern, and efficient ports in Africa.[4]

Goods Handled through Lourenço Marques[5] 1934–1962

Year	Metric Ton	Year	Metric Ton
1933	1,022,476	1941	2,019,496
1935	1,346,482	1942	2,343,099
1936	1,418,652	1943	3,303,896
1937	1,663,013	1947	2,989,289
1938	1,751,769	1949	3,304,852
1939	1,697,188	1953	3,537,269
1940	1,752,221	1954	3,890,623
1955	4,134,341	1959	5,300,000
1956	4,828,466	1960	5,807,000
1957	5,513,412	1961	6,694,000
1958	5,627,646	1962	7,093,310

Coal Exported through Lourenço Marques[6] 1934–1953

Year	Metric Tons	Year	Metric Tons
1934	299,415	1945	2,577,101
1937	506,305	1946	2,180,859
1938	611,660	1947	1,450,564
1939	487,129	1948	785,450
1940	517,693	1949	1,172,966
1941	579,921	1950	1,513,202
1942	1,044,486	1951	729,751
1943	1,303,999	1952	475,298
1944	2,410,129	1953	580,621

During the same period, however, the African labor force that moved the traffic worked harder for less money. The replacement of casual port labor with *shibalo* working around-the-clock shifts was designed in part to increase tonnage handled per worker. Tonnage handled between 1931 and 1933 increased by 52 percent at waterfront and 33 percent in the rail yards, over a period when African personnel in the entire port and rail complex was cut by 15 percent, and waterfront personnel was cut at least 21 percent.[7] A combination of mechanization and coercion contributed to the fairly steady increase in labor productivity.

Average Tonnage Handled per African Laborer per Day[8] 1929–1950

Year	Wharf Tonnage	Railway Tonnage
1929	2.6	5
1931	5.36	7.1
1948	7.0	14.5
1949	6.5	16.6
1950	8.5	29.9

In the immediate postwar period, the number of Africans employed at the port and railway complex increased 20 to 30 percent. The great majority were casual workers with no benefits beyond a day's wage. The basic day wage for port labor in the state sector remained unchanged from 1933 to 1957, but inflation picked up markedly in the war years and steadily eroded the real value of those wages. Workers at all levels could make a good case for wage increases by the late 1940s.

African Personnel at Port and Railway 1946 to 1950[9]

Year	1946	1947	1948	1949	1950
Subordinate	276	288	761	450	288
Minor	10,201	12,187	12,625	13,929	12,176

Different categories of port workers experienced the pinch a bit differently. The key difference, as usual, was between voluntary and *shibalo* labor. The state's position was always that their basic wage rate was equal, except that volunteers received their full wage in cash whereas *shibalo* received about half the value of their wage in kind for room and board. Both had access to overtime income at the same rate. During the war years, however, the cost of housing and food escalated so much that by 1949, even the municipality urged the state to raise wages for volunteer port workers, because the prices they paid for food and housing had increased sharply since 1938.[10] In theory, *shibalo* labor should have suffered less since they did not have to purchase room and board on the urban market. *Shibalo*, casual hod carriers, and the more specialized stevedores each felt the stress of increased production on a tighter budget and responded accordingly.

Port photograph.

Overtime Strategies—Casual Labor Binges

The revived traffic flow was the key to port labor strategies from recovery through the war years. Workers were once again able to work a six-day week and even earn overtime income. Coming from Depression conditions, when a man was lucky to work two days a week, the mere return to full employment alleviated part of the problem of falling real wages. It took more money to live at the same standard, but for a while at least, people could stay even if they could work more hours. Overtime strategies were central to casual labor's ability to sustain their living in this period.

With the completion of the rail link to Southern Rhodesia in 1955, traffic at Lourenço Marques increased dramatically, and the state was determined to see that freight handling kept pace. Despite the addition of a second line of track between Lourenço Marques and Manhica in 1955, congestion remained a problem at the waterfront. Workers, whose base wages had remained fixed while both taxes and the cost of living continued to climb, also had powerful incentives to work as much overtime as they could handle. By 1953 the African press complained that wharf labor was being worked to death, pushed to skip meal and rest times.[11] Roberto Tembe and

Joaquim da Costa, tally clerks at the port throughout this period, also emphasized the risk to worker health and safety from depending upon overtime income. Both told of workers being crushed to death because they had hidden under a temporarily stopped locomotive to grab some much-needed sleep.[12]

Although day wage rates stagnated, both the state and private companies raised overtime rates to keep up with the increasing traffic. Day-shift production almost inevitably suffered. Stretching the regular shift's load into overtime or preserving strength on the regular shift to take advantage of available overtime opportunities were common strategies. Slowdowns were particularly prevalent among *shibalo* gangs seeking overtime for cash wages. For the most part, headmen and production managers came to terms with this common strategy by developing an informal piece-work system. The rail yard *shibalo* gangs, for example, were assigned a specific number of cars to load or unload per day, but once those were finished they could wait around for overtime, sleep, work on their crafts, or do what they liked.[13] Port directors were aware of *shibalo* time bargaining, but tolerated it as long as it did not challenge authority and production kept pace with traffic.[14] Clearly a certain measure of inefficiency was a built-in cost for controlling conscripted workers whose contract wages provided little incentive for productivity, and even *shibalo* workers resisted overtime when it became excessive.[15]

Volunteer hod carriers and stevedores clearly also paced their work with one eye on the clock, but they were driven harder and were more frequently sanctioned for slowdowns.[16] Day laborers preferred to maximize their income by working "group binge" strategies to take advantage of the overtime rates. Ten or twelve men worked together as a binge gang for two or three days running. They worked and slept in shifts, with eight to ten men on and two to four men off.[17] Overtime rates were pegged to the nature of the job. For regular cargo in 1948, state hod carriers earned 12$00 per day shift, but they could earn 36$00 with a regular around-the-clock binge.[18] In the early 1950s volunteers in cold storage work earned 6$00 per daytime half-shift, and each overtime half-shift paid 11$00. Overtime at the caustic mineral wharves paid 8$50 per overtime half-shift and all others paid 7$50. By working an around-the-clock binge in cold storage, day laborers could earn almost a full week's regular pay.[19]

Workers were well aware of the specific danger in each zone, and the cost of serious injury to uninsured, unprotected people like themselves. Scrapes, slivers, and gashes from rough edges in the woodlots, for example, could lead to an infection, loss of work time, or worse. Some of the most serious damage to workers only took its toll after years of exposure. The higher overtime rates for sustained exposure to asbestos, caustic soda, and coal dust were eventually weighed against damage to workers' lungs and skin.

In August 1953 the state finally raised the issue of protective clothing, mandatory rest, showering time, and maximum overtime in the toxic material, caustic minerals, and cold storage zones. The state explicitly recognized the danger to its labor force, but continued to postpone investments in safety.[20] When the state finally decided to require some protection for labor working with toxic or caustic materials in 1954, it made the stunning decision to exclude itself from compliance—only private shipping and handling firms would be legally required to protect their workers.[21] Basic protective equipment, such as dust masks, was not provided to workers in the state-run port zones until the 1960s.

Only salaried Africans with more than fifteen years' service could be considered permanent employees eligible for a pension when unfit, ill, or elderly.[22] Since most Africans were casual labor, not part of the permanent staff, they remained excluded from coverage regardless of their years of service.[23] The best a disabled worker could look forward to was dispensation from his "moral obligation to work," followed by a life of begging in the street.[24] The only significant and sustained effort to assist the urban disabled was the "Fund to Assist the Poor," begun by Rufino de Oliveira.[25] In sum, up to a certain point, opportunities for overtime labor in the burgeoning port zone enabled workers to compensate for inflation. The cost of that strategy in terms of worker health and safety was paid almost exclusively by the workers.

Confrontations—Manual Labor
from the Bottom to the Top

Labor confrontations were few at the port and railway complex between 1933 and 1962. Several confrontations in the late 1940s reveal the narrow margins available to workers. *Shibalo* workers at the bottom of the manual labor hierarchy and stevedores at the top each confronted authorities in this period. Workers in each case were arguably seeking a return to the *status quo ante* rather than an actual improvement in their situation.

In 1947 *shibalo* workers in the port compound were involved in two incidents, which may have been related.[26] The first incident occurred in July 1947 and was corroborated with written documentation, whereas to date the second has emerged only in the oral record and the exact timing remains uncertain. The July incident was a refusal to work unpaid overtime and the other was a confrontation regarding the amount and quality of food *shibalo* received. The two may be related because, according to Roberto Tembe, who was put in charge of *shibalo* food supplies after the incident, part of the *shibalo* grievance was that the amount of food they received was insufficient to carry a man through the regular work day, even without the expected overtime load.

The incident in July 1947 involved a group of three hundred men who were assigned to shovel trainloads of fill for the railway projects at two locations on the rail line just outside the city. The men's regular day's task was to shovel six trains of fourteen cars each, but a seventh train was typically added to be handled at overtime rates. Despite the opportunity for overtime at double pay, the men grumbled because the work was exhausting and frequently kept them shoveling after dark. More important, although they had been told they would receive double pay for overtime work, they had received no overtime wages since May. Indeed, men who arrived in May had unloaded the extra train every day without ever receiving any overtime.

On July seventh, when the seventh train rolled into position, the workers looked at each other and simply leaned on their shovels. The port police were summoned. At first the workers simply looked on, but when the police began large-scale arrests the workers quickly resumed work and completed the job. Sixty-eight men were arrested, seven of whom were determined to be the leaders. In the end the alleged leaders were deported for two years to Niassa and the remaining sixty-one were sentenced to sixty days of correctional labor, unpaid *shibalo*.

Little is known of the incident beyond the names, ages, and ethnicity of those arrested and sentenced. The authorities noted that six of the seven leaders were *magaiça*, or returned mineworkers, and suggested that their action might have been influenced by the 1946 mine strike. Given the extent of mine migration from Sul do Save by mid-century, an equal proportion of the entire *shibalo* labor force were probably *magaiça*. The Portuguese usually attributed labor resistance to the pernicious influence of South Africa, rather than to intolerable conditions experienced at home. The pool of those arrested included men from every age group, but it is perhaps significant that over 80 percent of those arrested were Chopi and Bitonga, from areas that were chronically prey to *shibalo* conscription.[27] They or their relatives would probably be back working *shibalo*, and if that were the case, they wanted to be paid.

The arrests, prison labor, and deportations set an example of the state's iron-fist strategy with African workers. But it had not been a fruitless sacrifice. Along with the SNI's deportation order and prison sentences went a sharp reminder to the port and railway administration that overtime wages were to be paid no later than the fifth day of every month. As we have seen, workers at the port and rail yards shoveled to the tune of "The Portuguese live by stealing our wages, Heave that shovel, heave!" but in this case, they had let it be known that they were unwilling to work overtime *de graça*.[28]

The second incident was a further effort by *shibalo* to mediate the intensity of their exploitation, and again it was met with both force and reform. *Shibalo* were not only being forced to work paid or unpaid overtime, they were not being fed enough to endure the work load. Sometime in 1947, they rioted to protest their skimpy rations. The riot was firmly put down, but the SNI followed up with an effort to improve their situation.[29] The port authorities brought in Roberto Tembe, a tally clerk with almost twenty years' experience at the port. Tembe was to ensure that workers received proper rations, measuring the full amount of flour and groundnuts cooked daily. His instructions were that *shibalo* should never complain of hunger again. They were to work "with their bellies full, full, full of porridge" and anything else Tembe could arrange to fill their stomachs.[30]

Confrontation cost some of these *shibalo* workers a beating, others an extension of their contract term, and a small group of alleged instigators suffered deportation, but their efforts also shaped the conditions of their labor. They held the line against overtime without the requisite pay and sustenance. The quality of *shibalo* food and housing continued to be bad, but the state took precautions to ensure that it was not intolerable.

Casual port workers who negotiated their food and housing with cash were desperate for an increase in salary. The issue of declining wages was first confronted in early April 1949 by workers comparatively better off than the truly desperate hod carriers.[31] African stevedores working casual labor for the private firms, Renny, Delagoa Bay Agency, and Mann George, pressed for an increase in the basic shift wage.[32] The private stevedoring firms had increased overtime wages for both European and African workers in March as part of the general strategy to keep the traffic moving. Workers wanted the 20$00 per eight-hour basic shift increased to 50$00 per day.

On April first the workers sent a representative to the SNI, while they continued working. When their petition was rejected on April fourth, however, they went out on strike and blocked other workers' access to the port zone. The striking stevedores successfully shut down the port for two days. On April sixth the police intervened; *shibalo* from the port compound were sent in to unload the ships in port, and an undetermined number of workers were arrested and imprisoned. Four men who were identified as leaders were deported to São Tomé for three years. The 1949 strike by private stevedores was the last direct confrontation on the waterfront prior to the abolition of the *indigenato* in the early 1960s.[33]

Ducking the System

In response to the 1949 strike, the entire casual labor force, whether hod carrier or stevedore, was incorporated into a daily card system. It was designed to keep production up in the regular shift section and to counteract workers' tendency to sign up only for high-pay zones and work binge strategies to maximize their income per hour worked. Prior to the registration system, casual port workers could ascertain what kind of work was available on any given day and decide whether to seek work or not. If only general cargo or timber work was available, men might decide not to risk injury for that wage and seek opportunities elsewhere in the city.

The new system required all registered day laborers to work whatever jobs were available by the time they got to the front of the daily line—whether that meant stevedoring at 20$00 a shift, timber at 15$00, or general cargo at 12$00.[34] Furthermore, all casual laborers had to carry cards *(cartões de efectividade)* which were stamped daily to verify that they had actually checked in to work. If no work was available by the time their turn came, the attendance card was stamped to that effect and they were free to seek out other opportunities in the city without threat of arrest for vagrancy. Workers who failed to have their registration card stamped daily and could not produce a medical excuse were considered delinquent and subject to *shibalo* or fines.

Since thousands of workers signed on daily, monitoring such a system was clearly a bureaucratic nightmare. The administration generally limited itself to spot checks to ensure that workers were taking work as it came up. In April 1955, however, the ACLM undertook a systematic check of registered casual labor force. The check revealed that falsification of attendance among hod carriers and stevedores at both the port and the railway was a common strategy. If no attractive jobs were available, men arranged to get a card falsely showing they had been turned away for stevedoring work, when they had not. The men acquired the falsified cards to protect themselves from work they considered too costly to their health for the wage it paid.[35]

The 5 percent sample of the urban labor force during this period revealed that 16 workers were clearly caught in the sweep, and another 12 were probably involved. If one takes only those sample cases where the documents explicitly show arrest in April 1955 and mention falsified cards, the sample suggests that as many as 320 workers were apprehended. Most of those apprehended were sentenced to three months' *shibalo*, but the men thought to be the leaders were deported to São Tomé. Valente M. Vucuzana of Chibuto, one of the accused organizers, was sent off for nine years aboard the *Sofala*.[36]

Pride and Prejudice—Struggles in the Offices

Africans working unskilled jobs on the waterfront and rail yards were more concerned about increasing traffic and stagnant wages than about increased Portuguese immigration. The small group of Africans who typed, filed, tallied figures, and organized payrolls in the port and railway offices also struggled with stagnant or falling real wages, but their day-to-day strategies and challenges were usually more closely shaped by events in the European community. New State protectionism and advocacy of metropolitan educated civil servants made life increasingly difficult for educated Africans. It was only with Portugal's signature of the ILO agreement in 1957 and the African political challenge of the 1960s that the state began actively to promote selected Africans into middle- and upper-level office and management positions.[37] In the economic crisis of the 1930s, the best-educated and best-placed Africans had been sacrificed to the interests of the floundering white community, and had been hard pressed to hold their own, let alone regain lost ground.

Quantitative evidence for the 1933 to 1949 period is thin, but the systematic sample of registration records from 1950 to 1962 clearly shows that the one group of Africans to lose ground relative to other groups was the *indígena* elite.[38] In the late 1940s, top jobs for people considered *indígenas* paid between 900$ and 1,700$00 per month. By 1958 the top range was 1,200$ to 2,300$00, but by 1960 Africans could not earn over 2500$00 unless they became *assimilados*.[39] When the combination of economic expansion and state promotion of African mobility forced up wages between 1957 and 1962, middle-level wages increased much more rapidly than wages at the top. Furthermore, growing unemployment among the white immigrant population cramped African access to a whole range of attractive jobs. The result was that the differential between wages in middle-level and top-level African jobs narrowed by about 40 percent.

The dimming horizons for educated Africans were particularly frustrating because educational credentials had been acquired at such great expense. Before completion of Salazar High School in Lourenço Marques, only those who could afford to study in Portugal could acquire the qualifications for mid-level positions in the civil service. Tenured positions within the civil service were limited to those with a minimum of two or three years of secondary education. For most families it was a great sacrifice to see a child through primary school *(quarta classe)*. Living and travel expenses for an education in Lisbon were beyond the potential of all but a tiny handful, and clearly families with some Portuguese relatives were in a better position to consider secondary education.[40]

Families were much more likely to invest in education for sons, in part because there were few career opportunities for women outside of nursing. The sacrifice necessary to attain an education enhanced the graduate's frustration when racism denied him the opportunity to use it. Although doubtless many Mozambicans became discouraged and settled into a job quite irrelevant to their education, the patience of those who persevered despite the cumulative disadvantages of racism, patronage, language, and cultural differences was quite remarkable.

An appropriately deferential demeanor was as basic a qualification for any African in the port offices as an education and a typing certificate.[41] A *"bom rapaz"* (good boy) was respectful, punctual, cheerful, forever willing, and never confrontational or contrary. They trained incoming white workers who would be promoted while they would not. They could never arrive late or leave early. Only African office workers were also expected to sweep, serve, and clean.

Only an exceptional Mozambican managed to be hired or promoted without the support of a network of Portuguese *padrinhos* or *cunhas*. A *cunha*, literally "a wedge," was the generic term for a patron of any variety. A *padrinho*, a godfather, was a specific personal patron whom one had to cultivate formally. In the Portuguese system a *cunha* was virtually obligatory for any worker, but a patron was particularly important for those trying to bridge the divide between their own complexion and jobs considered the exclusive right of people with different complexions. José Cutileiro's classic study of Portuguese society captures the essence of patron-client relations and their reproduction. According to Cutileiro, ordinary people understand that:

> the number of things in life to which one may have access is very small, and . . . most of things to which one aspires are obtainable only through privilege. This privileged situation is, in its turn, attainable only through the protection of someone close to the ultimate source of the benefit needed. To secure such protection, a personal bond has to be created. A whole network of patronage is one of exchanged favors between private individuals often subsumed under the institutions of spiritual kinship and friendship. . . . Implicit in the general acceptance of patronage is the notion that society is wrongly organized in some basic way and that individual rather than collective efforts are the only means of attempting to avoid this predicament.[42]

Privilege, private individuals, and personal bonds are the key words here. A steady, well-paid job with potential for promotion was a white privilege and any African hoping to have access to it would have to identify someone as "close to the source of the benefit" as possible. The protocol for establishing such a bond ranged from informal gift giving and service, to a formal confirmation of spiritual kinship through godparenthood—usually at weddings or christenings. Under the New State regime, administrators were increasingly selected from among metropolitan immigrants; the power elite was increasingly all white, and all metropolitan. Mozambicans generally had to cultivate a string of *cunhas*, because one or another could always be on leave or repatriated to the metropole. As Cutileiro observed, "the need to find a patron [was] a frequent and recurrent phenomenon."[43]

Chibindji's Courtship

The experience of Bandi Albasini Chibindji provides a fine example of both the gap between qualification and employment and the courtship game aspiring Africans had to learn to play very well.[44] Chibindji was born in Chibuto, in the lower Limpopo Valley in 1910. In 1927 he left Chibuto to study at the Protestant Swiss Mission boarding school just outside Lourenço Marques. When he completed primary school in 1936, he was among the most educated Mozambicans of the time. His first reward for this accomplishment was to spend the next several years in the country's worst job— as a soldier earning 50$00 per month. He did not aspire to serve in the military. He volunteered to take the place of his brother who had been drafted, because his brother's earnings were the sole support for Chibindji's mother and younger siblings. His brother worked in South Africa's mines, and his repatriated wages had also helped pay Chibindji's school fees.

Chibindji's military service certainly did not make him rich, but it did enhance the "good boy" reputation necessary for future mobility. Chibindji then began the long process of sitting for every qualifying exam scheduled for placement or promotion at the port and railway complex. He passed the first exam, and was accepted as a counter for loading and unloading trains. Despite his qualifications, he was paid 12$00 a day, the same as a hod carrier who could neither read nor cope with mathematics. He continued to take and pass every exam, but despite his legally preferred status from military service, he only succeeded in increasing his burden of job responsibility, not his paycheck. His strategy of demonstrating his qualifications through success on qualifying examinations had brought few tangible gains.

Throughout the period Chibindji maintained an excellent work record and a glowing "*bom rapaz*" reputation, but he began to understand that his reputation and success on qualifying exams were insufficient. He decided to cultivate a patron, and identified Pinto Maior, an office manager, as the most promising candidate. He began to present Pinto Maior with unsolicited gifts of eggs, fresh chicken, and goat that Chibindji's family produced on their land in Marracuene. In 1956, when a position as office assistant opened, Chibindji passed the qualifying exam, and with the intervention of Pinto Maior, he got the job. The position paid 45$00 *escudo* a day, triple his former wage, and was clearly worth the chickens, goat, and eggs.

Unfortunately, Pinto Maior retired to Lisbon, so Chibindji began to make friends with a woman who worked in the port office. Her husband was an important figure at the port. Chibindji's family did the woman's laundry without charge, brought them eggs and meat, and did occasional jobs without pay. In return, she also sometimes passed along her husband's old shirts. In 1960, when a position opened as office auxiliary (one step up from assistant), she prevailed upon her husband to speak on Chibindji's behalf. He got the job, which paid 65$00 per day. Courtship had paid handsomely within the margins of black mobility, but it should not be viewed uncritically. Patronage courtship was an important investment, but it also confirmed and even reinforced the basic inequality that privileged whites and required blacks to serve whites in order to tap the benefits of the privilege. Despite Chibindji's skill and his promotion, he could never waver from the "*bom rapaz*" posture, and he was still expected to sweep up at the end of the day. On the one hand, Chibindji despised the system that rewarded him so minimally for his talents and efforts, but on the other hand he did not allow bitterness and anger to poison his life. He was a warm and cheerful person with a deep faith in a just God. He concluded that he had worked hard for little reward, and that whites who knew less and did less were paid more, promoted, and retired with full benefits, but "That was just the way it was then." He was well aware of the cost of challenging "the way it was."

Tembe's Pride

Chibindji's case demonstrated that skill acquisition and discipline were essential, but not necessarily sufficient, qualities to secure a good job. According to Guilherme de

Brito, who was a port and railway administrator for nearly forty years, passing a qualifying exam meant little if one did not have a powerful *padrinho* on the selection committee.[45] This powerful system taught Africans at the upper reaches to favor individual over collective strategies for mobility. Although whites controlled access to privilege throughout the colonial economy, some Africans managed to move up within the system without entertaining the courtship ritual of clientage. Manuel João dos Santos Tembe provides a case in point.

Tembe, whom we met in Chapter 3, had first-hand and largely positive experience with Portuguese individuals in a social context as a child. After he decided not to accompany his employer's family to Portugal, he studied at the Catholic mission school, San José Hlenguene, in Lourenço Marques. With financial support from an older brother, he was able to complete the third class. When his father died, however, the brother's obligation to the rest of the family increased and Tembe had to leave school and seek employment. Unlike Chibindji, however, Tembe was able to draw upon his own family networks to break into the state system. His uncle, António dos Santos Tembe, was an office worker in the commercial services of the port with a long and distinguished record of service—he retired in 1970 after fifty years.[46] Indeed, Tembe's family had several advantages. They were local, and although they did not have any Portuguese relatives, they shared a Catholic education and Catholic networks with the Portuguese. In 1934 a family member told Tembe about a job in the government's general stores area. He passed the qualifying exam and was hired. That was particularly impressive in the strongly protectionist atmosphere of 1934. In 1940 he was able to move from his job as office servant in general stores to a position as office worker in the port's commercial service section where his uncle worked.

Manuel João dos Santos Tembe also worked his way up the job ranks, passed all the exams, and maintained a vigilant personal posture. But Tembe never had to cultivate a Portuguese patron through services and gifts. He was protected by his family's exceptional reputation and his scrupulous work record. He took full advantage of every inch the law gave him, including the higher wage ceiling for assimilation. Although Tembe clearly considered assimilation a humiliating imposition, he nonetheless petitioned for and was accorded the status of *assimilado* in 1960. He explained his decision:

> I always carried native documents. I am obviously a native. [Pointing to the skin on the top of his hand] I'm a Negro. But, after a long while I decided to assimilate for the same reason most other natives decided to assimilate. I wanted to earn a bit more money—that was the only reason to do it. Because if you were an *assimilado*, you earned a little more, and if you were not an *assimilado* then you were a Negro, so of course you were paid only a pittance. That is why. When I married I realized that my circumstances had changed. If I wanted to keep my family together and educate my children, I would have to assimilate so that I could earn a bit more. . . . Some Africans [without assimilation papers] could earn what I earned, but only if they were *afilhados*. Those who had patrons could earn that much because their boss put them up for promotions. I did not have a patron. I never needed a patron. I could hold my own.[47]

Tembe's preference for the legal route, which freed him from courting favor suited his quiet, self-assured, and fiercely independent temperament. Chibindji was a warm and quite open person who expressed a genuine like for the various patrons who helped him along his way. Chibindji's strategy was characteristic and Tembe's exceptional, both pursued individual strategies, and the contrasts illustrate that personal temperament also shaped labor strategies.[48]

In short, office workers, like *shibalo*, stevedores, and hod carriers, could see that society was "wrongly organized in some basic way," but in their case "individual rather than collective efforts" seemed appropriate to mediate that unequal organization of society.[49] Casual labor and *shibalo* might both seek to curry favor with an overseer to secure a more attractive job assignment, but they usually mediated their way through group efforts. The weakest occasionally stood in solidarity, whereas the potentially most powerful usually made their way individually. Such patterns favored colonial strategies to sustain dominance through division and weakness within the urban African labor force.

Finally, the port case study demonstrates that although the port sector brought in strategic foreign exchange and was a quite profitable sector of the economy in this era, African labor at all levels was unable to benefit significantly from the added value their labor created and sustained. The value was redistributed to European workers who enjoyed wages and benefits disproportionate to those available to them for similar work in the metropole.[50]

Port and railway expansion, enhanced transit traffic, and a large and increasingly privileged white labor force were indeed all at African expense. The handful of labor confrontations that occurred in this period were over almost before they began. Workers claiming what was their legal due were met with force, arrest, and, in the case of leadership, deportation. But different groups of Africans paid different prices in different ways. Men working overtime without protection in the coaling and asbestos handling facilities to accommodate falling real wages paid one price, while aspiring office workers who worked weekends doing a patron's laundry or running errands paid another, casual labor organizers another, and exhausted *shibalo* workers yet another. The *indigenato*, as well as the structure of the workplace, shaped a hierarchy of struggle, encouraging some workers to combine in a group confrontation and others to make a way as individuals.

9

Accommodation, Mobility, and Survival Public Sector Labor, 1933–1962

Municipal Labor in the Urban Context

The men and women of the urban African community had as much to divide them as they had in common. Although virtually everyone in the community faced racist discrimination in the colonial era, the daily challenge varied greatly depending upon the individual's location in the hierarchy. Gender, ethnicity, education, class, lifestyle, and life cycle all shaped an individual's potential to make a living and a life in the city. Different groups encountered different problems, opportunities, and challenges. Different groups held different goals, expressed themselves differently, and forged different methods of working toward their goals.

The range between the wages and working conditions of the poorest and best-paid African urban workers was as wide as between black workers as a group and white workers as a group. The labor registration records revealed a ten-fold wage differential, for example, between *shibalo* or entry-level domestic service jobs and top "native" African jobs. Despite efforts by the New State bureaucracy to standardize wages and hold increases to a minimum, four-fold differentials among adult males were common, and the standard differential between steady unskilled or semi-skilled jobs for adult African men and women was at least two to one.[1]

Divisions within the city were not merely a matter of numbers. As we have seen, the insecurity, apathy, and disunity created in the critical Depression era were difficult to overcome. People "arranged the charcoal to grill [their own] sardine."[3] The city was ever fuller; competition for housing, markets, and jobs was intense; and individuals were keen to exploit their full strengths in order to survive and prosper.

Wage Rates for African Males in Lourenço Marques[2] 1933–1962

Year	Low/State	Mid/State	Factory	Professional	Casual
1933/35	100–300$	420–500$	240$	500–800$	140–325$
1936/39	100–300$	300–500$	280$	750–900$	208–325$
1940/45	125–375$	300–520$	300–400$	700–1,000$	350$
1946/50	180–300$	300–675$	300–700$	700–1,700$	200–700$
1951/55	180–300$	350–500$	350–700$	750–2,250$	312–500$
1956/60	220–375$	600–800$	420–850$	800–2,300$	390–780$
1961/62	300–800$	1,150–1,500$	650–1,600$	1800–2400$	400–775$

Natives of Lourenço Marques and newcomers alike typically depended principally upon family support networks.[4] Newly arrived migrants stayed with family if
at all possible, or with friends from their rural networks—language and cultural links
were therefore important. Three-quarters of the informants who came to Lourenço
Marques as migrants first stayed with family or friends.[5] About half the informants
either found their first job or were hired for a subsequent job through the interces-
sion of family or friends.

This chapter explores a range of accommodation, resistance, exploitation, leadership, and mobility patterns through case studies of municipal labor in the middle
and bottom ranks of the urban wage order. The first case study concerns the municipal slaughterhouse workers. It is developed as a window into the middle ranks of the
urban wage labor community during the postwar expansion. It considers African
patronage, job security, and the shift toward capital accumulation by Africans for
investment in urban rather than rural pursuits. The slaughterhouse workers were
typical of migrants with limited school education. Most had earned bridewealth at
the mines and then come to find steady work in the city.

The second case study looks at *shibalo* who worked on municipal contract
projects for the city's leading Portuguese entrepreneur, Paulino Santos Gil. It sheds
light on the special struggles experienced by those on the bottom ranks of this fast-
expanding economy, and reveals the extent of abuse and vulnerability characteristic
of work relations at that level. It also explores the tap-dance between the colonial
government and its leading citizens around labor legislation and abuse. The administration obviously wanted its settlers to prosper, but there were some limits on the
means they would tolerate to that end. For many workers on the bottom ranks, the
concern was less for mobility than for accommodation and survival. The Santos Gil
study also highlights the tensions between the re-emerging African urban leadership
and these most vulnerable workers.

Networks and Security in the Middle Ranks

Case Study: The Slaughterhouse

The municipal slaughterhouse developed as a classic example of European privilege
at African expense. The first municipal slaughterhouse was built in the late nineteenth century by *shibalo* laborers on land alienated from local people.[6] It was

designed to serve white customers, diminish the market share of African meat sellers, and drive up the price of meat for urban consumers—all under the familiar banner of "public health and safety."[7]

Upon completion of the slaughterhouse, the municipal council claimed monopoly control over the city's wholesale meat market and partial control over retail sales. By 1904 only meat slaughtered at the municipal facility could be sold legally in the city. Africans who formerly slaughtered their livestock and sold meat directly to urban customers were excluded from the promising urban market.[8] At the outset of the economic slump that became the Depression, the city council tried to privilege Europeans in the beef industry further by setting qualifications for certified meat cutters in retail shops. While stopping short of racist exclusion, the law gave whites sufficient advantage to discourage black competition.[9] By the late 1930s shops selling beef also had to be licensed.[10]

Europeans had long argued that they should be protected from competition with African farmers or ranchers, because Africans exploited usufructory lands and family labor.[11] In 1936 the powerful, settler-dominated Cattle Raiser's Cooperative (the Cooperativo da Criação de Gado, or CCG) successfully pursued that line to gain a monopoly to supply the municipal slaughterhouse. The CCG then further compromised its limited African membership with quotas to improve the market share of its "non-native" members.[12] The CCG quotas were then periodically readjusted "in order to permit European cattlemen to sell off . . . adult cattle ready for slaughter. . . ."[13]

Monopolies and quotas were obviously difficult to enforce, and when faced with market exclusion, African producers turned from the legal market to a system of mobile, flexible "clandestine" markets. Clandestine beef sales undercut the CCG strategy to push up retail beef prices throughout the 1930s. By the postwar era, however, the city implemented more effective sanctions on clandestine markets, and the result was a chronic shortage of moderately priced meat in the city.[14] In short, the history of the municipal slaughterhouse produced little benefit for Africans.

Be that as it may, the consensus among the twenty-five men who began work there between 1933 and 1961 was that the slaughterhouse provided good jobs for Africans who were willing to work hard.[15] First, unlike casual dock work, slaughterhouse jobs were not seasonal or irregular—they provided steady, predictable income and occasionally overtime work. Second, they were firmly "native" jobs, so workers did not have to worry that waves of unemployed Portuguese immigrants would displace them—they were doubly secure. The workers also had greater control over their work environment than other municipal areas. In 1952 a new and expanded workers' cafeteria was inaugurated. African workers had their own lockers, food storage, uniforms, bathroom, and laundry areas.[16]

Finally, their wages were paid on a monthly basis, and the consensus among workers at all levels was that monthly payment facilitated their efforts to accumulate savings. The pay was not sufficient to enable a young man to accumulate bridewealth, but it was enough to support the piecemeal purchase of construction materials that would eventually enable a mature, married man to build a house for himself and his family, and if he were lucky, perhaps to invest in urban rental housing for supplementary income. In sum, the slaughterhouse provided secure, steady, fairly well-paid jobs that suited adult, married males very well.

The labor chain began with assistants, who had the difficult and dirty job of pushing cattle along the runways to slaughter, and continued with operators, permanent salaried operators, and foremen. Head foremen or slaughter master were the top jobs held by Africans. By 1950 a total of sixty Africans were employed at the slaughterhouse: forty-two operators and assistant operators, about evenly divided, seventeen foremen, and one general foreman.[17] The jobs did not require an education or any special skills except physical strength and endurance, but the pay was a cut above most unskilled jobs.

Between 1950 and 1955 slaughterhouse operators earned 19$00 per day and assistants earned 16$00. That compared favorably with 12$00 for unskilled labor at the railway and 20$00 for an apprentice woodworker. *Shibalo* wages were 125$00 to 180$00 a month and basic African civil service jobs, like the police, paid about 300$00.[18] The overall urban African wage range in 1950 was from about 1,000$00 per month for trained and educated "native" professional jobs, such as chauffeur or interpreter, to 600$00 for trained practical nurses, to about 330$00 for ordinary workers.[19] Between 1956 and 1958 slaughterhouse operators earned 500$00 per month; from 1959 to 1961, 900$00; and then in 1962, 1,000$00.[20] By 1956 wages in private industries, such as soap, textile, rubber, and cement factories, were a bit higher, ranging from 520$00 in Caltex to 650$00 in the rubber plant, to 715$00 in Companhia União Fabril de Moçambique.[21] By 1961–1962 slaughterhouse wages were back in line with most others.[22]

The slaughterhouse was such a good place to work that entry became tied to a nod from a fellow-countryman, family member, or friend already employed there. Like many of the city's "good" African jobs, an opening was never really advertised; rather word would go out among the employees that an opening was imminent and workers would approach key African patrons to put forward their friends and family. The slaughterhouse labor cohort interviewed in 1977 was generally ethnically clustered around two mature patrons, Marcelino Welamo Mafuane (a Xitswa speaker) and Daniel Tene Nhangumbe (a Chopi speaker).[23] Each had been a policeman before entering the slaughterhouse in the late 1930s, and each had worked his way up from cattle pusher. At least two other workers had also been policemen, but the police link seems to have started with Marcelino Welamo Mafuane.

Mafuane arrived in Lourenço Marques in 1932, and at age twenty-two got his first job as a domestic servant.[24] Two years later, with his uncle's help, he was hired as a police aid, but in 1937 he was fired because the Portuguese supervisor didn't believe he had missed work due to illness. A white colleague, who knew for a fact that Mafuane had been ill, introduced him to the personnel manager at the slaughterhouse, and with his intervention Mafuane began as an ordinary worker at 350$00 per month in 1937. By 1949 he was a foreman earning 600$00 and in 1952 he became "mestre de matança" (slaughter master) with the impressive salary of 1,300$00. He was clearly the patron among this labor force.

By 1940, Mafuane's friend on the police force, Daniel Tene Nhangumbe, realized he was earning 75$00 less a month as a policeman than Mafuane earned at the slaughterhouse, so he signed on with Mafuane's help.[25] Nhangumbe began in 1941 as an assistant earning 375$00, and in 1943 was promoted to operator at 400$00, but he remained as salaried operator. Unlike Mafuane, he did not climb the promotion ladder to the top but remained as a salaried operator, where he sponsored the employment of other Chopi workers. Most workers attributed their original hire to either Mafuane or Nhangumbe, and the networks tended to correlate with language and home origin.[26]

The work could be physically demanding, but the money was steady and comparatively good. Those who were strong enough and well placed to take advantage of opportunities for overtime income earned enough to save. The workers received clean uniforms, but otherwise lived and ate on their own in the city, usually with their families.[27] Although their wives sometimes worked gardens in the peri-urban area or had jobs as seamstresses or saleswomen in the city, the salaries of these operators were potentially sufficient to support the entire family. In 1960, for example, rents for three-room houses in the municipal housing ranged between 100$00 for a long-time resident covered by rent control to 215$00 for new residents.[28] Operators at the slaughterhouse earned 750$00 to 1,000$00 a month without overtime, so they were comparatively well set.

Workers enjoyed relative protection in these middle ranks because whites did not covet their jobs, and *shibalo* gangs were unsuited for much of the work. The slaughterhouse workers occupied a fairly comfortable niche within the *indigenato*, but whites with similar skills and obligations in employment earned far better wages and could look forward to their children moving up the class ladder. Many of the slaughterhouse workers had originally come to the city seeking work to avoid *shibalo* in their home area. Although some still had family in rural areas, they clearly identified themselves as urban workers, and invested accordingly. The job security, steady income, and potential for overtime were all particularly attractive to mature men who had come to terms with city life. They may not have aspired to employment beyond that of slaughterhouse operator, but their investment of overtime income and savings in construction materials for rental income or for their personal homes indicated their commitment to the urban workplace and their strategies to build financial security in the city. They were able to combine a life and a livelihood in the middle ranks of workers in Lourenço Marques. That was not the case for the men who occupied the bottom ranks.

Exploitation and "Respect" in the Bottom Ranks

Throughout the century, conditions for state and municipal contract *shibalo* were among the worst.[29] *Shibalo* workers were legally entitled to two sets of work clothing, blankets, soap, and a contract clearly stipulating rights and obligations. Informants who had worked *shibalo* ridiculed the very idea of such legal niceties.[30] SNI and health records corroborate their cynicism. Inspections routinely revealed that, when it was issued at all, *shibalo* work clothing "would not last two months," blankets were underweight, and *shibalo* virtually never received soap.[31]

The state's capitulation to private employers regarding minimum standards during the Depression era set a stubborn precedent. A 1950 circular, issued jointly by the health department and the SNI, roundly condemned Sul do Save employers for their failure even to approximate their obligations under *shibalo* contract regulations,[32] a fact echoed in the 1960 report cited in the introduction.[33] Health reports on construction and sanitation *shibalo* on municipal contracts were the worst. *Shibalo* in these areas were housed in "true pigsties" and served food "of the worst possible quality."[34] Contractors provided "improper food, improperly cooked and improperly stored," and were further condemned for "failing to provide adequate sleeping and sanitation facilities."[35] Beyond these serious complaints with food and housing, *shibalo* were routinely overworked in dangerous conditions, and minors were placed in jobs too heavy for their growing frames.[36]

The record is quite clear, in short, that urban *shibalo* routinely failed to receive the legal minimum benefits they were due. Their wage packet was also set in law. By this period *shibalo* usually received their cash wages, but in comparison with the contemporary tax burden, full *shibalo* wages were as inadequate as their trimmed benefit package. From 1933 to 1962 *shibalo* wages increased as follows:

Shibalo Monthly Wages for Agriculture and Industry[37]
Lourenço Marques District, 1933–1962

Years	Agricultural Wage	Industrial Wage
1933–1938	100$00	125$00
1938–1944	100$00	125$00 to 80$00
1944–1949	100$00	125$00 to 200$00
1949–1958	125$00	180$00 to 200$00
1958–1959	180$00	220$00
1959–1960	180$00	250$00
1961–1962	205$00	280$00

The retail price index increased at about the same rate over the general period, but *shibalo* wages lagged for important intervals. The index moved from the reset base of 100 in 1939 to 180.77 by 1947, to 215.54 by 1958, and 213.55 for 1960.38 Although most urban construction workers qualified for the higher industrial wage, even at that rate a man had to work two months' *shibalo* simply to cover his tax burden. The usual wage in 1951 for unskilled volunteer construction labor in the city was about 335$00 per month, so *shibalo* earned just over half the volunteer cash wage.[39] The overall combination of cash income, non-cash compensation, overtime, and entrepreneurial potential all figured into the mix when assessing the differences between *shibalo* and voluntary labor, but whereas volunteer workers had a choice about the value relationship between their room, board, and wage, *shibalo* did not.

Municipal *Shibalo*: The Case of Santos Gil

The contemporary skyline of Maputo dates from the postwar expansion. All the high-rise buildings and many of the dominant central structures were built after 1945.[40] New permanent construction in Lourenço Marques increased just under 50 percent between 1925 and 1940, with a total of 1,104 buildings. Between 1950 and 1960 residential and public works construction was up about 33 percent, and spilled into the rapidly developing suburbs of Matola and Machava.[41] Construction employment tripled between 1940 and 1960.[42] The state undertook most of its construction projects with *shibalo* labor, and also supplied *shibalo* to some private contractors. The Roman Catholic Sé Cathedral, which forms part of city hall plaza, and the Salazar

High School, the city's largest public high school, were among the major projects undertaken with *shibalo* labor in this period. According to informants, the devil built the first and according to the written record the firm of Paulino Santos Gil built the latter; working and living conditions for the conscripts who did the actual labor on both sites were notorious.

Construction of the Sé cathedral evoked particularly bitter memories. Nearly thirty years after the Sé's construction, the lines on men's faces hardened and anger flashed in their eyes when they recalled the brutal and humiliating conditions experienced by the men and women who built the cathedral. Informants decried such hypocrisy and disrespect for both humans and God. Women, arrested for brewing or prostitution, hauled mud, concrete, and firewood to the construction area and prepared meals for their fellow workers and prisoners. Right in the heart of the city, *shibalo* and prisoners built the cathedral. Every day they were filthy, degraded, and shackled, working without minimum safety precautions or sanitation facilities.

Informants claimed that several workers were killed at the site when their chains became entangled in the primitive scaffolding on the church's graceful soaring spire. They fell, each toppling another, and became hung up on the lower scaffolding. Informants insisted that the dead were allowed to hang from the scaffolding until the end of the work day.[43] Those who witnessed its construction harbor anger and bitterness toward the cathedral right down to the present. Ernesto Machalucuane Muianga echoed the sentiments of many other informants: "The [Sé] cathedral was built for the devil himself! The prison built that church for the devil himself."[44]

The Salazar High School was built on contract with *shibalo* labor by one of the city's leading entrepreneurs, Paulino Santos Gil. Santos Gil's use and abuse of *shibalo* was on the same scale as Eduardo de Almeida Saldanha's, but whereas Saldanha never flinched when the African press pilloried him, Santos Gil courted the African press and even contested his reputation with the SNI. When we first met Santos Gil in Chapter 2, he was just coming into a position of power as the Republic displaced the Monarchy. In Chapter 3 he had just taken over the municipal sanitation contract from Carvalho and David in 1918. A true survivor, Santos Gil also vaulted from First Republic to New State in 1926, again landing nicely on his feet as a prominent Portuguese settler personality. By 1950 Santos Gil was an important shipping agent, importer, exporter, civil construction and public works contractor, and transportation agent.[45] Santos Gil indeed had "a finger in every pie."[46]

Throughout his career Santos Gil combined hard work, entrepreneurship, political acumen, and access to every manner of government patronage, concessions, and monopolies in order to prosper. He was a particularly shrewd entrepreneur of *shibalo* labor supplies. From his base in state and municipal contracting, supplies, and construction, for which his firm requisitioned regular supplies of *shibalo*, Santos Gil expanded into soap and oil processing, cement production, building supplies, lumber sales, woodworking, and furniture. Even incomplete statistics demonstrate that between 1918 and 1950 Santos Gil had a standing labor force of between two and five hundred *shibalo* laborers on rotating contracts just for sanitation and urban construction projects, and he often had many more.[47]

Santos Gil was the quintessential entrepreneur of *shibalo*, accumulating capital for expansion on the backs of *shibalo* workers. He clearly knew how to encourage a coerced, ill-paid labor force to perform like a better-paid volunteer force. He fine-tuned carrots and sticks to improve production, and took advantage of every opportunity to deny his *shibalo* workers their full non-cash due. He also maximized labor productivity by employing *shibalo* in creative combinations with volunteers on many of his projects. His heavily protected investments in the wood industry provide a good example of this technique. He was allowed to requisition *shibalo* to work his forestry concessions, but was supposed to hire casual volunteers to stack and load the timber from those concessions at his Lourenço Marques lumber yards. He clearly had to hire skilled labor for carpentry and woodworking jobs at his furniture-making plant which brought his wood industry full circle from sapling to dining room sideboard. The *shibalo* who worked Santos Gil's forest nurseries, road construction, or sanitation brigades, however, were allowed to work overtime as volunteers on his various other undertakings. He therefore often had overtime *shibalo* working among volunteer casuals at the timber lots or even in the woodworking shop.[48] Gil thus received overtime labor at volunteer wages, and got maximum productivity from workers whom he was required to house and feed anyway.[49]

Gil was successful with this tactic of *shibalo* manipulation, in part, because it worked to the advantage of some workers. Men who were conscripted for Gil's road gangs, for example, sometimes took advantage of overtime work toting lumber in the furniture factory to learn some woodworking skills and enhance their take-home pay. Some even returned to work for Santos Gil as volunteers if they made good contacts and built some skill base for better jobs in his many businesses.[50]

Santos Gil was creative in the opportunities he provided to *shibalo*, but he was equally creative in minimizing his expenditures on their well-being.[51] He repeatedly tried to avoid paying justified damage claims when his workers were injured on the job.[52] Workers who complained they were assigned to projects they were not hired for faced retaliation, such as unjustified pay discounts. One informant was threatened with a beating for insisting that a *shibalo* co-worker, who had been injured while working overtime at the timber lots, receive appropriate medical care.[53]

Santos Gil held the municipal sanitation contract from 1918 until 1949, when it became a municipal department.[54] As we have seen, Chopi sanitation workers exploited their exclusivity to gain greater control of the work process and opportunities for entrepreneurship. They were clearly less successful in their struggle to secure appropriate room and board. In 1937, the sanitation gangs housed around the municipal incinerator rioted. The municipal officer who investigated the incident concluded that the temporary housing Santos Gil had provided for these workers was "an embarrassment!"[55] Little was done to improve the situation, but by 1939 the SNI ordered Santos Gil to "immediately relocate" *shibalo* who were housed at the municipal stables or face stiff fines.[56] Santos Gil's *shibalo* workers continued to struggle with his failure to provide their legal minimum benefits, and he fought them every step of the way until his death in 1951.

An incident in 1944 illustrated Santos Gil's personal technique, and his tactic of victimizing workers who dared to complain to the SNI. Two sanitation workers complained of rotten, poorly cooked, and insufficient food, which was making them dangerously ill.[57] The sanitation foreman, Francisco António Sitoe, was ordered to bring the two sanitation workers to the SNI to be beaten for having a bad attitude toward food in the *shibalo* compound.

In this case, however, a particularly formidable SNI inspector seriously reviewed their complaint. Before the men were beaten, they were questioned about the situation. They claimed they had simply refused to eat rotten flour, poorly cooked and topped with equally rotten groundnuts. They refused because the worms in the rotten flour were making them too sick to work. If *shibalo* did not work, the boss discounted their pay. When the SNI official questioned foreman Sitoe, he claimed not to have direct knowledge of the flour they refused to eat, but he did know that the groundnuts served the previous week were rotten. They all acknowledged that the flour was often full of worms. This was obvious because when the workers mixed the flour with water to make their usual drink, mahéu, the worms floated to the surface. The inspector then made an on-site visit, which confirmed the rotten food.

Santos Gil countered the accusation himself. He claiming it was a temporary aberration and that Sitoe lied and misled the SNI, so he fired Sitoe. The SNI responded that Sitoe clearly had not lied. His careful and truthful answers were supported by other witnesses as well as the SNI's inspection. The SNI regretted that Santos Gil had fired Sitoe, since it was a "bad precedent to fire a man for honesty," and "other foremen would notice."[58] Santos Gil obviously hoped other foremen would notice, but he diplomatically responded that he too "regretted the incident," and hoped it would not hurt his "usual good relations" with the SNI.[59] This was a pattern of labor exploitation that consistently tested the limits of tolerance. The case was unusual in that the workers who dared to complain or speak up were merely fired and not beaten. Santos Gil's various firms and contract jobs were repeatedly warned by SNI and Health Department officials, but sanctions seldom went beyond threats to withhold labor or fines.

Despite Santos Gil's appalling reputation with municipal *shibalo* pay and treatment, his political status was such that he was awarded the construction contract for Liceu Salazar, the new high school. Conscription records are probably incomplete, but they demonstrate that his firm received at the very least 686 *shibalo* in 1946, 770 in 1947, 277 in 1948 and 250 in 1950.[60] Santos Gil was consistently in trouble with municipal inspectors on the Salazar site. *Shibalo* workers complained that legal work conditions "especially with regard to length of contract and quality of food had not been respected."[61] During a surprise inspection, they found the sleeping areas and latrines "deplorable," the food completely unacceptable, the blankets too thin, and only one faucet on the site for over three hundred men to drink and wash.[62] Inspectors finally threatened to refuse to guarantee further labor supplies unless Santos Gil brought the Salazar construction site into legal compliance within eight days. Nothing more came of it.

Santos Gil certainly fitted the image portrayed in Mozambican worksongs and testimony that Africans earned Europeans' money for them, while Europeans ate African blood.[63] But Santos Gil was as clever about distributing the money Africans "earned for him" as he was about requisitioning *shibalo* to earn it. He was careful to invest some of the pennies he pinched from *shibalo* in a courtship of the potentially troublesome African elites.

This was the era of clubhouse construction among the leading African and Portuguese social groups in Lourenço Marques. Social groups aspired to construct a headquarters that would project their prestige, wealth, and influence. The CANM and the AACM built their headquarters in this period, necessitating a good deal of fund raising. In 1946, in a flurry of public relations activity, Santos Gil presented a check for 20,000$00 to the committee funding construction of the CANM's headquarters.[64] That was the equivalent of more than eight years' wages for Gil's best-paid conscripts. The AACM could also always count on Santos Gil to make a contribution when tapped.[65]

When Santos Gil died in 1951, the *Brado Africano*'s obituary praised his contributions to the urban African community without so much as a hint that an important component of that fortune was built on the backs of conscripted Mozambicans. Certainly the elite leadership was well aware of labor conditions in Santos Gil's various enterprises. Perhaps they chose to accept Santos Gil's patronage rather than to challenge him. The urban African community included both those who made Santos Gil's money for him, and those who received his charity contributions. Such patterns took advantage of and exacerbated existing divisions in the city. The children of the *shibalo* conscripts who built Liceu Salazar were unlikely to attend it. In 1960, of the one thousand students enrolled in Liceu Salazar only thirty were Africans, and they were *assimilados*.[66]

The slaughterhouse workers in the middle ranks of the city's workers began as migrants, became permanent urban workers, and were able to build a sense of community and niche of material security for themselves. They could combine a life and a livelihood as adult males in Lourenço Marques. In contrast, municipal *shibalo* workers in the bottom ranks circulated in and out of the city. Although in the case of Chopi sanitation workers, the bottom-rung workers had carved a niche that offered them some autonomy and material advantage, the vast majority of municipal *shibalo* developed a sense of community more as part of their strategy to persevere and survive the grim conditions they had to tolerate. Chapters 8 and 9 have surveyed workers' situations and strategies from top to bottom ranks in the public sector. Chapter 10 returns to the private sector to pursue the development of urban domestic service.

10

Accommodation and Mobility—Strategies in the Private Sector Domestic Service, 1933–1962

> The natives are attracted to the cities by the higher living standards, and they come as vagrants to escape the uncomfortable existence in rural areas depopulated by contract labor. . . . These detribalized Africans work as domestics, restaurant help, specialists or permanent salaried workers. . . . The others form a fluctuating mass of irregular unskilled labor for whom idleness and vagrancy alternates with one or another day of work.
>
> Marcello Caetano, 1954[1]

The Portuguese concern with African idleness, vagrancy, and detribalization resonated in the upper echelons of state power. Under the reign of the redoubtable municipal curator of native affairs, Afonso Ivens Ferraz de Frietas, the Lourenço Marques labor force was registered, ordered, and organized in the late 1940s to the point that scarcely a niche was overlooked. Port labor was decasualized, and the entire urban labor force was registered and divided into specific contract categories. Eventually, Ferraz de Freitas, whom Africans called Malalanyana ("the skinny one"), even brought petty sales and service providers into formal groups sponsored by the municipality.[2] It was increasingly difficult for urban Africans to hide amidst the "fluctuating mass of irregular unskilled labor" or to work only "one or another day" in Lourenço Marques.

Malalanyana was a contradictory but undeniably powerful figure. Marvin Harris alleged that he directed the urban African labor force "with an iron hand" in the late 1950s.[3] According to Africans who worked in the city during his tenure, he was the terror of the local population. His name indicated that he was somehow able "to drink the blood of the city's African workers without ever gaining weight."[4] In the closing years of colonial rule he was reputed to be a viciously effective agent of the Portuguese secret police, PIDE.[5] At the mention of his name, many informants rolled their eyes to heaven, shuddered, and then laughed heartily with relief—despite all their other problems, at least they did not have to worry about him any more.[6] But Ferraz de Freitas's vigor also extended to investigating employer abuse of labor contracts, promoting wage increases for African women, and pursuing basic facilities for urban African markets. He left a particularly strong imprint on labor relations in the private sector, ensuring that employers and employees alike respected the municipal labor regulations.[7]

Domestic service was a crucial growth area in the urban economy overseen by Ferraz de Freitas. The growth of the European immigrant population and expansion of the tourist industry increased demand for personal service workers. The service labor force in the district more than doubled between 1950 and 1962.[8] The number of registered domestics increased from about 9,500 in 1940 to almost 14,000 in 1950, and to over 20,000 in 1960.[9] Despite the law requiring employers to register their domestic labor, servants were the most likely group to be under-registered, so the increase was probably even larger. The great majority of domestic workers in Lourenço Marques between 1933 and 1962 were African males under the age of twenty. In 1940, more than half that group was between the ages of ten and fifteen.[10] African women comprised the second largest group of domestics, and between 1950 and 1960 the proportion of females to males in domestic service increased from one in fourteen to one in three.[11] In contrast with male domestics, however, in 1940 two-thirds of females were over twenty.[12]

This chapter places domestic service in the context of post-1933 urban employment and specifically explores the constrasting alternatives open to male and female domestics in Lourenço Marques. It demonstrates that domestic service was typically an episode in the early wage labor career of males, a stepping stone to a better situation, whereas women domestics were usually older and for them domestic service was yet another dead end job. Finally, the chapter considers the New State's effort to promote the feminization of domestic service from the 1940s. What drove this effort? How was it perceived by employers and employees, and to what extent did it succeed?

Domestic Service in the Municipal Context

A house-to-house survey of the municipality in 1949 found that about half the registered urban labor force worked in domestic service.[13] In continuity with the earlier period, trust, skill, and intimacy remained central to the work relationship, and domestic service continued to include a range of skills. Wage and employment conditions still varied with the class location of the employer's household. Employers still wanted to be "well served," just as domestics wanted the position to serve their needs well.

Postwar economic conditions, however, produced a situation in which both domestic servants and their employers felt themselves worse off.[14] Based on the salary of a civil servant of the first rank, the usual wage for a domestic servant in 1939 cost that civil servant one-twentieth of his wage. The servant's salary in 1948, however, cost the same civil servant about one-thirteenth of his salary. Employers were angry because they were effectively paying more of their income for the same service. Domestic servants were equally unhappy, because postwar prices for bread, corn flour, and cloth had doubled, and even the servant who by 1948 managed to earn twice his 1939 wage still had less purchasing power. The boss was paying more for his servant, and the servant was getting less for his salary. Servants were only able to make marginal gains in relation to the cost of living index with the wage increases of the late 1950s.[15]

By 1949, the average household in Lourenço Marques employed 1.8 servants. White working-class homes often had one servant, but middle- and upper-class homes employed at least two and frequently three—a cook, a *mainato,* and one or two *criados.*[16] But whereas prior to 1933 domestic service had been an almost exclusively male occupation, the number of women employed in that sector increased sevenfold between 1950 and 1960. Females were still outnumbered by males three to one, but their entry into wage labor in this period was dramatic.

Registered Domestic Servants in Lourenço Marques District[17]
1940–1960

Year	Males	Females	Ratio
1940	8,832	648	14 to 1
1950	9,816	706	14 to 1
1960	14,792	4,962	3 to 1

The seven-fold increase in the female domestic service population between 1950 and 1960 was due to a combination of factors, including deteriorating conditions for some women farmers in rural and peri-urban areas, the crack-down on illegal petty sales and services in the city, the increased tax burden of the *mudende,* and the limited legal alternatives open to women to earn cash.[18] The *mudende* was a great burden to women who worked largely outside the cash economy. Within a year of its implementation, *Brado Africano* protested that African women, especially those who had been left behind by men who emigrated to Lourenço Marques or Johannesburg, fled the "uncertain bush country" for the relative safety of the city, only to find themselves forced to turn to prostitution to pay their tax.[19] Women often spent two or three days in the bush gathering firewood to make charcoal, which sold for 5$00 per bag in the city. They had to sell twenty bags, a two-month investment in time, just to pay their *mudende.*[20]

The predominance of divorced, single, or separated women in the urban wage labor force is an important theme in the administrative records for the period 1933 to 1962. An SNI study done in 1949 and Ferraz de Freitas's detailed study of 1957 revealed that the majority of women working for wages in the city did not live with or enjoy support from a husband.[21] Minimum wages for African women in Lourenço Marques, however, were set at half that of men on the assumption that urban women had accompanied their husbands into the city and enjoyed their support. Both studies urged that the minimum wage for women be raised.[22]

Nanny with baby.

Women usually only resorted to the long hours and low wages of domestic service because of the limited alternatives. Since the second decade of the century, a small group of local women had worked in the city's tobacco processing and stitching industries. By the late 1940s and 1950s the tobacco factories employed sixty to seventy women and girls, and the garment factory about the same number.[23] These "nimble finger" jobs were comparable to the slaughterhouse jobs at several levels. They were not particularly well paid or attractive, but since they provided steady, secure income with opportunities for overtime or piece work, they were seen as good jobs. Openings for these jobs tended to be filled by the urban family and friends of the workers, and were therefore less accessible to migrants.[24]

In the early 1950s opportunities for women to earn wages expanded significantly with the opening of cashew-processing factories in the Lourenço Marques area. When the Fábrica Industrial de Cajú, popularly known as Cajú, retooled and expanded production in the 1950s, it employed a predominantly female labor force. In 1956 Cajú employed 1,257 African women, and by 1962 that number had increased to 2,935.[25] Employment choices for women were largely limited to factory labor or domestic service. The better-paid factory jobs and professional opportunities tended to be dominated by local women with some education.[26] Migrant women dominated the cashew jobs.[27] The systematic sample of the registered labor force revealed that 59 percent of the city's female labor force worked at Cajú, about 14 percent worked at the city's other factories (garment, textile, rubber, tobacco, and soap), and about 24 percent worked as domestic servants.[28] Young males in Lourenço Marques enjoyed many more choices for employment.

Domestic servant with groceries.

Wage Rates for African Women in Lourenço Marques[29] 1933–1962

Factories*		Cajú	Domestic Service	Professional	Woodlots
1933/35	nd	nd	40–300$	300–900$	120$
1936/39	nd	nd	40–300$	300–900$	120$
1940/45	nd	nd	40–300$	300–900$	180$
1946/50	200–240$	nd	50–200$	400–800$	nd
1951/55	240–800$	240$	75–300$	400–1,000$	nd
1956/60	240–800$	245$	120–375$	550–1,300$	nd
1961/62	345$	330$	120–450$	550–1,800$	nd
*The wage range for factories reflects the availability of piece work.					

In the early 1950s, the development of the cashew industry provided important entry-level employment for thousands of Mozambican women. In the late 1940s and throughout the 1950s, casual labor on urban construction, extensive projects in transportation and communication infrastructure, and the rapid expansion of manufacturing and the upriver industrial port complex at Matola opened opportunities for unskilled, inexperienced African males. The range, potential, and depth of employment opportunities for young males was much greater—which is also to say that the demand for male labor was much greater. The heightened labor demand was one component in the state's growing campaign to replace males in domestic service labor with females; questions of discipline and immorality were the other components.

Domestic Disobedience, Immorality, and Disorder

Discipline and trust in the domestic service relationship were no less controversial after the Depression than they had been before. If the question seems more serious, it is probably only because the documentation is broader and more detailed, and the overall numbers are larger. The administration's attitude toward service labor was also reminiscent of the patronism characteristic of the earlier era. In the early 1940s, for example, Mozambique's governor general, José Tristão de Bettencourt, observed:

> Sometimes a servant refuses to do a chore and becomes contrary. In such a case an educative prod by the police, well oriented, and guided more by educational than repressive criteria, would improve the native's conduct somewhat and make him more adaptable to service and more convivial with European families.[30]

The police in fact intervened regularly to educate domestic servants to be more adaptable and convivial to European standards. Servants were not only seldom given the benefit of the doubt, they were assumed to be inherent scoundrels. Recalling Silvestre Zuana's quote from Chapter 7, the senhora's word was always golden, "it was no use to complain."[31] A regular column published in the *Lourenço Marques Guardian* in the 1940s and 1950s illustrated these common assumptions; the column was entitled *"A Molecagem e a Malendragem."* The title, which is as poetic in Portuguese as it is awkward in English, translates roughly as "A Bevy of Blackboys—a Bevy of Rascals." One of the column's stock images was that of a tricky youngster who used his privileged access to European homes and material goods to set himself up in a youth street gang fencing stolen goods.[32]

Minors Serving Correctional Labor in Lourenço Marques 1935 to 1942[33]

Year	Minors as % of Total	Year	Minors as % of Total
1935	2	1938	3
1936	3	1941	15
1937	< 2	1942	44

Some of the children who fled to the city in the postwar era might indeed have turned to theft or might simply have been caught as vagrants upon arrival. Either case may explain the puzzling statistics on "juvenile delinquency" during the early war years. After 1942 the statistics no longer distinguished minors among prison populations, and perhaps 1942 was merely a blip, but some other evidence suggests youth gang activity increased in this era, especially theft rings. Reports in 1946 and 1947 refer specifically to youth gangs fencing stolen goods, which they acquired in part through cooperation with or intimidation of domestic servants.[34]

In 1947–1948 the *Lourenço Marques Guardian* complained that once domestics became experienced in the city, they became unruly drunks. They allegedly pretended not to like wine or sugar, but then cleaned out the household's supplies of each. That clearly echoed the stereotype of domestics from the 1900–1933 era as crafty liars and thieves. The handful of humble, pious, and obedient mission youth who looked for work as domestics, the *Guardian* alleged, were soon corrupted by the others.[35]

The New State, however, knew just what to do with contrary or undisciplined domestics. Governor Tristão de Bettencourt's "educative prod" was in fact a *palmatória* beating. Records from this period starkly reveal the petty and pervasive use of such beatings to render domestic servants "adaptable" to service. The municipal registration records included incidents of beatings on the verso of the registration cards, and the municipal curator's office had tidy volumes entitled "Register of Corporal Punishment." Those volumes documented beatings legally administered at the ACLM between 1953 and 1957—just the sort of thing De Bettencourt advocated.[36] Beatings inflicted by employers at the workplace, of the sort Mabunda and dozens of others referred to, took place above and beyond the formal sort, so the documents obviously underrepresent the extent of violence deployed to keep domestic servants in order.

The register's entries probably represent only the tip of the iceberg. That tip, however, strongly corroborated informant claims that they were regularly and severely beaten for "any little thing." A rapid survey of these records for the period 1951-1957, for example, demonstrated that passive resistance, such as being tardy, slow, or unresponsive, regularly earned a worker twelve *palmatória* blows, but the usual beating was between twelve and twenty-five blows. Twenty-five *palmatória* blows could cripple the recipient for weeks, depending upon where the blows fell.

Fully three-quarters of the beatings were for simple disobedience, disrespect, or a "bad attitude." Between October 1952 and May 1953, for example, a child of thirteen from Bilene who worked as a *criado* received a total of sixty *palmatória* blows for failing to get properly washed and having a "bad attitude" toward his tedious chores. It is probably an exceptional thirteen-year-old boy who washes properly without the usual prodding or who carries out boring chores with a "good attitude." Since petty theft accounted for less than 2 percent of the offenses, the link between domestics and gangs of thieves was probably quite limited. Indeed, some of the instances the author has tallied here as "petty theft" included a child of eleven having taken an unripe orange from a backyard tree.[37]

The age and sex profile of the victims was a close reflection of the domestic labor force, and corroborated the link of *molecagem* and *malandragem*—about three-quarters were males under twenty, and many were between ten and thirteen. No one received more than twenty-five blows and, significantly, virtually all those beaten were males—only three women appeared among the thousands who were listed.[38] The Register of Corporal Punishment revealed the physical assertion of colonial domination and authority, particularly over young males. It was designed to impress upon very young black males who was boss—for any little thing.

As the economic, employment, and political situation changed, domestic discipline patterns also changed. Charting registered beatings year by year through the systematic sample, we find that the incidence of registered corporal punishment peaked in the early 1950s and then dropped precipitously after 1956. To some extent the decline in corporal punishment might reflect the increasing proportion of women in domestic service, which is documented in the year-by-year survey. Despite the downturn, however, in 1957 more than four beatings per weekday still took place at the municipal office.[39] The sharp decline in *palmatória* beatings more likely coincided with Portugal's decision to sign the ILO's Labor Convention as part of her strategy for closer integration in the European community. That decision enhanced the possibility of an international labor inspection, in which case such disciplinary procedures would be awkward.

The final consideration in the state's efforts to feminize domestic service was the question of sexual immorality. "Any little thing" regularly earned a domestic a beating, but an allegation of sexual "misconduct" generally resulted in deportation. Young African males had to negotiate the intimate spaces of a European household very carefully. When it was a matter of a European's word against an African, the African's testimony was usually dismissed if it was even aired—in the case of sexual allegations, the situation was exponentially more dangerous. A young boy caught peaking through the keyhole at a young girl in her bath was deported without a hearing or defense. The municipal officer asked for the "strong sentence" because of the boy's "lack of respect for European women."[40] An African youth who happened to glimpse a naked European female from outside the house was sent for deportation, with a note appended to the documentation saying, "[to allow him] to remain in the area of the municipality is dangerous to our native policy. I have the honor to propose that Your Excellency deport him."[41]

The files on alleged sexual misconduct by domestic servants from the 1940s to the 1960s clearly demonstrate that an allegation of wrongdoing was sufficient to bring almost immediate deportation, and little effort was made to substantiate or refute the charge. Incidents between servant boys and European children were handled in a similar manner, although in the case of a very young servant, the boy was sent off to a mission school outside the district. Despite protests from the missions, their boarding schools served the administration as juvenile delinquent detention centers. Supporting correspondence strongly indicated that African male sexuality was a charged subject. Whether it was a matter of adolescent sexual curiosity, happenstance, or attempted sexual assault, any incident was met with summary and severe sanctions.[42]

Toward Feminization

De Bettencourt hoped to improve discipline and hold down wages for domestic service labor by promoting the feminization of domestic service. The great majority of "contrary" and undisciplined domestics, or at least those whom their employers chose to discipline, were teenage boys. African women, whether youthful or adult, were assumed to be more accustomed to obedience and therefore more docile and respectful. De Bettencourt's promotion of female domestics was framed in terms of advancing the New State's civilizing mission in cooperation with Catholic mission training: "It has been our mistake to ignore the native women with respect to domestic service."[43] The polite construction was that service would ease unsophisticated rural women into the ways of civilized society.[44] Later, Colonial Minister Vieira Machado put it more bluntly: domestic service was "properly a woman's job" anyway.[45]

The discourse was patently hypocritical. De Bettencourt, Machado, and everyone else knew that African women disliked employment in domestic service, and Portuguese women disliked hiring African female domestics, and they knew why. Both groups of women shared the same concern: the male head of household's attitude toward sexual access as part of the servant's job description.[46] The long hours and live-in arrangements of domestic service made it very difficult for African women to sustain important social links with their families, but the threat of sexual harassment was an important additional burden for women.[47] African male and female sexuality elicited quite different responses.

Despite strong New State promotion, the feminization of domestic service failed to attract African women who had other choices, largely because for them domestic service was not a bridging step into a better paid job, it was a dead end. The African women who registered as domestic servants between 1950 and 1962 typically worked as *criadas* (nannies) or *lavadeiras* (washerwomen). These women domestics not only did not experience upward mobility through domestic service, they emerged as the only group in the survey actually to experience a decrease in cash wages over time. Women who worked as domestics and left for the birth of a child typically reentered the labor force at the same wage, but sometimes they had to begin again at a lower wage.[48]

The sample data revealed that turnover among female domestic servants was high, even though the women did not seem to experience wage gains with each change of employer. That pattern for domestic service was in sharp contrast with that of women in factory labor, especially at Cajú. Despite the low wages and absence of annual increments for most of the 1950s, turnover at Cajú was among the lowest in the city.[49] The regular hours, fairly predictable income, and live-out conditions of factory work were clearly preferred to domestic service if women were in a position to make a choice.

By 1960 the feminization of domestic service had succeeded only among mulattos and whites. According to the census, it was exclusively a female occupation among mulattos, and white women outnumbered white men in domestic service by

Charcoal and firewood seller.

Charcoal and firewood seller.

the same ratio that African men had outnumbered African women a decade earlier.[50] The Asian population more closely reflected the African ratio, with four men to every woman, but the total number of Asians in domestic service according to the 1960 census was less than seventy.[51]

Domestic Service and Male Youth

The majority of both native and migrant informants first worked as domestic servants, and provided a body of testimony from their vantage point, some of which we have already heard.[52] Gabriel Mabunda's experience fleeing his jealous, knife-wielding employer was among the more colorful, but strong themes emerged amidst the range of experiences. The majority took a job in domestic service because it was easy entry, and the majority left because there was no hope of earning any "real money" in domestic service. Some, like Mabunda, were ambitious and hoped to use their base in domestic service to attend night school, get a typing certificate, or simply penetrate networks into the city's more desirable employment opportunities.[53] Even those who sincerely liked their employers and their work situations found the cash wage was always very little. "Não pagava nada!" (it paid nothing) was most people's summary explanation of why they left.[54] All expressed an appreciation of the twin dangers and benefits of living intimately with Europeans, but people had quite different experiences. Many felt unfairly harassed and virtually all eventually chafed under the long hours, inappropriate living space, and absence of personal freedom.

Domestic service provided rural youths quick entry into wage labor, but after that it could come down to a matter of luck and chemistry. How well did the employer and employee get on? How honest was the employer? Most informants went through several employers before ending up with what they considered a reasonable situation. Good situations could be very good, and sympathetic employers could be very helpful in the city's patronage-steeped employment networks. Manuel Sihalo Inguane began as a dishwasher at the Escola Instituto Mousinho de Albuquerque in the city. His boss was sufficiently impressed to recommend him for a very desirable job as a cook in the wealthy Polana residential area. Inguane remained satisfied in that position from 1933 to 1938 until his boss was to be transferred. Before leaving, his boss went out of his way to have Inguane placed in a secure and fairly well paid position at Câmara Municipal de Lourenço Marques, where he worked for the next forty years. Although Inguane only worked in domestic service five years, for him it was an immediate stepping-stone for a satisfactory lifetime career.[55]

Cumbiane Macaneo had a similar experience with domestic service between 1939 and 1944. He enjoyed his job taking care of a family's home and their small stock, but he was getting older and would soon need higher cash wages if he hoped to marry and have a family. When an opening came up at the slaughterhouse, Macaneo's employer brought it to his attention and supported his application.[56] Other informants had similar experiences, with varying emphasis on the utility of a patronage connection, the quality of a personal relationship, or the pay and accommodations in the job.[57]

Bad situations could also be very bad. Mabunda's story stood out in part because he told it with such style, but many informants had similar experiences. Many were fired as an excuse for nonpayment or left because they were unfairly punished.[58] In the late 1930s Silvestre Zuana, then a youth of sixteen, worked as a servant for 40$00 per month. One evening he was so homesick for his family that he decided to stay overnight with his aunt who lived in Ximpamanine. Upon arrival at work the following morning, he was reprimanded for disobedience and taken off to the ACLM office for a *palmatória* beating, which he never forgot. He left for his home the following day and did not return to Lourenço Marques for the next thirty years.[59]

Zuana's experience highlights a key bias in the oral sample. For the most part informants represent those who persevered in the city. The registration sample provides a slight corrective for that bias by providing a cross-section of people who left employment in the city for one reason or another. Although it was difficult to identify consistent patterns when the registration record often simply indicated "abandonou" (quit and left), one pattern emerged strongly. Zuana was not the only urban worker to decide that one undeserved beating was enough. Many workers who experienced *palmatória* beatings subsequently left, and did not return.[60]

João Boavida Macaringue worked as a domestic in the 1950s because he wanted to try to complete his education through the Swiss mission school, and had no relatives in the city. He combined domestic service and evening school, but he was always very uncomfortable with the Portuguese: "Even when I heard someone speaking Portuguese, I would get the same feeling one gets when one comes across a snake in the pathway."[61] Macaringue returned to Gaza as soon as he finished the second class, and only returned to the city fifteen years later when he was mature and strong enough to work day labor at the port—at an arm's length from the European community.[62]

Finally, domestic service was sometimes just another unremarkable job that people kept or left for reasons that had little to do with the pay or the employer. Zagueu Muianga's first domestic service job was with a mulatto woman whom he quite liked, but she made her living brewing and he was always getting drunk—he finally decided it was an occupational hazard, pulled himself together, and went off to work in the South African mines.[63] For all the male informants, however, domestic service was only a stage in their early lives, part of their experience as youths in the city. Whether they liked their work situation or not, they left as adults because "It paid nothing."

Informant complaints that domestic service didn't pay anything were supported in the registration sample. The only group to receive less than what male domestics referred to as "nothing" were female domestics. From 1946 to 1962 women consistently received the lowest recorded wages, from 50$00 to 75$00 per month in the late 1940s to 200$00 a month in 1962—at both junctures that was less than wages for industrial *shibalo*. But male domestics working in private households or boarding houses regularly earned the next lowest wage, ranging from 75$00–150$00 from the late 1940s, depending upon the worker's age, to about 300$00 in the late 1950s and early 1960s.[64] So male informants were correct to say that domestic service "paid nothing." Documents also corroborated that males moved fairly quickly from the bottom wage of beginning domestic servant to higher paid positions as gardeners, *mainatos,* or caretakers, receiving annual wage increments in recognition of their experience, age, and assumed family responsibilities.[65] They left domestic service when their expenses and aspirations as adults were no longer covered within the range of possible promotions and wages.[66]

Conclusion

With the development of an African labor surplus in the late 1950s and 1960s, an administrative classification emerged that seemed most unlikely in the urban historical context: that of "unemployed domestic servants." For the first time, domestic servants were not in short supply, they were a surplus. The flight of women and children from the rural south certainly contributed to this novel phenomenon. The unemployed were all young male migrants, mostly from Chibuto, Muchopes, Bilene, and Gaza administrative districts. Ninety percent were unskilled *criados.*[67] African women were more mature and experienced and yet worked for the same wage or less than young males, and were generally perceived to be more obedient than young men. The question of discipline was one of the major reasons for state intervention in the city's backyards, but women's seeming inability to command higher wages commensurate with their experience also probably contributed to the growing proportion of women in domestic service.

While domestic service remained an ill-paid occupation for men and women throughout the period to 1962, the men earning the low wages in 1946, for example, were not the same men earning them in 1953 or in 1962. It was clear from oral testimony, the registration sample, and the census that young males constantly replenished the category of male domestics as older men moved to more lucrative positions.

Again, that was not the case for women. It remains unclear at this point if high absenteeism related to female fertility or child care responsibilities was a negative factor that counterbalanced women's positive reputation as obedient and disciplined workers. It is clear, however, that to the extent that women participated in the wage labor economy of Lourenço Marques before 1962, the great majority occupied unpromising, ill-paid positions, and experienced little if any upward mobility.

In conclusion, we have seen that gender, luck, individual drive, and networks all played a role in African experience as domestic servants in this period. The occupation was closely monitored by the registration and native affairs system because of its intimacy with European families. The specific behavior of individual workers was much more closely monitored than in most other unskilled or semi-skilled jobs in the city. Despite the clearly positive relationships some informants developed, all fell within the patron/client or father/son categories, which confirmed European male authority and tutelage over African males. Perhaps nothing more clearly illustrates the parental aspect of domestic service better than the *palmatória* spanking received by "disobedient" domestics. The domestic service relationship could sustain benevolence and advocacy, but even when people knew and basically liked one another, the *indigenato* and the social system it created and reproduced was intolerant of man-to-man equality. In the case of domestic servants, there was less need for hypocrisy.

Conclusion: African Workers and Colonial Racism Images, Groups, and Individuals

> The man who did well here was the white man. He ate the
> blood of other people. I sweated; he didn't, but he had a five-
> story house and I didn't.
>
> Valente Pande Nhabanga[1]

The *indigenato* ensured that Africans sweated and white men did not, that white men
could achieve comfort and security, whereas Africans could not. The whites who
really "did well" in Lourenço Marques, like Paulino Santos Gil, achieved their success with a hefty infusion of African sweat and blood. Joaquim da Costa, an *assimilado*,
made his career at the port as a tally clerk. He had gone as far as Africans of his generation were allowed under colonial racism. He was not a member of the urban elite
associations that received Santos Gil's charity checks, but he was of the same social
class. From the perspective of unskilled laborers like Nhabanga, Da Costa was also
included among those who "did well" during the colonial era.[2] Da Costa had his own
perspective. He watched thousands of Portuguese, who made their careers at the
port and railway complex like he had, build "houses" and enjoy comfortable retire-
ments, whereas at eighty-two he still went to work every day:

> We were the ones who worked here. We did every job, and as the railway
> and port traffic increased, we were the ones who moved it. I can honestly
> say that all this has been at my expense! I'm not ashamed to say so, not even
> in front of the big shots. . . . And I earned what? What have I earned up to

today? Had I been white I would have been made an inspector. By now I would have been relaxing in my home.[3]

The *indigenato* allowed Portuguese at every level, common laborer, *cantineiro*, contractor, bureaucrat, and planter, to exploit their racial advantage to accumulate at African expense, in big ways and small. Economists refer to the process as the extraction of absolute or relative surplus value, but in a very real sense Portuguese colonists fed themselves on African blood, whether Nhabanga's, Da Costa's, or others'. The *indigenato* ensured that value flowed from Africans to Europeans and that Africans were prevented from interfering with or diverting that flow.

The structures and mechanisms that created, sustained, and reproduced European advantage and African disadvantage spanned the class spectrum, shaping African class formation in Lourenço Marques from top to bottom. The overall tendency was to encourage the growth of a scrapping, marginalized working class. Workers enjoyed little security and less mobility up the class ladder, but neither were they allowed to escape wage labor by producing a livelihood on their own land and with their own labor. Despite the fact that most Mozambicans continued to have access to land and labor throughout the century, they were forced into minimum-condition wage labor. The voluntary flow was strong and volunteer workers clung to unattractive situations because the level of exploitation experienced by conscript labor was so high. In most of Mozambique, *shibalo* extracted labor from men and women who were forced to use their own tools, bring their own food, and build their own shelter. Eventually (in different places and at different times) *shibalo* were provided with tools, but food and shelter usually remained insufficient. Indeed, in places like Saldanha's *matadouro*, *shibalo* were worked to death, or worked so hard and in such poor conditions that they subsequently died. That certainly qualifies as extraction of absolute surplus.

The *indigenato* not only ensured that a very large group of Africans became trapped in the struggles of the working poor, it also blocked the ability of the most competent African entrepreneurs, professionals, and skilled workers to attain, sustain, and reproduce middle-class status. Lídia Felizmina Tembe's case is a fine example. Structural barriers frustrated her efforts to acquire the credentials for middle-class status, to attain that status once she had qualified, and then to transmit her limited social and material gains to her daughters. Just like her uneducated mother and grandmother, this professional nurse-midwife had to resort to illegal income generation, not only to sustain herself and her daughters, but to provide the education necessary for her daughters to have access to professional opportunities.

The formidable structures of the *indigenato* were exploited, accommodated, challenged, mediated, circumvented, and explained in different ways by different groups and individuals. Structures are important, individual agency is important, family and group mutual support is important, and so are the wild cards like luck, health, and personality. This study introduced contrasting individual and group perspectives to the relationships and structures of the *indigenato* in an attempt to highlight the variety and textures that developed around it. Although the *indigenato*'s structures eventually weighed heavily on all "people of the Negro race and descendents thereof," perspectives and strategies varied through time and by individual.

When Mussongueia Samuel Mussana became painfully ensnared in the developing *indigenato*, he sustained his spirit through song and mischief. He explained his experience saying he had the ill luck to become involved in the evil and foolish ways inspired by the growing European presence. He felt it had very little to do with him. His challenge was to avoid it more successfully in the future. For the most part he was successful. Unlike Mussongueia Samuel Mussana, João dos Santos Albasini's class and social position placed him beyond the reach of most of the *indigenato*'s snares, yet he approached its development with a markedly different attitude from Mussongueia's. Albasini felt the *indigenato* had a great deal to do with him. He realized that every law that distinguished citizens on the base of race impinged upon his rights and human dignity even if he were not immediately subject to them. He therefore brought his considerable intellect, energy, and imagination to a spirited effort to abort the *indigenato* before it came into full bloom.

By the time Bandi Albasini Chibindji became a young adult, the *indigenato* was fully developed. Chibindji wended his way amidst the *indigenato*'s formal and informal labor control structures with grace, serenity, and patience. He carefully cultivated the paths he hoped would ease his way to promotion and greater material security for his family. His personal generosity of spirit seemed to encourage flexibility within the barriers. Chibindji saw the *indigenato* as an unjust burden, but he also saw it as a structure much greater and more powerful than himself. He coped with it as best he could, without malice or self-recrimination. In the same period, however, Manuel dos Santos Tembe drew focused energy from the simmering anger those same structures kindled in his proud and dignified carriage. The petty daily assaults the *indigenato* meted out to Africans did not slide easily off his back. He gave the system no opportunity to undercut him, and he persistently and carefully pushed the space open to him as far as it would go. Both Chibindji and Tembe were patient in their quite different ways, and patience eventually paid off for each.

Gabriel Mabunda first confronted the *indigenato*'s structures a generation after Chibindji and Tembe. He was neither particularly patient nor especially angry—he was ambitious. Mabunda brought energy, wit, and a touch of humor to his daring interplay with the *indigenato*'s formidable structures and sanctions. It was almost as though he enjoyed the challenge of a dangerous game. His drive and courage were scarcely daunted in the fray. He was not brash, however; he knew enough to walk away from a month's pay rather than confront a white employer determined to defraud him, but he risked a whole range of sanctions to acquire the skills and technical credentials he needed to pursue his career goals. Mabunda was lucky. As we have seen, Samuel Chipoco Miuanga also took risks in a dangerous game, but luck was not on his side.

Between 1877 and 1962 the colonial construction of inequality in Mozambique developed piece by piece. Its effectiveness and the challenges raised against it ebbed and flowed, shaped by events in the economic and political arenas. After the shock of conquest and the boom years around the turn of the century, the colonial government set about the task of subordinating and directing the region's labor force. Between 1900 and the mid-1920s, Mozambicans in Sul do Save vigorously contested such subordination and channeling, ironically while subsidizing the state's efforts through their taxes, registration and criminal fees, fines, and unpaid labor contributions. By the mid-1920s the colonial administration had successfully deflected virtually all direct confrontations by warriors, workers, and intellectuals. Confrontation had become too costly.

The economic crisis of the early 1920s and early 1930s, in combination with prior defeats and the racist retrenchment of the New State regime, broke the will of the mature generation which had led the confident and vigorous, if ultimately failed, struggles in the press, the neighborhoods and workplaces. Disunity and apathy plagued the African urban community from the 1930s into the late 1940s, despite the economic recovery. The post–World War II generation of leadership failed to gain a firm foothold, in part because it faced both government censorship and the hostility of the rapidly increasing white immigrant population. The flood of new settlers clustered in and around Lourenço Marques and threatened to claim for themselves whatever gains urban Africans had made since the depression. By the late 1950s political trends in Africa, the economic reorientation of Portugal's dominant classes toward Europe and pent up frustration among a whole range of African and European groups in Mozambique combined to promote at least the partial dismantling of the *indigenato*. Even so, groups in the urban African community remained largely cautious and inward-looking. Major Choque's deportation for insisting a young person accord him the dignity of a proper address suggests the wisdom of such caution.[4]

Between 1877 and 1962, however, the articulation, implementation and perpetuation of *indigenato* structures had, directly and indirectly, fueled the flow of Mozambicans into wage labor. The arbitrary and potentially life threatening vulnerability to *shibalo* was nowhere taken lightly. Contract or clandestine flows to neighboring South Africa were the most familiar and best paid alternative to *shibalo* harassment. The great majority of Mozambicans who were old enough, fit and willing tried that route. The "moral obligation to work . . . ," with its racist and culturally arrogant prescriptions of what constituted work and morality, forced a secondary flow of Mozambicans into Lourenço Marques. They accepted the low wages and poor conditions typical of many urban jobs, in part because they were a far sight better than *shibalo*.

Shibalo futher warped urban labor conditions and relations due to the state's policy of displacing unskilled casual labor in key sectors of the economy with *shibalo* gangs working in shifts. Labor demand for entry level positions was therefore not allowed to push up wage rates. Finally, the state increasingly and systematically deployed *shibalo* gangs to undermine volunteer labor action throughout the urban economy. Men and women who challenged the mechanisms which constrained their ability to participate as full competitive adults in the urban economy were also punished by sentences of *shibalo*. Workers who tried to get around the constraints of registration, or women who brewed popular alcoholic drinks in competition with Portuguese *cantineiros*, faced three months of *shibalo* if apprehended. At virtually every corner the *indigenato* curbed and curtailed African aspirations to material and social security.

This study has charted the interaction of regional, rural and urban challenges and constraints on African work seekers. It has explored the labor structures and relationships Portugal developed to direct and control African labor, and has tried to identify patterns and diversity of African perspectives on those processes. Mozambicans "of the Negro race or descendent therefrom . . ." had a great range of experiences under the *indigenato*, but the *indigenato* denied all "natives" and *assimilados* their basic adulthood, security, and human dignity. Karel Pott, a middle-class mulatto with a Coimbra law degree, and Valente Pande Nhabanga, an unskilled, uneducated municipal worker, were arguably at the polar ends of African urban experiences in Lourenço Marques, yet both were denied full authority and participation, and both brought similar imagery to their colonial experience. Nhabanga claimed the white-man "ate the blood of other people," and Pott accused the colonial state of sustaining itself on revenues ". . . generated virtually in full by the product of our labor, by our blood!"[5] The refrains of waterfront worksongs echoed a similar theme, ". . . Portu-guese live by stealing our wages." The Ross report emphasized that Africans seldom received the full value of their wage packet, and Pinto de Fonseca, on the threshold of the system's abolition confirmed that it condemned people to "enormous moral and material prejudice."[6]

Portugal always took great pains to vigorously deny anything but the most benevolent intentions in her colonial labor policy and practice. The historical record, however, clearly demonstrates that the Portuguese engineered and fine tuned Afri-can inequality. They developed barriers to prevent Africans from developing their skills and capital to make a better life and livelihood for themselves. The barriers were in part a response to the fears of white immigrants, in part the state's perceived need for certain kinds of African labor, and in part its perception of other kinds of African labor as inconvenient. Skilled and "lettered" African workers were always suspect.[7] Ironically, of all the sources exploited for this study, the colonial power's own archives provided the most irrefutable evidence that the *indigenato* was specifi-cally designed to define Africans as lesser beings, who "did not have two legs like they did," in order to prevent them from successfully competing with whites, and to allow whites to prosper on African "blood."[8]

The perspectives on labor history articulated by male informants for this study and by the male journalists who wrote in the African press in its most open period challenged economistic and managerial interpretations of colonial labor relations. Colonial constructions of meaning around African labor are important and tell us a great deal about labor relations. Socioeconomic criteria that shaped the nature, pace, ebb, and flow of capital investment, labor demand, and strategies for labor exploita-tion are also crucial. Labor historians have made great strides in these areas.[9]

African experience as articulated and interpreted by African actors, however, should be at the center of historical analysis. African perspectives on colonial racism, and on the process and meaning of moving into lifetime wage labor in an urban area highlighted material, social, and physical security, adult authority, and personal human dignity. Mozambicans frequently experienced and explained colonial labor relations in terms of black men/white men and dignity/indignity. These were not simple metaphors for different types of capitalist development. Virtually all white Portuguese could exercise very real social, material, and physical power over virtu-ally all Africans, whether those Portuguese were illiterate, unskilled laborers, petty bureaucrats, household heads, or capitalist magnates. By the same token, Africans were vulnerable to white injury whether they were gang laborers, well-educated, experienced office workers, or at the top of the permitted black mobility scale. Histo-rians must rework our analytical and theoretical frameworks to better accommodate and interpret human dignity, personal security, and adult authority in colonial labor relations. Such concerns were at the heart of colonial racism and African interpreta-tions of their experience as urban workers.

NOTES

INTRODUCTION
African Workers and Colonial Racism

1. Oral Testimony [OT], S. L. Chichongo. Informants are identified in notes simply by initials and surname. If informants were interviewed several times, the specific interview is identified as (a), (b), etc. All informants are listed in alphabetical order with their full name, date of birth, and place and date of interview(s) in Annex I.
2. *Shibalo* is used as both noun and adjective, to refer both to forced labor and to those required to perform it. Alternative spellings include *xibalo, chibaro,* and *chibalo.*
3. Quotations in this paragraph were echoed by many informants. Only the most explicit are noted here: OT, G. Mabunda, J. da Costa (a), S. Tembe, F. Zavala.
4. OT, E. Langa.
5. OT, J. da Costa (a), P. Faleca, I. Jeque, S. Muianga.
6. Mozambique's song heritage has been fruitfully explored by several historians, but see especially Leroy Vail and Landeg White, *Power and the Praise Poem: Southern African Voices in History* (Charlottesville, 1991).
7. Song OT, J. Kuamba.
8. Xai-Xai, alternate spelling Chai-Chai; during the New State era it was Vila João Belo. It is again Xai-Xai.
9. Song OT, M. Cossa.
10. Worksongs also addressed tensions between male workers competing for the services and attention of the women they left behind. These are raised later in the text, but are not the focus of this study. See Celina in Annex II.
11. Song OT, F. Muconto.
12. *Ibid.*
13. Many informants sang versions of this song. The most complete recording was in OT, J. Machanga.
14. "It is time to pay taxes to the Portuguese, the Portuguese who eat eggs and chicken." Edward A. Alpers, "The Role of Culture in the Liberation of Mozambique," *Ufahamu,* 12, 3 (1983), 155; Vail and White, Power and the Praise Poem, 45–46, and 126–30.
15. Language compiled from the preface and text of the dominant labor codes and regulations of the century. See J. M. da Silva Cunha, *O Trabalho Indígena: Estudo de direito colonial* (Lisbon, 1949).
16. James Duffy, *A Question of Slavery: Labour Policies in Portuguese Africa and the British Protest, 1850–1920* (Oxford, 1967), 5.
17. Marvin Harris, "Race, Conflict, and Reform in Mozambique," in Stanley Diamond and F. G. Burke, eds., *The Transformation of East Africa: Studies in Political Anthropology* (New York, 1966).

160   African Workers and Colonial Racism

18. Song OT, F. Zavala.
19. Luciano Maia Pinto da Fonseca, Inspector Administrativo, "Relatório da Direcção dos Serviços dos Negócios Indígenas e da Curadoria Geral . . . Periodo de 7 Junho de 1958 a 31 Dezembro 1959," 25 June 1960, Fundo do Governo Geral [FGG], Rel. 721, Arquívo Histórico de Moçambique [AHM], Maputo.
20. *Ibid.*, 16–17, 19.
21. *Ibid.*, 19.
22. *Ibid.*, 8.
23. The *escudo* (written 1$00) was the unit of currency in Mozambique from the beginning of the second decade of the twentieth century through Independence. It replaced the *reis* (written $001). One *escudo* equaled one thousand *reis* or one *milreis*. (written 1$000). A *conto* equaled a thousand *escudos* (1,000$00).
24. Câmara Municipal de Lourenço Marques [CMLM], *Anais da Câmara Municipal de Lourenço Marques, 1950* (Lourenço Marques, 1952), quadros, 18–21.
25. Petition, "Comissão Organizadora do Sindicato Nacional dos Motoristas Africanos de Moçambique," dated 26 January 1948, with 110 signatures appended. Fundo Direcção de Secretaria de Negócios Indígenas [SNI], Caixa [Cx] 2, AHM.
26. *Ibid.*, 18–21.
27. Although this point is more fully documented throughout the text, the following reports provide essential corroboration. "Relatório, 21 Maio 1909," SNI Cx 104, AHM. "Relatório," 1 April 1950, Cx MM ACLM.
28. Henri A. Junod, *Manuel de Conversation et Dictionnaire—Ronga—Portugais—Français— Anglais* (Lausanne, 1896).
29. *Ibid.*, 13–17. The dialogues are explored more fully throughout the book.
30. Pinto de Fonseca, "Relatório . . . 1959," 7–8, FGG, Rel. 721, AHM.
31. The quote is from OT, P. Faleca, but at least thirteen informants expressed the same sentiments. Discussions of hegemony and counter-hegemony among History Workshop members of the University of the Witwatersrand, Vail and White's essays on forms of resistance, and the work of James C. Scott all confirm an implicit acknowledgment of exploitation between exploiter and exploited. They do not diminish the fact that the limits and rules of exploitation were in constant negotiation. See, for example, Belinda Bozzoli, comp. and ed., *Labour, Townships and Protest* (Johannesburg, 1978), *Town and Countryside in the Transvaal: Capitalist Penetration and Popular Response* (Johannesburg, 1983), *Class, Community, and Conflict: South African Perspectives* (Johannesburg, 1987); Vail and White, *Power and the Praise Poem*; James C. Scott, *The Moral Economy of the Peasant: Rebellion and Subsistence in Southeast Asia* (New Haven, 1976), and *Weapons of the Weak: Everyday Forms of Peasant Resistance* (New Haven, 1985).
32. The specific wording to include Negros and mulattoes was not made explicit until the 1920s. See Jeanne Penvenne, " 'We Are All Portuguese!' Challenging the Political Economy of Assimilation, Lourenço Marques, 1870 to 1933," in Leroy Vail, ed., *The Creation of Tribalism in Southern Africa* (Berkeley, 1989), 255–88.
33. Jeanne Penvenne, "Attitudes toward Race and Work in Mozambique: Lourenço Marques, 1900–1974," *Boston University African Studies Center Working Paper*, 16 (1979). The term "pocket white" from OT, E. Langa, N. Macaringue, M. Tembe, T. Comiche (a).
34. Vail, *The Creation of Tribalism*, introduction.
35. The source base for the case studies is explained in more detail below.
36. James C. Scott, *Weapons of the Weak*, and *The Moral Economy of the Peasant*. For Mozambique, Allen Isaacman's *The Tradition of Resistance in Mozambique: Anti-Colonial Activity in the Zambesi Valley, 1850--1921* (Berkeley, 1976) focuses on a range of peasant resistance and rebellion, and Leroy Vail and Landeg White's work addresses diverse and everyday forms, "Forms of Resistance: Songs and Perceptions of Power in Colonial Africa," *American Historical Review* 88 (1983), 883–919 and *Power and the Praise Poem*, especially Chs. 1, 2, 4, and 6.

37. Bill Freund's *The African Worker* (Cambridge, 1988) charts the path of African labor history over recent decades.
38. The term "engender" is now in general usage thanks to the explosion of African women's history over the past fifteen years. That scholarship is surveyed in Nancy Rose Hunt, "Placing African Women's History and Locating Gender," *Social History* 14 (1989), 359-79; and Cheryl Johnson-Odim and Margaret Strobel, "Conceptualizing the History of Women in Africa, Asia, Latin America, the Caribbean and the Middle East," and reviews of their "Restoring Women to History" in *Journal of Women's History [JWH]* I (Spring 1989), 31-62, 120-22. See also Sharon Stichter, *Migrant Laborers* (Cambridge, 1985).
39. Comparative works by Gareth Steadman-Jones, E.P. Thompson, Eric Hobsbawm, George Rudé, James C. Scott, and António Gramsci have been particularly important for African social history. They have inspired pioneering probes into Africa's past such as John Iliffe's inspiration from the literature on poverty in Europe to document life for Africa's poor. *The African Poor: A History* (Cambridge, 1987).
40. See especially, "Kinship, Ideology and the Nature of Pre-colonial Labour Migration: Labour Migration from the Delagoa Bay Hinterland to South Africa up to 1895," in Shula Marks and Richard Rathbone, eds. *Industrialisation and Social Change in South Africa: African Class Formation, Culture and Consciousness, 1870-1930* (London, 1982).
41. Charles van Onselen, *Chibaro: African Mine Labour in Southern Rhodesia, 1900-1930* (London, 1976); van Onselen, *Studies in the Social and Economic History of the Witwatersrand, 1886-1914*, 2 vols. (London, 1982).
42. See Bozzoli references in note 31 above and her book with the assistance of Mmantho Nkotsoe, *Women of Phokeng, Consciousness, Life Strategy, and Migrancy in South Africa, 1900-1983* (Portsmouth, N.H., 1991). Terence Ranger and Cherryl Walker reflect on the ways in which History Workshop publications have shaped southern African history in their respective essays: "Audiences and Alliances," *Southern African Review of Books* (May/June 1991), 4-5, and "Women and Gender in Southern Africa to 1945: An Overview," in Walker, ed., *Women and Gender in Southern Africa to 1945* (London, 1990), 1-32.
43. Cooper, *On the African Waterfront: Urban Disorder and the Transformation of Work in Colonial Mombasa* (New Haven, 1987).
44. Luise White, *The Comforts of Home: Prostitution in Colonial Nairobi* (Chicago, 1990); Stichter, *Migrant Laborers*; Iris Berger, *Threads of Solidarity: Women in South African Industry, 1900-1980* (Bloomington, 1991).
45. Vail and White, *Power and the Praise Poem*, and *Capitalism and Colonialism in Mozambique; A Study of Quelimane District* (Minneapolis, 1980).
46. Vail and White, *Power and the Praise Poem*; Tim Keegan, *Facing the Storm: Portraits of Black Lives in Rural South Africa* (Athens, 1988), 159ff; Belinda Bozzoli, *Women of Phokeng*, introduction.
47. Personal Narratives Group, *Interpreting Women's Lives: Feminist Theory and Personal Narratives* (Bloomington, 1989).
48. José Capela, *O Movimento Operário em Lourenço Marques, 1898-1927* (Porto, 1981); Simon E. Katzenellenbogen, *South Africa and Southern Mozambique: Labour Railways and Trade in the Making of a Relationship* (Manchester, 1982); Alexandre Lobato, *Lourenço Marques, Xilunguine; Biografia da Cidade*, I—A Parte Antiga (Lisbon, 1970); Maria Clara Mendes, *Maputo Antes da Independência: Geografia de Uma Cidade Colonial* (Lisbon, 1985).
49. There is some confusion regarding the date of the last issues of *O Africano*. Various sources note it as 1918, 1919, and 1920. The last issue that exists in the most complete collection (Biblioteca Nacional de Lisboa) is dated 1919. According to Dr. António Sopa of the AHM, who has worked extensively on Mozambican newspapers, the paper ceased publication in 1920, according to references in *Notícias da Beira*, 13 January 1920; *Brado Africano*, 10 January 1920. Thanks to personal communication from Dr. Sopa, 15 January 1993.
50. Several recent published and unpublished works focus on these newspapers. Olga Maria

Lopes Serrão Iglésias Neves, "Em Defesa da Causa Africana: Intervenção do Grêmio Africano na Sociedade de Lourenço Marques, 1908-1938" (Master's thesis, Universidade Nova
de Lisboa, 1989); Paulo Soares and Valdemir Zamparoni, "Antologia de textos do jornal 'O
Africano' (1908-1919)," *Estudos Afro-Asiáticos*, 22 (September 1992), 127-78; Valdemir Zamparoni, "A Imprensa Negra em Moçambique: A Trajetoria de 'O Africano' (1908-1920),"
Africa: Revista do Centro de Estudos Africanos (São Paulo), 11, 1 (1988), 73-86; Jeanne Marie
Penvenne, "Principles and Passion: Capturing the Legacy of João dos Santos Albasini,"
[*Boston University African Studies Center*] *Working Papers in the African Humanities*, 12 (Bos-
ton, 1991). José da Silva Moreira, "A Imprensa dos Albasinis" (licenciatura thesis, Universidade Eduardo Mondlane, 1982).

51. See Ilídio Rocha, *Catálogo dos Periódicos e Principais Seriados de Moçambique* (Lisbon, 1985),
     and the more complete and detailed work by António Jorge Diniz Sopa, "Catálogo dos
     Periódicos Moçambicanos Procedido de uma Pequena Notícia Histórica: 1854-1954"
     (licenciatura thesis, Universidade Eduardo Mondlane, 1985). Capela, *O Movimento Oper-
     ário*, details the Portuguese working-class press.

52. Five Europeans were also interviewed as part of the project, two long-established South
     African entrepreneurs, one elderly Portuguese port worker, and two former Portuguese
     administrators. See Annex I.

53. The author completed transcription and translation of all tapes recorded in Portuguese.
     Tsonga, Chopi, Zulu, and Bitonga songs and testimony were translated with the assistance
     of Alpheus Manghezi, Gaspar Guevende, and Paulo Zombole. Bento Sitoe and José Katu-
     pha clarified several issues relating to orthography and linguistics during the final revision
     of the study.

54. Augusto de Castilho, *O Distrito de Lourenço Marques, no Presente e no Futuro*, 2nd ed. (Lisbon,
     1881); Eduardo de Noronha, *O Distrito de Lourenço Marques e a Africa do Sul* (Lisbon, 189⬚);
     António Enes, *Moçambique: Relatório Apresentado ao Governo* (Lisbon, 1946); A. A. Freire de
     Andrade, *Colonisação de Lourenço Marques: Conferência feita em 13 Março de 1897 pelo sócio hon-
     orário A. A. Freire de Andrade* (Porto, 1897); Freire de Andrade, *Relatórios sôbre Moçambique*,
     I-IV (Lourenço Marques, 1907-1910); Freire de Andrade, "As Terras da Coroa," in Eduardo
     Borges de Castro, *Africa Oriental: Portugal em Africa* (Porto, 1895); Josê Tristão de Betten-
     court, *Relatório do Governador Geral de Moçambique: Respeitante ao Periódo de 20 Março de 1940
     á 31 de Dezembro, 1942* (Lisbon, 1945).

55. Frederick Cooper, Jack R. Warner, David Sousa, and the academic support section of uni-
     versity computing at Boston University kindly advised and assisted in the definition of a
     significant sample and manipulation of the data through a Soft Programming for the Social
     Sciences program. Data generated from this source base is referred to as ACLM Sample.

CHAPTER 1

Context and Chronology: The Metropole, the Region, and
the Hinterland

1. For the formation, development, and dissolution of the Gaza state and the Luso—Gaza wars
    of the 1890s, see the works of Gerhard Liesegang and Patrick Harries, especially Gerhard
    Liesegang, "Notes on the Internal Structure of the Gaza Kingdom of Southern Mozam-
    bique, 1840-1895," in J. B. Peires, ed., *Before and After Shaka: Papers in Nguni History* (Graha-
    mstown, 1981),178-209; Patrick Harries, "Slavery amongst the Gaza Nguni: Its Changing
    Shape and Function and Its Relationship to Other Forms of Exploitation," in Peires, ed.,
    Before and After Shaka, 210-29. See also René Pélissier, *Naissance du Mozambique: résistance et
    révoltes anticoloniales (1854-1918)* (Orgeval, 1984); Eduardo de Noronha, *A Rebellião dos In-
    dígenas de Lourenço Marques* (Lisbon, 1894); Lisa Ann Brock, "From Kingdom to Colonial
    District: A Political Economy of Social Change in Gazaland, Southern Mozambique,

1870–1930" (Ph.D. thesis, Northwestern University, 1989); Douglas L. Wheeler, "Gungunhana," in Norman R. Bennett, ed. *Leadership in Eastern Africa: Six Political Biographies* (Boston, 1968).

2. Mashaba, quoted in Alfredo Henrique de Silva, *Um Error de Justiça de que se Tem Sido Victima Roberto Ndevu Mashaba . . .* (Porto, 1897), 25.

3. For Mozambican labor migration to South Africa and the struggle between Portugal and the mining industry over Mozambican labor, see the following: Jonathan Crush, David Yudelman, and Alan Jeeves, *South Africa's Labor Empire: A History of Black Migrancy to the Gold Mines* (Boulder, 1991); Selim Gool, *Mining Capitalism and Black Labour in the Early Industrial Period in South Africa: A Critique of the New Historiography* (Lund, 1983); Patrick Harries, "Labour Migration from Mozambique to South Africa: With Special Reference to the Delagoa Bay Hinterland" (Ph.D. thesis, University of London, 1982), and his recent study in this series, *Work, Culture, and Identity: Migrant Laborers in Mozambique and South Africa, c. 1860-1910* (Portsmouth, N.H., 1993); Alan H. Jeeves, *Migrant Labour in South Africa's Mining Economy: The Struggle for the Gold Mines Labour Supply, 1890–1920* (Kingston, 1985); Montague George Jessett, *The Key to South Africa: Delagoa Bay* (London, 1899); Katzenellenbogen, *South Africa and Southern Mozambique*; M. D. D. Newitt, "Mine Labour and the Development of Mozambique," *Societies of Southern Africa in the 19th and 20th Centuries*, 4 (1974), 67–76; Leroy Vail and Landeg White, *Capitalism and Colonialism in Mozambique*; Charles van Onselen, *Studies in the Social and Economic History of the Witwatersrand*; Philip R. Warhurst, *Anglo-Portuguese Relations in South-Central Africa, 1890–1900* (London, 1962); David Yudelman and Alan Jeeves, "New Frontiers for Old: Black Migrants to the South African Gold Mines, 1920–1985," *JSAS*, 13 (1986), 101–24; Ruth First et al., *Black Gold: The Mozambican Miner, Proletarian, and Peasant* (New York, 1983); Luis António Covane, "A Emigração Clandestina de Moçambicanos para as Minas e Plantações Sul-Africanas, 1897–1913," *Cadernos de História: Boletim do Departamento de História da Universidade Eduardo Mondlane* [*Cadernos*], 8 (October 1990), 91–102; Covane, *As Relacões Económicas Entre Moçambique e a Africa do Sul, 1850–1964: Acordos e Regulamentos Principais* (Maputo, 1989).

4. Tito de Carvalho, *Les Colonies Portugaises au Point de Vue Commercial* (Paris, 1900), 42. Carvalho details Portugal's colonial trade in the late nineteenth century and the dramatic role of Lourenço Marques's trade in that context; see 61–62, 96.

5. Noronha, *O Distrito de Lourenço Marques*, 132–43.

6. Telegraph, water, electricity, and tramways were eventually undertaken with foreign capital. Delagoa Bay Development Corporation, Ltd., had purchased the controlling interest for power, water, and the tramline by 1903–1904. "Processos Relativo das Obras Públicas no Porto de Lourenço Marques," Maço 2475, Direcção dos Caminhos de Ferro Ultramarinos [DCFU], Arquivo Historico Ultramarino [AHU], Lisbon. *Delagoa Directory* [becomes *Anuário de Lourenço Marques*] follows the development of the city's utilities, especially 1914, 58–59. See also Salamão Vieira, "Os Electricos de Lourenço Marques I: 1900-1920," *Arquivo* (Maputo) 9 (April 1991), 5–44; Mendes, *Maputo*, Ch. 2. Vail and White present the best overview in *Capitalism and Colonialism*, 200–244.

7. Gervase Clarence-Smith, *The Third Portuguese Empire, 1825–1975: A Study in Economic Imperialism* (Manchester, 1985), Ch. 5.

8. See Chapter 5.

9. The key legislation for this process is outlined in Silva Cunha, *O Trabalho Indigena*, 200–208.

10. See Chapter 5.

11. Penvenne, "We Are All Portuguese!" 278–81, and Chapter 6.

12. See Chapter 6.

13. Manuel Pereira dos Santos divides his study of industrial development in Mozambique at 1946. He considers basic agricultural processing industries which were established by 1928. He then studies industrial change from 1937 to 1946, and the diversification and growth from 1947 to 1954, the date the study was published, *A Indústria em Moçambique* (Lourenço

Marques, 1956). See also Moçambique, Repartição Ténica de Estatística [RTE], *Estatística Indústrial* (annual from 1947 to 1973) (Lourenço Marques, 1950–1974).

14. See Chapter 7.

15. Historical research for the 1960s and 1970s is still quite limited. The Thomas Henriksen's *Revolution and Counter-revolution: Mozambique's War of Independence, 1964–1974* (Westport, 1983) is the most complete study of Portugal's specific response in Mozambique. Clarence-Smith explores the economic shifts leading up to and accompanying the outbreak of hostilities in Mozambique in his *Third Portuguese Empire,* Ch. 7.

16. Malyn Newitt, *Portugal in Africa: The Last Hundred Years* (Essex, 1981), 219ff.

17. U.S. consular despatches on the economy and labor situation in Mozambique from 1950 to 1974 chronicle the changing economic situation, the debate over foreign investment, and especially the mixed impact of labor and economic reform throughout the period. The despatches are contained in the United States National Archives [USNA], Washington, D.C. They were obtained by the author through the Freedom of Information Act [FIA]. Copies of the despatches were deposited at the Boston University African Studies Library and the Arquivo Histórico de Moçambique. They are cited below by despatch number, date, and FIA/BU.

18. For commoditization and industry replacement, see Chapter 2.

19. Elizabeth Colson, "African Society at the Time of the Scramble," in L. Gann and P. Duignan, eds., *Colonialism in Africa,* I (Cambridge, 1968), 27–65.

20. Henri Philippe Junod, quoted in E. Dora Earthy, *Valenge Women: The Social and Economic Life of the Valenge Women of Portuguese East Africa* (London, 1933), 9.

21. Charles E. Fuller, "An Ethnohistorical Study of Continuity and Change in Gwambe" (Ph. D thesis, Northwestern University, 1955), 6–21; Earthy, *Valenge Women,* 9; Cruz, *Terras de Gaza,* 161; Vail and White, *Power and the Praise Poem,* 113.

22. Vail, "Introduction," *The Creation of Tribalism;* Patrick Harries, "The Roots of Ethnicity: Discourse and the Politics of Language Construction in South East Africa," *African Affairs,* 87, 346 (January, 1988), 25–52; Patrick Harries, "The Anthropologist as Historian and Liberal: H.-A. Junod and the Thonga," *JSAS* 8 (1981), 37–50.

23. Alternative spellings include Muchopes, Chope, Mchope, and Thonga.

24. Shangaan is also spelled Shangana or Machangaan.

25. Mozambican scholars have recently undertaken a series of research projects on language and ethnic groupings throughout the country. This paragraph reflects current analysis according to linguistics specialists. Personal communication from J.M.M. Katupha, 31 October 1992; Bento Sitoe, 27 September 1992.

26. Correlations among environment, out-migration, and adaptive production techniques in Sul do Save were raised in the scholarly debate between António Rita Ferreira and Marvin Harris in the 1960s. Subsequent research by scholars including Sherilynn Young, Patrick Harries, José Fialho Feliciano, and Gerhard Liesegang has explored them in greater detail. António Rita Ferreira, "Labour Emigration among the Moçambique Thonga: Comments on a Study by Marvin Harris," *Africa,* 30 (1960), 141–52; Rita Ferreira, "Labour Emigration among the Moçambique Thonga: Comments on Marvin Harris's Reply," *Africa,* 31 (1961), 75–77; Marvin Harris, "Labour Emigration Among the Moçambique Thonga: Cultural and Political Factors," *Africa,* 30 (1959), 50–66; Harris, "Labour Emigration Among the Moçambique Thonga: A Reply to Sr. Rita-Ferreira," *Africa,* 30 (1960), 243–45; Patrick Harries, "Labour Migration from Moçambique"; Harries and Liesegang in Peires, *Before and After Shaka;* José Fialho Feliciano, "Antropologia Económica dos Thonga do Sul de Moçambique," two vols. (Ph.D. thesis, Universidade Técnica de Lisboa, 1989); Sherilynn Young, "Fertility and Famine: Women's Agricultural History in Southern Mozambique," in Robin Palmer and Neil Parsons, eds., *The Roots of Rural Poverty in Central and Southern Africa* (Berkeley, 1977), 66–81. Three very important but unpublished papers by Young are particularly valuable for

this question: "Changes in Diet and Production in Southern Mozambique, 1855–1960," paper presented at the British African Studies Association Conference (Edinburgh, 1976); "Women in Transition: Southern Mozambique, 1975–1976," paper presented at the Conference on the History of Women (St. Paul, 1977) " 'What Have They Done with the Rain?' 20th Century Transformation in Southern Mozambique with Particular Reference to Rain Prayers," paper presented at the African Studies Association Annual Meeting (Baltimore, 1978). I am grateful to Sherilynn Young for sharing unpublished rainfall, soil quality, vegetation, and fauna maps of Sul do Save, which she painstakingly constructed from a wealth of primary sources on the late nineteenth and early twentieth century. Her unpublished works are both meticulous and important.

27. República Popular de Moçambique, Ministério de Educação, *Atlas Geográfico*, I, 2nd ed. revised (Stockholm, 1986), 13, 16, 17.

28. *Ibid.*

29. Fialho Feliciano, "Antropologia Económica dos Thonga," I, 74–76.

30. Young, "What Have They Done with the Rain?" 17. Megan Vaughan's *The Story of an African Famine* (Cambridge, 1987) also highlights gendered access to community resources and options to migrate.

31. The concept of the household has generated an extensive literature which cannot be adequately addressed here. The concept and experience of a household, much like that of ethnicity, was fluid and adaptable. The ideal household described by elder males was probably a minority amidst many adaptive variations. The essential point is that claims on and access to resources, including labor, were frequently shaped by an individual's place within a social unit, which is most conveniently described as a household. See Jane I. Guyer, "Household and Community in African Studies," *African Studies Review*, 24, 2/3 (1981), 87–138; Pauline E. Peters and Jane I. Guyer, "Conceptualizing the Household: Issues of Theory and Policy in Africa," *Development and Change*, 81, 2 (1987), 197–213; Jean Koopman Henn, "The Material Basis of Sexism: A Mode of Production Analysis," in Sharon B. Stichter and Jane L. Parpart, eds., *Patriarchy and Class: African Women in the Home and the Workforce* (Boulder, 1988), 27–59.

32. Henri A. Junod, *The Life of a South African Tribe*, I (New York, 1962), 15; St. Vincent Erskine, "Journey to Umzila's, South—East Africa, in 1871–1872," *Journal of the Royal Geographical Society [JRGS]*, 45 (1875), 45–128; Cruz, *Em Terras de Gaza*, 41–53; David Webster, "Migrant Labour, Social Formations, and the Proletarianization of the Chopi of Southern Mozambique," *African Perspectives*, 1 (1978), 156–63; António Rita Ferreira, "Ethnohistory and Ethnic Groupings of the Peoples of Moçambique," *South African Journal of African Affairs*, 3 (1975), 58-59.

33. Young, "Women in Transition," 1–5; Webster, "Proletarianization of the Chopi," 169–70; Martha Binford Morris, "Rjonga Settlement Patterns, Meaning and Implications," *Anthropological Quarterly* 45 (1972), 228; Junod, *Life of a South African Tribe*; and Earthy, *Valenge Women, passim.*

34. "A woman taken in marriage without the payment of bridewealth is not bound to the marriage. She can go away when it pleases her and leave her husband in grief." H. P. Junod and Alexandre A. Jacques, *Vutlhari bya Batsonga (Machangana): The Wisdom of the Tsonga—Shangana People*, 2nd ed. (Johannesburg, 1957).

35. Literature regarding the concept and practice of *lobolo* is both extensive and contentious. At its poles *lobolo* is presented either as the barbaric sale of a woman into virtual slavery or the sole legitimate seal of a marriage bond, without which the bride is no better than a prostitute. John Wesley Haley, a missionary at Mabile station near Inhambane from 1902 to 1920, took the position that *lobolo* confirmed the value of women in society and provided a strong incentive to keep marriages intact, *Life in Mozambique and South Africa* (Chicago, 1926), 42–50; interview with "old Pachisso" in *Brado Africano*, 24 September 1949.

36. This is explored in detail in the Harris/Rita Ferreira debate, note 26 above.

37. H. A. Junod, "The Fate of Widows amongst the Ba—Ronga," *Annual Report of the South African Association for the Advancement of Science* (Grahamstown, 1909), 3. The entire question of *lobolo* as an empowering, leveling, or enslaving practice falls outside our principal concerns here, but it merits fundamental reanalysis privileging African women's views.

38. Patrick Harries, "Slavery, Social Incorporation, and Surplus Extraction: The Nature of Free and Unfree Labour in South-East Africa," *Journal of African History [JAH]*, 22 (1981), 309–30.

39. Quoted in Amadeu Cunha, *Mousinho e Sua Obra e Sua Época* (Lisbon, 1944), 438–40, translated and quoted by Wheeler in "Gungunhana," 219. The term Vátua was used by the Portuguese to describe the ruling elite of the Gaza state, in contrast to ordinary people of Gaza and Lourenço Marques who were sometimes called Landim. The terms have no linguistic significance.

40. Harries, "Slavery, Social Incorporation," 311, 318–20.

41. Fialho Feliciano, "Antropologia Económica dos Thonga," I, for emphasis on the construction of social dependency relations.

42. OT, M. S. Mussona.

43. The most complete statistics on the proportion of Mozambican migrants in the mine labor force are provided in Jeeves, *Migrant Labour*, 188–89; Yudelman and Jeeves, "New Labour Frontiers," 123–24; Crush, Jeeves, and Yudelman, *South Africa's Labor Empire*, Chs. 1–3.

44. First et al., *Black Gold*, Parts II and III; Moçambique, Circunscrições de Lourenço Marques, *Relatórios das Circunscrições: Distrito de Lourenço Marques, 1909–1910, 1911–1912, 1912–1913* (Lourenço Marques, 1911–1915); *Respostas aos Quesitos Feitos pelo Secretaria de Negócios Indígenas, Dr. Francisco Ferrão, para a Confecção do Relatório Sòbre o Distrito de Lourenço Marques* (Lourenço Marques, 1909); J. R .P Cabral, *Relatório do Governador de Inhambane, Anno 1911–1912* (Lourenço Marques, 1913); Daniel da Cruz, *Em Terras de Gaza* (Porto, 1910); OT, the fathers of the majority of informants born before the late 1920s had worked at least one mine contract. About half went as Wenela contracts and half walked as independents (thirteen informants).

45. According to the 1912 census, the entire African population of Lourenço Marques was under 6,000. That year nearly 76,000 southern Mozambicans were contracted at South African mines. *Recenseamentos da População e das Habitações da Cidade de Lourenço Marques e seus Subúrbios, Referidos á 1 de Dezembro de 1912* (Lourenço Marques, 1913), and Jeeves, *Migrant Labour*, 189.

46. "Politica indígena" in the series of "Elementos para o Relatório da Sua Ex. o Governador Geral de Moçambique, Relativo ao Ano de 1951," SNI, Cx 121, and similar reports for the period 1943 throughout the 1950s, SNI, Cx 124, 125, AHM.

47. Junod, *Manuel de Conversation*, 31, 33.

48. The relationship between famine strategies and migrant labor in Sul do Save is explored by several scholars, Alpheus Manghezi, "Ku Thekla: Estratégias de Sobrevivência Contra a Fome no Sul de Moçambique," *Estudos Moçambicanos*, 4 (1983), 19–40; Kenneth Hermele, *Contemporary Land Struggles on the Limpopo: A Case Study of Chokwe Mozambique, 1950–1974* [AKUT, 34] (Uppsala, 1986); Otto Roesch, "Migrant Labour and Forced Rice Production in Southern Mozambique: The Colonial Peasantry of the Lower Limpopo Valley," *JSAS* 17, 2 (June 1991), 239–70.

49. Although referring to a later era, Stephanie Urdang's quote from a Mozambican informant applies as well to the earlier era: "It is not for nothing that fathers wish their daughters to marry South African miners. It is because of Hunger." "Rural Transformation and Peasant Women in Mozambique." *International Labour Office Working Paper* (Geneva, 1986).

50. Jeeves, *Migrant Labour*, and First et al., *Black Gold* on Wenela recruitment.

51. Statistics compiled from SNI Docs. 3–120, and 3–121, AHM; *Relatòrio da Secretaria Geral, 1910*, 16.

52. First et al., *Black Gold*, 32–33; Jeeves, *Migrant Labour*, 188; Alvaro de Castro, *Africa Oriental Portuguesa: Notas e Impressões* (Lisbon, 1918), 43.

53. OT, E. Zavala.
54. OT, I. Jeque, M. Inguane, J. Gulele, S. Tembe.
55. *O Progresso*, 24 October 1907, quoting the 1907 governor's report.
56. Frederick Elton, "Journal of an Exploration of the Limpopo River," *JRGS* 42 (June 1873), 38; O. W. Barrett, "Impressons and Scenes of Mozambique," *The National Geographic Magazine*, 21 (October 1910), 812–13; OT, J. Manguese, E. Zavala.
57. Quote from Junod, *Manuel de Conversation*, 61; Mashaba in Silva, *Um Error de Justiça*, 25.
58. This pattern emerges in the labor requisitions files throughout the century; see, for example, 1915–1926 in SNI 3–196.
59. Distrito de Inhambane. *Relatório do Governador, 1911–1912* (Lourenço Marques, 1912), 159–61.
60. Variously entitled the Secretaria de Negócios Indígenas, Intendência de Negócios Indígenas, and Repartição Central de Negócios Indígenas.
61. "Relatório, Distrito de Lourenço Marques, 27 December 1909," SNI to Secretaria Geral de Lourenço Marques [SGLM], SNI Doc. 3–359, AHM. The SNI periodically sent questionnaires to each administrative unit regarding the overall status of "native affairs." These always included a section on *régulos* and for various reasons the majority of *régulos* were acknowledged to enjoy "little respect." *Respostas aos Quesitos . . . Ferrão, passim*, and "Respostas ao questionário da Inspecção de Servisos Administrativas e das Negócios Indígenas [ISANI] ao Governo Geral . . ." are peppered with phrases like "little prestige" and "weak," SNI Cx 134, AHM.
62. OT, S. Uinge.
63. OT, A. Nhaposse.

CHAPTER 2
Creating a White Man's Town

1. Mendes, *Maputo*, 81–82; António Pacheco, "Lourenço Marques na Última Década do Século XIX," Boletim da Sociedade de Estudos de Moçambique [BSEM], 31 (1962), 20; Castilho, *O Distrito de Lourenço Marques*, 11–12; Alexandre Lobato, *Lourenço Marques— Xilunguine: Biografia da Cidade I–A Parte Antiga* (Lisbon, 1970).
2. The legal definition of native and non-native developed piecemeal from wording in the criminal code of the late nineteenth century. Eventually it included "all people of the Negro race and descendent therefrom," as per New State legislation, Law 36 of 12 November 1927. Subsequent legislation in 1954 (Decreto Lei 36,999 of 20 May 1954) interpreted assimilation as a personalized, non-inheritable status. Pinto de Fonseca, "Relatório da Aplicação do Estatuto dos Indígenas Portugueses, Decreto Lei 36,999 of 20 May 1954," 25 July 1960, FGG, 722, AHM.
3. Alternative spellings, Mahambachleca, Maambatabili, Mafambatchéch. Biographical data from Ilídio Rocha, *Das Terras do Império Vátua as Praças da República Boer* (Lisbon, 1987); Julião Quintinha and Francisco Toscano, *A Derrocado do Império Vátua e Mousinho d'Albuquerque*, 3rd. ed. (Lisbon, 1935), 56, 74; Ferreira Martins, *João Albasini e a Colónia de S. Luis: Subsídio para a História da Província de Moçambique e as Suas Relações com o Transvaal* (Lisbon, 1957).
4. Quote from Rocha, *Das Terras do Império Vátua*, 187.
5. Alternative spellings Gimo, Jim Boy [Mabhay] and Jim Boy Chinunga. See Noronha, *Distrito de Lourenço Marques*, 168; Jan van Butselaar, *Africains, missionnaires et colonialistes: les origines de l'église presbytérienne du Mozambique (mission suisse) 1880–1896* (Leiden, 1984), 50 n66, 93, 102.
6. Quote from *Lourenço Marques Guardian*, 8 July 1907; *O Progresso*, 11 July, 26 August, and 5 September 1907; Letter of António Gabriel Gouveia to unknown, 21 September 1862, Códice 1299, Manuscritos Ultramarinos da Biblioteca Pública Municipal do Porto [BPMP],

Oporto, Portugal. From the inedited census of 1894, Bengalena's household seems to have consisted of nine people, eight women and girls and a three-year-old boy. Carlos Santos Reis, *A População de Lourenço Marques em 1894: Um Censo Inédito* (Lisbon, 1973), facsimile census sheet.

7. The social composition and background of these groups are treated in more detail in Penvenne, "'We are all Portuguese!'" G. Liesegang and A. Lobato both discuss *caseiras*, African common-law or civil law wives of foreigners and the process of registering property claims in freehold. Liesegang, introduction, in Anonymous, *A Guerra dos Reis Vátua do Cabo Natal do Maxacane da Matola . . . de Lourenço Marques* (Maputo,1986), 17ff; Alexander Lobato, "Lourenço Marques, Xilunguine: Pequino Monografia da Cidade," *Boletim Municipal [Lourenço Marques]*, 3 (1968), 12.

8. The Câmara de Comércio de Lourenço Marques [CCLM] was one of the first such associations. Its original membership included Portuguese, Englishmen with strong South African links, and Indian merchants who held British passports. Within a few years, the Indian merchants and small-scale Portuguese and Chinese merchants had formed separate organizations. Constantino de Castro Lopo, *Câmara do Comércio de Lourenço Marques, 1891–1966* (Lourenço Marques, 1966), 63–82; Associação Comercial de Lourenço Marques, *Relatório da Direcção [1891–1904]* (Lourenço Marques, 1892–1905). See also social and business news in the Lourenço Marques Guardian.

9. Castro Lopo, *Câmara do Comércio*, 66ff; Vieira, "Os Electricos de Lourenço Marques," 7, 12–13; Harries, "Labour Migration from Mozambique."

10. OT, quote from R. Tembe (a). Similar statements by M. Mussana (b), J. da Costa (a), and F. de Brito (a).

11. OT, M. Mussana (b), R. Tembe (a), J. da Costa (a), and F. de Brito (a).

12. *O Africano, Almanaque Humorístico e Ilustrado*, 1912, 17. João Tomaz Chembene and his sons, important figures in Lourenço Marques, worked in the offices of Allan, Wack, and Shepard in Beira. SNI Doc. 3-141; SNI Doc. 3-408, Log 28, October 1919, both AHM; *Brado Africano*, 20 May 1933.

13. Castro Lopo, *Câmara do Comércio*, 51–54; *Actas do Concelho do Governo, 1914–1915* (Lourenço Marques, 1915–1916); *O Progresso*, 21 January 1909; Capela, *O Movimento Operário*, 12.

14. Quote from the Portuguese press in Vieira, "Os Electricos, 21."

15. "Delagoa Bay is the dustbin of the Transvaal and South Africa," Crowe to Bertie, 16 May 1900, Foreign Office [FO] 2/365/1900, Public Record Office [PRO], London; U.S. Consular Despatches 150, 31 December 1895, and 173 of 24 October 1896, USNA.

16. Clemente Nunes Silva, *Lourenço Marques: Escandalos da Administração Municipal por um Municipe* (n.p., 1897); *Vanguarda*, 4 December 1903; *O Progresso*, May to September 1904; *O Mignon*, April and May 1905.

17. Angela Guimarães, *Uma Corrente do Colonialismo Português: A Sociedade de Geografia de Lisboa, 1875–1895* (Lisbon, 1984), 226.

18. José Capela, *O Vinho para o Preto: Notas e Textos sôbre a Exportação do Vinho para Africa* (Oporto, 1973), and Capela, *A Burguesia Mercantil do Porto e as Colónias (1834–1900)* (Porto, 1975).

19. Eric Axelson, *Portugal and the Scramble for Africa: 1875–1891* (Johannesburg, 1967), 13–15.

20. António Pacheco, "Lourenço Marques na Última Década," 19–20; António Pacheco, "Lourenço Marques—Difficuldades do Passado—Responsibilidades de Hoje—Problemas do Futuro," *[Collected Papers of the] Congresso da Sociedade de Estudos da Colonia de Moçambique*, III (1947), 13, 18, 20; Margaret Elizabeth Northey, *General Joaquim José Machado: A Selective Bibliography* (Johannesburg, 1970), vi.

21. Alfredo Pereira de Lima, *O Palácio Municipal de Lourenço Marques* (Lourenco Marques, 1967), 102; Pereira da Lima, "Para um Estudo da Evolução Urbana de Lourenço Marques," *Boletim Municipal*, 7 (December 1970), 7–16; Lobato, *Lourenco Marques, Xilunguine*; Mendes, *Maputo*.

22. Lyons McLeod, *Travels in Eastern Africa with the Narrative of a Residence in Mozambique* (London, 1860), I, 155.
23. St. Vincent Erskine, "Journey to Umzila's," 48–49.
24. Wallis Mackay, *The Prisoner of Chiloane: or, with the Portuguese in South East Africa* (London, 1890), 19.
25. *Ibid.*, 21–24.
26. Sra. Manuel Fernandes da Piedade's account published in Alfredo Pereira da Lima, *História dos Caminhos de Ferro de Mocambique [História dos CFLM]* (Lourenço Marques, 1971) I, 22–23; Monteiro, *Delagoa Bay*, 262ff; Captain Manuel Gomes da Costa, *Gaza, 1897–1898* (Lisbon, 1899), 129–31, 146–48.
27. George Agnew Chamberlain, *African Hunting Among the Tongas* (London, 1923), 10.
28. *Ibid.*,10–11. See also *Transvaal Leader*, 23 May 1910.
29. Alys Lowth, ed., *Doreen Coasting* (London, 1912), 216–17.
30. *Ibid.*, 218.
31. Warhurst, *Anglo-Portuguese Relations*, 129–35, 137, 150–51; Hollis to Department of State [DS], "Annual Report," 20 August 1896 and Despatch [Desp.] 252, 7 July 1902 with enclosed, USNA.
32. The press and minutes of meetings of the CMLM and groups follow most of these struggles. See, for example, Relatórios da Associação Commercial de Lourenço Marques, 1891–1893.
33. Castilho, *Distrito de Lourenço Marques*, 9.
34. *Ibid.*, 29.
35. *Delagoa Directory*, 1914, 58–59; Cawthra Woodhead, "Natal á Moçambique," in Borges de Castro, ed., *Africa Oriental: Portugal em Lourenço Marques* (Oporto, 1895), 36; Joquim Mouzinha de Albuquerque, *Moçambique, 1896–1898* (Lisbon, 1913), 212, Documents 4, 3, 8, 11, and 12; N. L. C. Meneses Abrantes *et al.*, *Concessão de Terrenos, Moçambique: Catálogo* (Lisbon, 1989); Noronha, *Distrito de Lourenço Marques*, 92.
36. The story of the Lourenço Marques railway has been detailed by Warhurst, Axelson, Hammond, and Pereira de Lima. The most recent study is Katzenellenbogen, South Africa and Southern Mozambique.
37. Pereira da Lima, *História dos CFLM*, I, 205. Corroborated by T. V. Bulpin, *Lost Trails of the Transvaal*, 2nd ed. (Cape Town, 1969), 259–65.
38. Pereira da Lima, *História dos CFLM*, I, 205.
39. *Ibid.*, I, 134–95; Hammond, *Portugal and Africa*, 236; Warhurst, *Anglo-Portuguese Relations*, 112; Manuel Barnabe Lopes, "Panorama Económica e Política dos Caminos de Ferro de Moçambique," *Revista do Gabinete de Estudos Ultramarinos*, I (1951), 8.
40. Data for this paragraph from *Relatório da Direcção do Porto e Caminho de Ferro de Lourenço Marques [RPCFLM]* (Lourenço Marques) for the years 1905 to 1912, and Ministério das Colónias, Caminhos de Ferro e Portos, *Estatística dos Caminhos de Ferro e das Colónias Portuguêsas de 1888 á 1910* (Lisbon, 1912); Freire de Andrade, *Relatórios sôbre Moçambique*, II, 143–45, 154–55.
41. Moçambique,"Relatório de Serviço de Saude de Lourenço Marques ao Anno de 1886," *Archivos Médicos Colónães*, I, 4 (1890), 45–86; "Registo de Mappa Estatística," scattered data for 1890s and 1901, Doc. 15/16, ACLM.
42. Monteiro, *Delagoa Bay*, 3.
43. Castilho, *O Distrito de Lourenço Marques (l880)*; 9–10; Mendes, *Maputo*, 32–84; *Delagoa Directory*, 1906, 1925; *O Futuro*, 16 November 1907; *Boletim do Porto, Caminhos de Ferro e Transportes de Moçambique*, Supplement (July 1970), 78.
44. Monteiro, *Delagoa Bay*, 260–61.
45. *Delagoa Directory* follows the development of the tourist industry throughout this period.
46. *Delagoa Directory*, 1921, 43.
47. *O Progresso*, 21 July 1904; *O Africano*, 25 December 1908; Noronha, *Distrito de Lourenço*

Marques, 58–59; Abrantes *et al.*, *Concessão de Terrenos*, revealed fewer than twenty concessions to people with African clan names or people identified as "indígenas." The only other concessions to Africans were grants to about a dozen men designated "régulos" or chiefs.

48. *RPCFLM*, 1906, 6.
49. Correspondence on *shibalo* landfill throughout SNI 3–196, SNI File 3–196, especially SNI to Empreiteiro do Aterro, 9 and 23 October 1918, AHM; "Projecto de Regulamento para a Exploração dos Cais de Lourenço Marques," and "Relatório das Obras do Porto de Lourenço Marques," 29 August 1910, both in DCFU, Moçambique, Caixa [Cx] 237, AHU.
50. Pereira de Lima, *História dos CFLM*, I, 22–23, 205–206; Jessett, *The Key to South Africa*, 68; Pacheco, "Lourenço Marques—Dificuldades," 161; Pacheco, "Lourenço Marques na Última Década," 51–52; Lobato, *Lourenço Marques*, I, 138–39.
51. Census of commercial and industrial establishments in Lourenço Marques in "Registo de Mappa Estatística," Doc. 15/16, ACLM.
52. Sugar-based brews were developed earlier and more extensively in Inhambane. The classic and most detailed references are in Enes, *Moçambique*, 3d ed., and Freire de Andrade, *Relatórios*.
53. Capela, *O Vinho para o Preto*.
54. OT, R. Tembe (b), J. da Costa (b), G. Guevende. Sá Nogueira's Ronga dictionary confirms the term means a Portuguese person, but speculates it may derive from the frequent use of *mas* (but) in Portuguese conversation. Rodrigo de Sá Nogueira, *Dicionário Ronga-Português* . . . (Lisbon, 1960), 303.
55. Quoted in P. Harries, "Labour Migration from the Delagoa Bay Hinterland," 9. See also Rose Monteiro, *Delagoa Bay: Its Natives and Natural History* (London, 1891), 75–77; Jessett, *Key to South Africa*, 66.
56. Enes, *Moçambique*, 45.
57. Van Onselen, *Studies*, I, Ch. 2.
58. van Onselen, quoting E. Perry, in *Studies*, I, 95.
59. *O Futuro*, 15 December 1906, 6 June, 9 July, 10 October 1907; *Actas do Conselho do Governo*, 30 September 1914, 26 January 1916, 20 January 1917, 28 July 1927; SNI Cx 61, 62, 106; SNI Docs. 3-344, 3-351, AHM.
60. Gregory Pirio, "Commerce, Industry, and Empire: The Making of Modern Portuguese Colonialism in Angola and Mozambique, 1890–1914" (Ph.D. thesis, University of California at Los Angeles, 1982), 178ff; *O Futuro*, 8 June 1907, 31 January 1908; *O Progresso*, 27 October 1904; Katzenellbogen, *South Africa and Southern Mozambique*, 59–60, 74–75, 91–92, 108.
61. "Registo de Mappa Estatística," Doc. 15/16, ACLM.
62. Van Onselen, *Studies*, I, Ch. 2, esp. 94–96.
63. Desp. 3310, 5 September 1908, FO 363, PRO.
64. The SNI, the Câmara de Comércio, and the Câmara Municipal all periodically sent delegations to Durban or Johannesburg to study their solutions to African worker housing and drinking. The politics of housing in Lourenço Marques is well covered in "Actas das Sessões de Bairros Indígenas" and "Informação," 9; "Projecto Diploma Legislativo Respeitante as 'Vilas Indígenas,'" A. A. Montanha, Chefe, RCNI, 3 April 1951, SNI Cx 258, AHM.
65. Computed from "Registo de Mappa Estatística," Doc. 15/16, ACLM.
66. See especially between 1907 and 1911, SNI Cx 106 and 161, SNI Doc. 3-361, AHM.
67. The quote is from *Westminster Gazette* [1910?], enclosed in "Liquor Traffic at Lourenço Marques," File 41,662, FO 367-188, PRO; Jeanne Penvenne, "Labor Struggles at the Port of Lourenço Marques, 1900–1933," Review, 8, 2 (1984), 252–61.
68. *O Africano*, 25 December 1908.
69. Junod, *Manuel de Conversation*, 33.

CHAPTER 3
"Work for the White People, You Will be Able to Get Money"

1. Junod, *Manuel de Conversation*, 33.
2. Pereira da Lima, *História dos Caminhos de Ferro*, I, 92–93; *Estatística dos Caminhos de Ferro . . . 1888 á 1910; Delagoa Directory* 1899 to 1910 provides annual descriptions of port construction and statistics on port and rail handling and revenue.
3. Work informants referred to as *cais, quintais,* and *obras.* "Registo de Certificados dos Indígenas," 1891, registered 424 people. Some 38 percent of those with stated occupations were domestics (87) and 62 percent worked at the port. Most had no listed occupation (192), ACLM Doc. 3/A/4. A municipal survey of urban labor conducted door to door in 1947 revealed that 80 percent of the labor force outside the port and conscript labor sectors were employed in domestic service, hotels, boarding houses, and restaurants. ACLM Doc. 234/147, AHM.
4. Junod, *Life of a South African Tribe*, II, 130.
5. H. A. Junod, *Les Chantes et les contes des BaRonga de la Baie de Delagoa* (Lausanne, 1897), 49.
6. Junod, *Manuel de Conversation*, 15–17.
7. The following all based on OT, Mussana (a) and (b). These interviews were conducted in Shangaan and Portuguese with the help of Gaspar S. Guevende. Because of his advanced age, Mussongueia used many words and phrases that are no longer commonly used. Transcripts of the taped portions of the interviews were further clarified with the assistance of Paulo Zombole.
8. OT, C. Capitine, S. Chichango, A. Cumbe, M. Inguane, and P. Faleca, 7 July 1977.
9. *Distrito de Lourenço Marques*, 17 August 1889, claimed that at least 750 *shibalo* had escaped upon arrival in Lourenço Marques that year to make their way to the Transvaal.
10. OT, M. Mussana, (a), (b). His descriptions of road and landfill *shibalo* corroborated by OT, A. Cumbe, and *O Africano*, 1 March and 23 December 1909.
11. *O Africano*, 1 March 1909.
12. Song, F. Muconto.
13. OT, V. Mainga, A. Cumbe, J. Sumbane, P. Faleca, and F. Nhauche.
14. "Casos de Peste em Lourenço Marques, 10 Dezembro 1907," *Relatórios e Investigações Anexxo ao Boletim Official* (Lourenço Marques, 1908), 229.
15. *Ibid.*
16. OT, M. Mussana (b).
17. Tape A contains at least seven versions of this song, the most complete by J. Machanga. Two-thirds of the municipal labor informants offered to sing it.
18. OT, M. Mussana.
19. CMLM, *Anais, 1950* (Lourenço Marques, 1952),117–23; *Anais, 1953–54*, 275–306.
20. Struggles to acquire and hold sanitation labor can be followed through the municipal correspondence logs, CMLM logs "Correspondência Entrada/Expedida," 1899–1920, File 01.03/2/ also documents the steady flow of African prison labor to work on the municipal sewerage system. All in library, Câmara Municipal de Maputo [CMM].
21. Governador Geral de Lourenço Marques [GGLM] to Intendência de Emigração [IE], 4 September 1906, SNI Cx 68, AHM.
22. *O Commércio de Lourenço Marques*, 8 October 1892, 4 February 1893; *O Futuro*, 30 August 1895; *Jornal de Commércio*, 12 November 1904; *O Progresso*, 27 October 1904, 3 November 1904.
23. *O Futuro*, 30 August 1895.
24. *O Futuro*, 19 November 1908.
25. The following paragraphs are based on incomplete documentation on sanitation contracts for 1905–1927 contained in SNI Cx 104, SNI Files 3–59, 3–60, 3–67, 3–120, 3–121, 3–142, 3–196, 3–357, 3–359, 3–361, 3–406, 3–407, 3–464, all AHM; OT, C. Capitine; A. Cuambe; C. Tambajam; E. Zavala; F. Zavala; V. Mainga.
26. Vail and White discuss the Chopi reputation in *Power and the Praise Poem*, Ch. 4.

26. This is the author's theory, and it is admittedly speculative. It was not stated by any informant, but one informant mentioned Chopi rural investments. The more extensive involvement of Chopi males in agriculture and tree crops emerges broadly from the colonial administration and ethnographic literature. OT, V. Mainga.

27. Quelimane to SNI 5 July 1907, 13 September 1907, SNI Doc. 3–357. See also Rita Ferreira, "Os Africanos de Lourenço Marques," 329.

28. SNI to Sub-Intendência de Negócios Indígenas, Inhambane, 96/24, 23 January 1923, SNI Cx 28, AHM.

29. CMLM logbooks and minutes of the CMLM board meetings document the problem extensively; but see, for example, Log 1248 of 5 November 1912, CMLM.

30. See Chapter 9.

31. Many informants whose urban experience dated from the later period mentioned that, although sanitation was a disagreeable chore, the Chopi had set it up so that it was not a taxing job. Others also mentioned the part-time, odd-job strategies they developed on the side. Vicente Pande Mainga mentioned the "tip" system and suggested the network between homeowner and odd jobs in gardening. OT, V. Mainga, 12 November 1912, AHM.

32. Eduardo Medeiros, "A Evolução Demográfica da Cidade de Lourenço Marques (1895–1975), Estudo Bibliográfico," Revista Internacional de Estudos Africanos 3 (1985), 231–39; Moçambique, Recenseamento da População e das Habitações da Cidade de Lourenço Marques e seus Subúrbios, Referidos á 1 de Dezembro de 1912 (Lourenço Marques, 1913); Repartição Técnica de Estatística [RTE], Anuário Estatístico, 1928; RTE, Censo da População em 1940 (Lourenço Marques, 1944). 68 n13.

33. ACLM Doc. 15/16 contains statistics for 1899 and 1904, AHM; Recenseamento . . . 1912.

34. Anuário Estatística, 1932 (Lourenço Marques, 1933), 317.

35. O Progresso, 14 April 1904, 16 February 1905; Jornal de Commércio, 11 January 1905; Relatório da Secretaria Gêral (1910), 192.

36. For the period under consideration, the great majority of general household workers and laundry workers were males. Rather than consistently include the masculine and feminine version of each job category, I have selected the masculine form.

37. OT, J. Machanga.

38. ACLM Doc. 15/16, AHM; Monteiro, Delogoa Bay, 22..

39. This paragraph based on Monteiro, Delagoa Bay, 22; O Futuro, 5 November 1898; O Progresso, 26 November 1903; USACLM, 362, 1 June 1904; Relatório, Secretaria Geral de Moçambique (1910); O Intransigente, 1 November 1911; Manhica to SNI, 2 September 1912, SNI 3–67, SNI 9 September 1922, SNI 3–407, AHM; AHM; OT, Z. Muianga, V. Nhabanga, F. Nandje, J. Mahumane, M. Mafuane, and F. Mondlane, 4 July 1977; Brado Africano, 14 January 1922.

40. O Futuro, 5 November 1898; O Progresso, 26 November 1903; USACLM, 362, 1 June 1904; O Intransigente, 1 November 1911.

41. Brado Africano, 28 December 1925; OT, A. Guambe, J. Machanga, V. Macuacua, M. Mafuane, J. Mahumane, J. Manguese, S. Manhiça, and V. Nhabanga.

42. Delagoa Directory, 1899; O Progresso, 26 November 1903, 14 April 1904; Relatório da Secretaria Geral (1910), 192; O Intransigente, 1 November 1911; Actas do Conselho do Governo, 9 March 1915; A Cidade, 22 April 1916.

43. A Cidade, 22 April 1916.

44. OT, V. Nhabanga.

45. Monteiro, Delagoa Bay, 16, 17, 22–23, 32.

46. Ibid., 16.

47. Ibid., 23.

48. Ibid., 17.

49. Ibid., 22.

50. Ibid., 23.

52. *Ibid.*, 32.
53. The municipal press contains a good deal of commentary on domestic service: *O Futuro*, 19 January 1895, 5 November 1898; *O Progresso*, 26 November 1903, 14 April 1904; *Jornal de Commércio*, 1 January 1905; *Relatório da Secretaria Géral (1910)*, 192; *Actas do Conselho do Governo*, 9 March 1915, and *Delagoa Directory* feature articles in 1899 and 1906.See also ACLM Doc. 35/37, Employer—Employee complaints from May 1909 to December 1912, AHM.
54. Evidence of sexual tensions between domestics and family members is clear for the 1940s through the 1960s, but thinner and more veiled for the early twentieth century. See Junod, *Manuel de Conversation*, 23–29; *O Futuro*, 5 November 1898; Hospital Miguel Bombarda to SNI 17 October 1916, AHM.
55. Junod, *Manuel de Conversation*, compiled from pp. 21–29.
56. *O Intransigente*, 1 November 1911, enclosed in Cx 18, Moçambique, Segunda Repartição, AHU.
57. *Brado Africano*, 22 January and 30 September 1922, 28 December 1925. See also Van Onselen, *Studies, II, Ch.1.*
58. OT, A. Guambe, J. Machanga, V. Macuacua, M. Mafuane, J. Mahumane, J. Manguese, S. Manhiça, and V. Nhabanga.
59. OT, J. Machanga.
60. OT, J. Nhabanga.
61. OT, M. Tembe and J. Nhabanga.
62. OT, M. Tembe.

CHAPTER 4
The Components and Costs of Inequality

1. *Distrito de Lourenço Marques*, 17 August 1889.
2. Freire de Andrade, *Relatórios sôbre Moçambique*, II, 15.
3. Freire de Andrade cited the case of 200 workers in one such situation. He demonstrated that the workers who quit, unpaid after 120 days were better off than their colleagues who worked an additional 60 days to complete a fraudlently adjusted contract, only to be refused payment at the end. *Ibid.* 15.
4. *Journal das Colónias*, 23 December 1882.
5. *O Progresso*, 14 April 1904, SNI to Chefe de Gabinete, 11 September 1908, SNI Doc. 3–359, AHM; *O Africano*, 25 December 1908; Cruz, *Em Terras de Gaza*, 46, 147, 221.
6. Smith-Delacour to Secretary of State for Africa [SOSFA], 4 April 1892, FO 84, 2224, PRO.
7. Secretaria do Governador de Lourenço Marques [SGLM] to Secretaria Civil do Governo do Distrito, "Confidencial," 22 December 1902, Cx 16, Moçambique, AHU.
8. *Ibid.*
9. Silva Cunha, *O Trabalho Indígena*, 372–98; "Relatório, 21 May 1909, ACLM," SNI Cx 104, AHM; *Journal de Commércio*, 1 March 1905; *Delagoa Directory*, 1907.
10. The original language is from "Orientacão de Regulamento de 1878," Art. 1, but is repeated with little change until the abolition of the *indigenato*, Silva Cunha, *O Trabalho Indígena*, 151, 153, 200, 203, 206–208.
11. Penvenne, "We are all Portuguese!" *passim.*
12. SNI Files 3–141 and 3–408, AHM.
13. Penvenne, "Principles and Passion: Capturing the Legacy of João dos Santos Albasini," Discussion Papers in the African Humanities, 12 (Boston, 1991); Penvenne, "We are All Portuguese!" 262–63, 274–81.
14. Zamparoni, "A Imprensa Negra;" Soares and Zamparoni, "Antologia de Textos."
15. *O Africano*, 27 January 1917.
16. *Brado Africano*, 4 January 1919; Penvenne, "Principles and Passion," Appendix B.

17. OT, M. Tembe, R. Tembe (a), A. Nuvunga, E. Matusse, G. Mabunda, J. da Costa (a), and B. Chibindji.
18. Exchange rates compiled through newspaper quotations in *Lourenço Marques Guardian*, *O Progresso*, *O Africano*, and *O Brado Africano*. After 1928 exchange values were published in *Anuário Estatístico [AE]*.
19. *O Africano*, 19 June 1920; *A Cidade*, 29 August 1919.
20. *O Incondicional*, 13 and 17 April 1917; *Diário de Notícias*, 2 November 1917.
21. *A Cidade*, 29 August 1919; *O Africano*, 19 June 1920.
22. *Brado Africano*, 3 September 1921.
23. Raul Bernardo Honwana, *Memórias* (Rio Tinto, 1989), 82.
24. OT, M. Tembe.
25. *Brado Africano*, 19 April 1919; 22 August through September 1922.
26. Assimilation records for the first wave of applications in 1917 and 1919 are contained in SNI Docs. 3–141 and 3–408. Later records are in ACLM Doc. 1517/1, all AHM.
27. Penvenne, "'We are All Portuguese!'" 279–81.
28. Honwana, *Memórias*, 72–75; OT, R. Tembe (b) and J. da Costa (b).
29. "Petition," Comissão Organizadora do Sindicato Nacional dos Motoristas Africanos de Moçambique to Governador Geral de Moçambique, 26 January 1948, SNI Cx 2, AHM. The implications of such linkage is clearly revealed in this document.
30. *O Africano*, 7 April 1909. Even by the close of the *indigenato*, there were few Africans in middle-level civil service jobs and virtually none in upper levels. See especially OT, M. Tembe, R. Tembe (a, b), A. Nuvunga, E. Matusse, G. Mabunda, B. Chibindji, J. da Costa (b, c), and G. de Brito (a, c).
31. *Relatório da Secretaria Geral de Moçambique, 1910* (Lourenço Marques, 1911), 191; Álvaro de Castro, *Africa Oriental Portuguêsa: Notas e Impressões* (Lisbon, ca. 1916), 37–98; *O Heraldo*, 5 February 1910; "Petition from Merchants and Forwarding Agents" to ACLM, enclosed in ACLM to Gov. Distrito de Lourenço Marques, 6 September 1911, and ACLM to Intendéncia de Negócios Indígenas e Emigração, 20 December 1911, both in SNI Cx 249, AHM.
32. *O Africano*, 22 August 1912; "Relatório," 21 May 1910, ACLM; in SNI Cx 104, AHM.
33. The struggle for municipal services is extensively documented in the African press: for example, *O Africano*, 24 December 1908, 24 April 1909, 5 June 1909, 8 December 1911, 13 January 1912, 21 June 1912, 12 September 1912, 14 June 1913, 7 November 1914, 15 April 1916, 5 January 1916, 11 March 1916, 16 March 1916, and 24 January 1917.
34. *O Africano*, 22 August 1912.
35. *O Africano*, 7 November 1912.
36. Portoria Provincial, 1098, September 1913. "Relatório do Serviço de Saude de Lourenço Marques . . . 1886," 49–0; "Casos de Peste em Lourenço Marques," 229; SNI to CFLM, 27 November 1920, SNI Doc. 3–201, AHM.
37. *O Africano* regularly reported the amount of money in the RSTI fund; see, for example, 16 December 1914 and 26 February 1916.
38. *O Africano*, 16 December 1914, 5 May 1915, 26 February 1916, 24 May 1916.
39. "Relatório, Comissariado do Polícia Civil de Lourenço Marques, in *Relatórios de Distrito de Lourenço Marques, 1915–1916* (Lourenço Marques, 1918), 16–20. Albasini's official role at the time was as head (*encarregado*) of "native services" at the railway complex.
40. The censuses of 1912 and 1927 revealed African urban populations of 5,695 and 28,568, respectively. Ten thousand is author estimate. Moçambique, *Recenseamento da População . . .1912*, and *Anuário Estatística 1926–1928* (Lourenço Marques, 1929).
41. *O Africano*, 5 January, 4 May, 5 June, 17 July, 31 August, 27 November 1918, and 25 January, 19 April, and 2 May 1919; *Brado Africano*, 26 April and 27 September 1919.
42. *O Africano*, 17 July 1918, 25 October 1919.
43. *O Africano*, 25 January 1919.
44. *O Africano*, 20 June 1917.

Notes   175

45. Census and "Movimento de Mão d' Obra" reports in SNI Cx 65, AHM.
46. "Relatório" SNI, 11 April 1930, SNI Cx 105, AHM. The contrast between the 1909 and 1930 reports strongly supports this point.
47. "Lavrarem as Actas das Reuniões da Comissão de Construção de Pousadas ou Bairros Indígenas" [hereafter "Actas das Reuniões"], SNI Doc. 3–410, 1923–1941, AHM.
48. Penvenne, "We are all Portuguese," 278—81.
49. "Para o Inglês Ver!" was a familiar phrase in the contemporary Portuguese and African press in Lourenço Marques. Brado Africano, 12 January 1929.
50. E. A. Ross, Report on the Employment of Native Labor in Portuguese Africa (New York, 1925), 58.
51. The official Portuguese rebuttal to Ross is in "Algumas Observações ao Relatório do Professor Ross . . . ," Boletim da Agência Geral das Colónias [BAGC] Ano 1, 6 (December 1925), 179–90; Ano 2, 7 (January 1926), 149–62; Ano 2, 8 (February 1926), 152–64.
52. Brado Africano, 14 October 1922.
53. The following paragraph is based on Ross, Report on Employment, Part II "Portuguese East Africa," 40–60.
54. Ross, Report on Employment, 40–60, "sheer terrorism" quote 58; O Africano, 9 July, 23 September, and 28 October 1911; 15 June, 12 July, and 7 November 1912; 13 February, 3 August 1913; 18 February, 18 March 1914; 25 March 1915; 23 February 1916; 24 January 1917; 31 August 1918; 4 June 1919; Brado Africano, 26 April and 2, 15, 22 November 1919; 10 December 1920; 14 May and 18 June 1921; 14 October 1922; 30 April 1923.
55. Ross, Report on Employment, esp. 42.
56. As far back as the 1860s, D. F. das Neves took up hunting and trading in the interior to escape the corrupt government in Lourenço Marques, Itinerário, 4–10. See also Noronha, Distrito de Lourenço Marques, 108; Pacheco, "Lourenço Marques na Ultima Década," 10; Enes, Moçambique.
57. O Incondicional, 24 March 1911.
58. Ross, Report on Employment, 50.
59. J. A. Lopes Galvão, "O Regime de Mão de Obra Indígena em Moçambique," BAGC 3 (September 1925), 116–28.
60. Eduardo d'Almeida Saldanha, published Jornal de Comércio in Lourenço Marques. Collections of his editorials in that paper were republished as Questões Nacionais: O Sul do Save (Lisbon, 1928) and O Problema de Moçambique: Artigos Publicados pelo Journal de Commércio e das Colónias de Setembro á Novembro 1923 (Lisbon, 1923).
61. SNI 6 January 1917, 8 August 1917, SNI 3–323; SNI to CFLM, 27 November 1920, SNI 3–210; SNI to DPW, 3 December 1921, SNI 3–326; SNI to CFLM, 12 January 1921, SNI 3–196; no. 1204, n.d. [May 1922] SNI 3–407, and files between SNI and Caminho de Ferro de Gaza, SNI 3–56, all AHM.
62. SNI to Governador Geral, 7 January 1930, "Propostas e Informação," SNI correspondence of December 1915 in SNI Cx 249, AHM.
63. SNI correspondence, 17 December 1915, SNI Cx 249, AHM.
64. SNI to Magude administrador, 14 August 1924, SNI 3–364, AHM.
65. SNI to Governador Geral, 7 January 1930, "Propostas e Informação," SNI Cx 249, AHM.
66. SNI to Governador Geral, 7 January 1930, "Propostas e Informação," SNI Cx 249, AHM; Vail and White, Capitalism and Colonialism, 235, on death of João Belo.
67. SNI to Governador Geral, 7 January 1930, "Propostas e Informação," SNI Cx 249, AHM.
68. Compare the rhetoric in Questões Nacionais and O Problem de Moçambique with Francisco Gavicho de Lacerda, "O Trabalho Indígena em Moçambique," BAGC, 5 (April 1926), 9–13.
69. "Relatório do Director dos Serviços e Negócios Indígenas, 1928" [Relatório, DSNI, 1928], SNI Cx 1311, AHM.
70. Relatório DSNI, 1928, SNI Cx 1311, AHM.
71. Total shibalo 1928 from Distrito de Lourenço Marques [DLM], 20,429; total population men, women, children DLM, 442, 261; total men from DLM working in South Africa, 41, 421;

total healthy males, 85,504. After the number of emigrants is subtracted (44,083), the number of *shibalo* conscripts expressed as a percentage of the number of remaining healthy males is just over 46 percent. Relatório DSNI, 1928, SNI Cx 1311, AHM.

72. Confidential circular 120/C, 10 August 1925, in Repartição Central da Colónia, 25 August 1925, SNI 3–464, and Relatório DSNI, 1928, SNI Cx 1311, AHM.
73. "Código do Trabalho dos Indígenas nas Colónias Portuguesas de Africa," published in *Boletim Oficial de Moçambique*, 1a Series, No. 2, 16 January 1929, Suplemento; Silva Cunha, *O Trabalho Indígena*, 203–206.
74. United States, American Consul at Lourenço Marques [USACLM], Despatch [Desp.] 146, 7 June 1927.
75. USACLM, 64, 1 January 1929; "Portuguese Colonies," *Annuaire de Documentation Coloniale Comparée*, I (1928), 469–775.
76. *Brado Africano*, 12 January 1929.

CHAPTER 5
Port Complex Struggles through to the End of an Era

1. From worksong "Loku vaku lanja," OT, F. Zavala. Annex II.
2. OT, R. Tembe (a); *Brado Africano*, 10 December 1932, 28 October 1933; 20 December 1920, SNI 3–201, Delagoa Bay Agency [DBA] employing women and children in woodlots; Jessett, *The Key to South Africa*, 81.
3. Direcção dos Portos e Caminhos de Ferro de Moçambique, *Relatório dos Portos e Caminhos de Ferro de Lourenço Marques* [later called, *Relatório dos Portos e Caminhos de Ferro de Moçambique*; both, RPCFLM], 1907.
4. Charts of port and railway personnel in the reports of 1907 (Mappa 2), and RPCFLM (1934–1935), 546–547 illustrate this point.
5. The process can be followed annually in RPCFLM, but is summarized in *Boletim dos Portos, Caminhos de Ferro e Transportes de Moçambique*, Supplemento, July 1970.
6. *Jornal de Comércio*, 1 March 1905; *Delagoa Directory*, 1907.
7. OT, R.Tembe (c), J. da Costa (c), and F. de Brito (b); RPCFLM (1929–1930), 17, 51.
8. OT, F. de Brito (a and b), R. Tembe (b and c), J. da Costa (c), and B. Chibindji.
9. MacDonell to SOSFA, 17 November 1916, "Confidential" 152, File 263258, FO 368, 1591; File 136, F10108, FO 368, 1799; File W7593;/5933/36, FO 371 15032, all PRO; *O Africano*, 25 June 1915, 24 February 1917, 20 June 1917, 8 June 1918; *O Brado Africano*, 4 October 1919; Saldanha, *Questões Nacionais*, I, 130.
10. OT, J. da Costa (b and c), R. Tembe (b and c); RPCFLM (1929–1930), 17, 51.
11. For example, John Iliffe, "The Creation of Group Consciousness among the Dockworkers of Dar es Salaam, 1929–1950," in R. Sandbrook and R. Cohen, eds., The *Development of an African Working Class* (Toronto, 1975), 49–72.
12. Direcção de Obras Públicas,"Comunicação Portos e Caminhos de Ferro de Lourenço Marques [PCFLM]," 11 January 1909, Cx 23, DCFU, AHU.
13. SNI to Comissariado de Polícia Civil de Lourenço Marques [CPCLM], "Confidencial," 42, 23 November 1909, SNI Log 3–358, also Entry 18 November 1909, SNI Log 3–357, AHM.
14. *O Emancipador*, 7 January 1929; *Brado Africano*, 19 January 1929.
15. RPCFLM (1929–30), 17.
16. *Ibid.*, 17; RPCFLM (1930–1931), 15; (1931–1932), 29; (1934–1935), 485.
17. Grêmio Africano to SNI, 29 April 1929, SNI Cx 69, AHM.
18. OT, R. Tembe (b and c), J. da Costa (b and c).
19. Quote from *O Emancipador*, 7 January 1929. See also Grêmio Africano to SNI, 29 April 1929, SNI Cx 69, AHM.
20. Pereira de Lima, *História dos CFLM*; Capela, *O Movimento Operário*.

21. Capela specifically considers racial divisions and labor solidarity in *O Movimento Operário*, Introduction.
22. *O Africano* , 5 January 1918.
23. The outstanding exception was the Associação de Artes Gráficas [AAG], see below.
24. *Brado Africano*, 29 January 1927.
25. What little is known about the initiative comes from *O Simples*, 24 June, 13 July, and 25 November 1911.
26. The following paragraph on the AAG based on José Capela, *O Movimento Operário*, 123–28; Raul Neves Dias, *A Imprensa Periódica em Moçambique, 1854-1954* . . . (Lourenço Marques, 1956); Neves Dias, *Quatro Centenários em Moçambique* . . . (Lourenço Marques, 1954).
27. Neves Dias, *A Imprensa Periódica, and Anuário Estatístico, 1954*.
28. *Os Simples*, 25 November 1911.
29. Consensus, but see especially OT, J. Cossa (a and b).
30. OT, R. Tembe (a, b, and c), J. da Costa (a, b, and c), F. de Brito (b).
31. RPCFLM (1929–30), 5, 154, 269 and (1931–1932), 274–75; *O Africano* , 18 March 1916; *O Brado Africano* 7 May 1918, 10 January, 12 June, and 23 July 1920.
32. *O Africano* , 4 May 1918; *Brado Africano*, 24 January, 10 May, and 22 November 1919, 24 January, 5 June, 4 September, and 25 November 1920, and 28 February 1921; *Lourenço Marques Guardian*, 17 September 1925; DBA to SNI 2 March 1921, SNI 3–408, AHM.
33. For Lingham Timber strike, 1905, and Delagoa Bay Agency strike, 1906, see *O Mignon*, 1 May 1905, 19 May 1905; *Diário de Notícias*, 27 March 1906.
34. *O Incondicional*, 13 May 1919.
35. RPCFLM (1929–1930), 5, 154, 269.
36. The correct title of the group was the Associação do Pessoal do Porto e dos Caminhos de Ferro de Lourenço Marques, but it was popularly known as União Ferroviario. The latter is preferred here because that name was regularly used in the workers' press and strike banners. Mathias Tullner, "Apontamento sobre a Greve de 1917 no Porto e Caminho de Ferro de Lourenço Marques," *Arquivo*, 9 (April 1991), 45–58; Pereira de Lima, *História dos CFLM*, I, 231.
37. *O Africano* throughout June 1917, and Pereira de Lima, *História dos CFLM*, I, 243.
38. The following paragraphs on the 1917 strike are based on *O Africano* coverage of 6, 7, 20, 23, and 30 June 1917, and Pereira de Lima, *História dos CFLM* , I, 243. See also Tullner, "Apontamento sobre a Greve de 1917."
39. Tullner, "Apontamento sobre a Greve de 1917," 53.
40. Details on the 1919 strike are from *O Africano*, 7 and 10 May 1919; *Lourenço Marques Guardian*, 4 and 10 May 1919; *O Indoncicional*, 6, 13 May 1919; *Brado Africano*, 10 May 1919.
41. The following paragraphs are based on press coverage of the strike, *O Indoncicional*, 13 May 1919; *O Africano*, 10 May 1919; *Lourenço Marques Guardian*, 8 May 1919.
42. *O Indoncicional*, 13 May 1919; *O Africano*, 10 May 1919; *Lourenço Marques Guardian*, 8 May 1919.
43. "Circular 199," 20 January 1920, SNI 3–196, AHM.
44. *Brado Africano*, 6 November 1920.
45. Quote from *Lourenço Marques Guardian*, 8 May 1919.
46. *Brado Africano*, 22 November 1919.
47. CCLM to SNI, 14 July 1920, "Auto de Averiguações," 27 July 1920; Manuel de Brito to SNI, 28 July 1920, all SNI Cx 51, AHM.
48. CMLM to SNI with "Autos de Investigação e Averiguações," 12, 14 and 27 July 1920 and throughout SNI Cx 51, AHM.
49. Circular, SNI to Distritos de Lourenço Marques, 18 May 1920, SNI 3–196, AHM.
50. Chibuto to SNI 11 September 1924, SNI 3–464, with corroboration from Sabié to SNI, 5 July 1924, SNI 3–464, AHM.
51. OT, F. de Brito (a and b).

52. Pereira de Lima, *História dos CFLM* , I, 231–234; USACLM, 6 April 1926, Record Group 84, USNA.
53. This strike received heavy press and diplomatic coverage. *O Emancipador*, the union's paper, published under a series of titles to evade proscription. Eduardo Saldanha's *Correio de Lourenço Marques* provided regular, hostile coverage, and both the *Brado Africano* and the U.S. consular despatches gave it fairly unbiased coverage. USACLM, 10 December 1925 and 6 April 1926, Record Group 84, USNA.
54. Minutes of the government council, printed in *Lourenço Marques Guardian*, 1 September 1927.
55. *Lourenço Marques Guardian*, 3 May, 1 September, 13 December, and 15 December 1928, and 1 January, 11 July 1929.
56. *O Africano*, 19 July 1911.
57. *Ibid.*
58. *O Africano*, 18 March 1914, 5 February 1916; *Relatório Anual dos Serviços da Exploração do Caminho de Ferro e do Porte, 1914*.
59. *Brado Africano*, 27 October 1927.
60. *Brado Africano*, 19 January 1929.
61. Quote from Khosa's letter to editor in *Lourenço Marques Guardian*, 4 April 1929. See *Brado Africano*, 26 January 1929, for Khosa on Kadalie.
62. *Lourenço Marques Guardian*, 4 April 1929.
63. Grêmio Africano to SNI, 23 March 1929, SNI Cx 69; AHM; *Brado Africano*, 26 January, 29 April 1929.
64. *Brado Africano*, 29 April 1929.
65. CFLM to SNI, Informação, 6 May 1929, SNI Cx 69, AHM.
66. The case of Matola is documented in "Requerimento" to SNI, 9 February 1929, SNI Cx 69, AHM.
67. *Ibid.*
68. The following paragraphs are based on *Brado Africano*, 14 May, 27 October 1929, 19 January, 26 January 1929; OT, R. Tembe (b and c), J. da Costa (b and c), and F. de Brito (a and b).
69. RPCFLM (1927–1930), 17, 51; OT, R. Tembe (b and c), J. da Costa (b and c), and G. de Brito (a and b).
70. RPCFLM (1933–1934).
71. What follows is based on RPCFLM reports for the period 1929–1934.
72. The *Quinhenta* strike was covered in *Brado Africano*, 9 September 1933; *Emancipador*, 11 September 1933; *Lourenço Marques Guardian*, 29 August 1933, 5 September 1933; *Notícias*, 28 August 1933.
73. *Brado Africano*, 9 September 1933.
74. *Ibid.*; *Emancipador*, 11 September 1933.
75. *Lourenço Marques Guardian*, 29 August 1933, 5 September 1933; *Notícias*, 28 August 1933.
76. The incident, its causes, and implications were debated by José Cardozo, writing in the New State's press mouthpiece *União*, and José Albasini, writing in *Brado Africano*, between January and March 1934. See especially *União* 13 and 27 January 1934; OT, J. Cossa, R. Tembe (b), and J. da Costa (a and b).
77. OT, J. Cossa, R. Tembe (b), and J. da Costa (a and b).
78. OT, J. Júlio, J. da Costa (a and b), R. Tembe (b), and J. Cossa.

CHAPTER 6

The New State—"For the Good of the Nation" 1926–1961

1. For analysis of corporativist structures in Mozambique, see Michel Cahen, "Corporatisme et colonialisme, approche du cas mozambicain, 1933–1979, I: Une genèse difficile, un mouvement squelettique; II: Crise et survivance du corporatisme colonial, 1960–1979," *Cahiers d'Etudes Africaines* 92, XXIII-4 (1983), 383–417, and 93, XXIV-1 (1984), 5–24.

2. New State economic policy and practice is currently being reassessed in both published and unpublished work. See, for example, the debate between Michel Cahen and Gervase Clarence Smith in Michel Cahen, "Lénin, l'impérialisme portugais, Gervase Clarence-Smith," *Cahiers d'Etudes Africaines* 107–108, XXVII 3-4 (1987), 435–42, and especially the important doctoral dissertation of Joana Pereira Leite, "La Formation de l'économie coloniale au Mozambique. Pacte Colonial et industrialisation: du colonialisme portugais aux réseaux informels du sujétion marchande—1930/1974" (Ph. D. thesis, University of Paris, Ecole des Hautes Etudes en Sciences Sociales, 1989); Newitt, *Portugal in Africa,* and Vail and White's *Capitalism and Colonialism* remain fine overviews of the shifts and tensions from 1926 to 1962.

3. Vail and White, *Capitalism and Colonialism,* Ch. 5.

4. Pereira Leite's thesis closely details the shifts in industrial and trade relationships. Pereira Leite, "La Formation de l'économie coloniale."

5. *Brado Africano,* 21 May 1932; 4 February 1933; 11 March 1933;1, 8, 15 September 1935; 27 May 1939; 19 January 1946; 28 May 1949.

6. *Brado Africano,* 24 July 1924; 24 December 1932.

7. Ilício Rocha, *Catálogo dos Periódicos,* 19, 21–23.

8. Tenente Mário Costa, *Cartas de Moçambique,* (Lisbon, 1934), 196–203; Quintinha and Toscano, *A Derrocado do Império Vátua,* II, 144–48.

9. Although the record is not clear, it seems that in 1907 Aguiar purchased the estate of Especiosa da Conceição Gouveia or Bengalena, either to protect or exploit her many African and European heirs. *O Progresso,* 11 July, 26 August 1907; *Lourenço Marques Guardian ,* 8 July 1907.

10. *Respostas aos Quesitos . . . Ferrão,* 136; Costa, *Cartas de Moçambique,* 196–203; *Brado Africano,* 14 January 1933; Quintinha and Toscano, *A Derrocado do Império Vátua,* II, 144–48, and *Brado Africano* social news throughout the 1920s and obituary, 14 January 1933.

11. The term "friend of the natives" is in Costa's *Cartas de Moçambique,* 196–219.

12. Roque de Aguiar was a member of the exclusively European government body, Commission for Aid and Native Support.

13. The names of original subscribers published in the first issue of the paper strongly reflected clan names of the local African population, whereas Grêmio group photographs and membership lists of in the early 1930s reveal a predominance of mulatto leadership.

14. Penvenne, "Principles and Passion," 9, 17–21.

15. *Brado Africano,* 28 April, 4 May 1935, 13 and 27 February, 30 October 1937; Quintinha and Toscano, *A Derrocado do Império Vátua,* II, 98.

16. *Brado Africano,* 30 October 1937.

17. *Brado Africano,* 26 August 1933.

18. *Notícias,* 9 April 1949, and *Brado Africano,* 2 April 1949.

19. See photo in Ch. 4, page 67. Photo from *Brado Africano,* 24 December 1935.

20. This paragraph is based on social news in *Brado Africano,* 30 June 1923, 9 May 1931, 4 July 1931, and 24 December 1954; Honwana, *The Life of Raúl Honwana,* 100–101; OT, R. Tembe (b) and J. da Costa (b).

21. Honwana, *The Life of Raúl Honwana,* 101.

22. "Basta," *Brado Africano,* 27 February 1932.

23. Honwana, *The Life of Raúl Honwana,* 100–101.

24. Penvenne, "We are all Portuguese," 274–81.

25. Pott and Cantine debates in *Brado Africano,* 30 September to December 1933, 31 March 1934, 19 June 1937, 13 November 1937, 18 March 1939, 10 January 1948, 15 and 29 January 1949, 26 February 1949, 25 August and 1 December 1951; OT, J. da Costa and R. Tembe (c) and J. da Costa (d), V. P. Mainga (a and b), and B. T. Navess.

26. *Brado Africano,* 14 June, 23 August, 1 November, and 20 December 1930, 26 September 1931, 3 October 1931, 30 December 1933, 17 February, 25 August 1934, 27 March 1936.

27. *Brado Africano,* 26 November, 3, 10, and 31 December 1932, 15 May and 19 June 1937.

28. OT, A. Muiane, J. da Costa (c and d), R. Tembe (c and d), G. de Brito (b), and M. Tembe; and *Brado Africano*, 30 December 1939 and 24 December 1948.
29. Edward A. Alpers, "The Role of Culture in the Liberation of Mozambique," *Ufahamu*, 12, 3 (1983), 143-89; Gerald Moser and Manuel Ferreira, *Bibliografia das Literaturas Africanas de Expressão Portuguesa* (Lisbon, 1983), 177-208, esp. 190-191, 206.
30. Moser and Ferreira, *Bibliografia das Literaturas*, 191, 326.
31. Fatima Mendonça placed this resurgence in the period 1945-47 to 1964. *Literatura Moçambicana: A História e as Escritas* (Maputo, 1988), 33-35; Alpers, "The Role of Culture"; Moser and Ferreira, *Bibliografia das Literaturas*.
32. "Cada um puxa a brasa para a sua sardinha," *Brado Africano*, 27 August 1949.
33. Alpers, "The Role of Culture," *passim*.
34. This paragraph is based on: *Brado Africano*,13, 20, and 27 February 1932, 4 February 1933, 14 January 1934, 12 January 1935, 11 and 18 January 1936; British Consul Kay, "Report on the Economic Situation in Portuguese East Africa," March 1937, enclosed in FO 371/21279; "Economic Conditions in Portuguese East Africa," October 1938, FO 371/22599/W15678/667/36, PRO.
35. From 37,766 in 1926/27 to 16,581 in 1931/32, *Anuário de Lourenço Marques*, 1928-1933.
36. Yudelman and Jeeves, "New Labour Frontiers for Old," from Appendix, 123-24.
37. Vail and White, *Capitalism and Colonialism*, Ch. 5; Clarence-Smith, *The Third Portuguese Empire*, Chs. 6 and 7.
38. *Anuário de Lourenço Marques*, 1933.
39. *Anuário de Lourenço Marques*, 1930.
40. The AFA's position is well stated through the New State's press mouthpiece, *A União*. See especially pieces by José Cardosa throughout 1933 and correspondence between SNI and AFA in SNI Cx 69.
41. Cardosa was clearly using the legal language of the contemporary legislation. The *Código de Trabalho dos Indígenas nas Colónias Portuguêsas de Africa, aprovado pelo decreto no. 16199, 6 December 1928* was later incorporated as the *Regulamento do Trabalho dos Indígenas na Colónia de Moçambique: Aprovado por Portaria no. 1,180 de 4 de Setembro de 1930* (Lourenço Marques, 1930) [hereafter RTI, 1930]. José Cardosa, "A Crise da Agricultura na Colónia de Moçambique," *BSEM*, 1, 5 (October, 1932), 9-36.
42. *Ibid.; Anuário Estatístico*, 1929 to 1949, includes figures for agricultural labor in Lourenço Marques, but the figures are very irregular and the criteria for selection unclear.
43. "Rel. DSNI, 1928," SNI Cx 1131, AHM.
44. The history of "clandestine" recruitment was detailed in "Informação," No. 8, 4 February 1948, ACLM; "Inquérito, Mão de'Obra Indígena, Manhiça," RCNI to Governador Geral da Colónia de Moçambique [GGCM], 4 February 1948, ACLM Cx CC; Circular 566/D/7 and correspondence in ACLM Cx CC,FF, HH ACLM, AHM; OT, A. Cumbe, J. Sumbane, M. Muchanga, E. Muianga, V. Nhabanga, A. Senete, S. Uinge, E. Zavala, F. Zavala, and M. Zonda.
45. Quote from USACLM, 64, January, 1929; USACLM, Stanton to DS, 29 April 1930, "forced labor . . . abolished in law, not in fact." USNA.
46. Maputo Subdistrict to SNI, n.d., 1929, SNI Cx 68, AHM.
47. For the impact of forced rice and cotton schemes in Sul do Save, see Roesch, "Migrant Labour and Forced Rice Production," and Allen Isaacman et al., "Cotton is the Mother of Poverty: Peasant Resistance against Forced Cotton Cultivation in Mozambique, 1938-1961," *International Journal of African Historical Studies [IJAHS]* 13, 4 (1980), 581-616.
48. Emphasis added; "Informação," No. 8, 4 February 1948, ACLM.
49. OT, A. Cumbe.
50. Chapter 5, p. 79.
51. *Anuário de Lourenço Marques* and RPCFLM, both 1929-1933, and Chapter 5.
52. See chart on registered unemployment p. 98.

53. See price charts in Chapter 4, page 68.
54. *Anuário Estatística*, 1941–1946.
55. *Anuário Estatística*, 1941–1946.
56. *Brado Africano*, 8 March 1930.
57. "Economic Report on Portuguese East Africa," 21279/W2874/2862/36, FPO 371, PRO.
58. Compiled from *Anuário Estatístico* (1926–28, 1936); *Brado Africano*, 20 August, 8 October, and 5 November 1927, 14 January 1928; *Delogoa Directory* (1929, 1930, 1932–36); Ford to SOSFA, 7 April 1933, W4856, No. 42, F/17416, FO 371, PRO.
59. *Actas do Concelho do Governo*, 11 February 1932, 139–165; Lindley to Hendersen, 2 November 1930, W11781/5933/36 FO 371, and Ford to SOSFA, 42, 7 April 1933, W4856/5/33/17416, FO 371, both PRO; Álvaro dos Santos e Silva, "Problema do Desemprêgo e da Colonização de Moçambique," *Boletim da Sociedade de Estudos de Moçambique [BSEM] 1, 3 (1932), 5–15.*
60. Ford to SOSFA, 42, 7 April 1933, W4856/5/33/17416, FO 371, PRO.
61. See table on "Portuguese Settlers Entering at Lourenço Marques" below, and *Anuário Estatística*. 1931–1938.
62. *Brado Africano*, 1 September 1934, and prior pressure in *Brado Africano*, 8, 15, 29 November 1919, and 16 April 1921.
63. *Actas do Concelho do Governo*, 11 February 1932, 139ff; see also "Atestados de Pobreza," August to December 1946, ACLM, Cx R, ACLM, AHM.
64. *Anuário Estatístico*, 1931–1947.
65. See Chapter 7.
66. *Lourenço Marques Guardian*, 13 January 1927 and 12 February 1927.
67. The specific nature and impact of Depression-era protectionist and quota legislation are detailed in American and British consular despatches throughout the era. See, for example, USACLM, Desp. 135, 3 December 1930; USACLM, Ebling to DS, "Current Wages in Portuguese East Africa," 29 August 1936, Record Group 84, USNA; Pyke telegram to FO, 17 May 1930, 15032/1930/W5933/36 FO 371; Pyke to SOSFA, No. 71, 10 May 1930, 1244/27A, FO 371; J. J. Wills to SOSFA, "Regulations Governing Immigration and Unemployment in the Portuguese colonies," 27 February 1933, W2285, O 371, PRO.
68. *Brado Africano*, 3 November 1935.
69. *Brado Africano*, 6 July 1935.
70. ACLM to DPAC, 25 August 1937, 8 Dember 1937, both ACLM Doc. 88/73; "Diário de Serviço," 16 August 1937, 8 November 1937, 22 December 1937, ACLM Doc. 92/78, ACLM, AHM.
71. "Diário de Serviço," 22 December 1937, ACLM Doc. 92/78, ACLM, AHM; *Brado Africano*, 15 January 1938, 12 March 1938; Ribeiro, *Sumários*, 245.
72. Enclosure in Sir W. Selby to Viscount Halifax, 9 February 1939, 31E, 24/107/W3266/36, FO 371, PRO.
73. *União*, reprinted in *Brado Africano*, 23 May 1942.
74. See the case of Manuel dos Santos Tembe, discussedin Chapter 4.
75. Pinto de Fonseca, "Relatório da Direcção ... 1959," FGG 721, AHM and USACLM labor reports throughout the 1950s.
76. Vail and White, *Capitalism and Colonialism*; Chapter 5.
77. *Compilation of Legislation Affecting Labour . . . Immigration* (Lourenço Marques, 1939).
78. Dec. Lei 38,200, 10 March 1951, "Povoamento do Ultramar," Ribeiro, *Sumários*.
79. *Anuário Estatístico* (1926/28 to 1962).
80. Circular 3707/50, Direcção Provincial, Administração Civil [DPAC] to ACLM, 1944, ACLM, Cx Q, ACLM, AHM; Roberto Saboia de Medeiros Fernandes, "Portugal and its Overseas Territories: Economic Structure and Policies, 1950–1957" (Ph. D. thesis, Harvard University, 1960), 178.

81. *Anuário Estatístico* (1926/28 to 1962) and Província de Moçambique, Repartição de Estatística, *Recenseamento Geral da População*, 1950 and 1960 "População Civilizada", *Censo da População em 1940.*
82. Oral communication, António Rita Ferreira, 20 July 1989; USACLM 170 and 242 of 1961; G. Edgar Vaughan, *Portuguese East Africa: Ecoomic and Commercial Conditions in Portuguese East Africa [Mozambique], October 1951* (London, 1952), 41.
83. DPAC toACLM, Circular 3707A/50, ACLM Cx Q, ACLM, AHM; USACLM 127 (1952); 141 (1952); 136 (1954).
84. USACLM, 127 (1952), 149 (1953).
85. Consular reports and the local press presented the problem in terms of unskilled immigrants unable to compete for skilled employment opportunities. Statistics show that registered unemployed were largely commercial and office workers. In 1959, however, there were 114 unemployed carpenters. *Anuário Estatístico*, 1956–1963.
86. *Ibid.*
87. ACLM sample correlating increasing white unemployment with a slowdown in black employment mobility in the best-paid "native" jobs. See also Chapter 7.
88. See Pereira Leite on shifting coordination of Portuguese industrial development, "La Formation de l'économie coloniale."
89. Industrial change is charted through: *Anuário de Moçambique* (1945–1960); Moçambique, RTE, *Estatística Industrial* (1947–1962); Mendes, *Maputo antes de Indepência;* Manuel Pimental Pereira dos Santos, *A Indústria em Moçambique* (Lourenço Marques, 1956); Rui Martins dos Santos, *Uma contribuição para a Análise da Economia de Moçambique* (Lisbon, 1959); António Rita Ferreira, *Evolução de Mão de Obra e das Remunerações no Sector Privado em Moçambique desde 1950 á 1970* (Lourenço Marques, 1971); Clarence-Smith, *Third Portuguese Empire;* Fernandes, "Portugal and its Overseas Territories," and USACLM annual economic and labor reports for the period.
90. Pereira dos Santos, *Indústria*, 25, 51.
91. *Anuário Industrial* for the period; USACLM reports, especially 148 (1957); Armando Castro, *O Sistema Colonial Português em Africa (Meados do Seculo XX)* (Lisbon, 1978), 299; Keith Middlemas, *Cabora Bassa: Engineering and Politics in Southern Africa* (London, 1975) is an essential study of the politics of industrial investment in what Clarence-Smith called "late colonialism." Clarence-Smith, *The Third Portuguese Empire,* Ch. 7. Cahora Bassa is the name more commonly used since independence.
92. This paragraph based on Mendes, *Maputo antes de Independência*, Ch. 4.
93. David Hedges and Aurélio Rocha, "Moçambique Durante o Apogéu do Colonialismo Português, 1945–1961: A Economia e a Estrutura Social," *Cadernos de História* 6 (1987), 50–53.
94. *Ibid.,* 50.
95. Confidential USACLM, Lourenco Marques, to DS, 16 September 1963, USNA. For the changing climate of the 1960s, see Clarence-Smith's final chapter in *The Third Portuguese Empire.*
96. South African promotion of tourism in Lourenço Marques from 1899 to 1940 is best followed in the yearbook *Delogoa Directory*, with its subsequent title changes to *Anuário de Lourenço Marques* and *Anuário de Moçambique.*
97. Compiled from *Anuário Estatística* and USACLM economic reports from 1950 to1965.
98. Rita Ferreira, *Evolução de Mão de Obra*, 80, 84, 89, 108.

CHAPTER 7
Tailoring Labor Control in the Postwar Economy

1. Preamble to Portaria 5,565 of 12 May 1944, ACLM to Chefe do Gabinete, Repartição do Governador Geral, 1197/B/15 of 11 December 1950, ACLM, AHM.
2. OT, S. Zuana. See discussion of *palmatória* below p. 108ff.

3. The ISANI reports from the late 1940s and Pinto de Fonseca's reports in the late 1950s are particularly clear on this point.
4. ACLM ficha 12061, further corroboration, Marvin Harris, "Raça Conflito e Reforma em Moçambique," *Política Exterior Independente*, 1 (1966), 32; OT, A.G. Tembe (a and b).
5. See Mabunda's case below p.111ff and Chapter 8.
6. *Brado Africano*, 29 August and 26 September 1953.
7. Quote from OT, T. Comiche; explicit corroboration from OT, J. Cuna, B. Chibindji.
8. As per Circular 818/D/7 of 7 October 1942 and "Inquiry" 4 February 1948, Cx CC, ACLM, one contingent of the SNI administration felt conscription had been "much abused." DPAC, however urged rapid expansion of conscription for postwar public works DPAC to ACLM 4100/B/15/3, 18 October 1946, Cx G, ACLM, AHM.
9. DPAC to ACLM 4100/B/15/3 18 October 1946, Cx G, ACLM, AHM.
10. DPAC to ACLM, 4623/B/15/3, 25 November 1946, Cx G, ACLM, AHM.
11. ACLM to RCNI, 3 August 1950, 782/B/15; RCNI to ACLM, 23 August 1950, Cx FF, ACLM, AHM.
12. USACLM, "Confidential," 3, 3 July 1958, USNA.
13. Circular, 23 October 1959, ACLM, AHM.
14. Most informants mentioned this process. Lázaro Amosse Bié, for example, recalled that he was almost "sold" to a Mwamba settler on a year contract when he became unemployed, but quickly took a poorly paid job as a domestic to escape. O.T., L. Bié.
15. *Ibid.*
16. *Estatuto . . . 1954*, Art. 26, 13.
17. "Registo de *Shibalo*/Desempregos," 1960, ACLM, AHM.
18. *Anuário Estatístico*, 1929-1964.
19. "Relatório," 1 April 1950, Cx MM, ACLM, AHM.
20. *Ibid.*
21. See Chapter 10.
22. USACLM, 105, 1951, USNA.
23. José Tangwizi's woodcut reproduced in Bertil Egero's *Mozambique: A Dream Undone, The Political Economy of Democracy, 1975-1984* (Uppsala, 1990), 51, is an excellent example. See also Alpers,"The Role of Culture;" Vail and White, *Power and the Praise Poem*; and songs in Appendix I.
24. Confidential Circular 3,635/B/6, 9 November 1943, DPAC, lists the offenses and defined the procedure, ACLM CxGG, AHM.
25. OT, S. Chichongo.
26. USACLM, 151 (1955), USNA.
27. Quote from OT, D. Nhangumbe, with explicit corroboration from the following informants: P. Faleca, S. Zuana, M. Zonda, E. Muiaga, F. Tinga, E. Zavala, S. Chichongo, A. Guambe, I. Jeque, J. Machonga, S. Manhica, C. Miuanga.
28. OT, A. Cumbe, C. Macaneo, and J. Machanga.
29. Allegations of sexual misconduct between African domestic servants and European women and children comprise one of the most important offenses leading to deportation throughout this period. ACLM files B/7 and M/4, Caixas T, X, DD, and II, ACLM, AHM. For details see Chapter 9.
30. Vail and White, *Power and the Praise Poem*, Chs. 2, 4, 6, and "Forms of Resistance," *passim*.
31. OT, S. Zuana.
32. ACLM ficha 10161.
33. ACLM ficha 23041.
34. Many informants used the term *inveja* (envy, grudging, or jealousy) with regard to Portuguese exclusiveness.
35. The following based on OT, R. Tembe (e), and with her father R. Tembe (f).
36. *Ibid.*, and *Brado Africano*, 8 April 1950, 29 April 1950.

37. The following is based on correspondence, reports, and marginal notes contained in Posto Administrativo de Munhuana (PAM) to ACLM, 23 March 1949, and throughout File 53/M/ 3 in Cx T, ACLM, AHM.
38. Very occasionally one finds a sharp SNI official responding to an inquiry about an *assimilado* to the effect that such matters should be directed elsewhere because the SNI only deals with *indígenas*.
39. OT, R. Tembe and J. da Costa (c), and ACLM assimilation file, 1517/1, AHM.
40. Biographical information on Nhaca culled from *Brado Africano*, 20 August 1927, RCNI log 1938 for assimilation, membership lists of Instituto Negrófilo, in *Brado Africano*; OT, R. Tembe and J. da Costa (c) recounted that Nhaca was a prominent member of the Wesleyan mission-educated group and a landowner in Catembe, Mafalala, and Alto Mahé.
41. RCNI to ACLM, 12 January 1949, 20/M3 and PAM to ACLM, 12/M/3, 29 January 1949, ACLM, AHM.
42. PAM to ACLM, 12/M/3, 29 January 1949, ACLM, AHM.
43. *Ibid.*
44. Portaria 5,553 of 3 June 1944; PAM to ACLM, 23 March 1949, 53/M/3, Notation on Magaia investigation RCNI to ACLM, 11 July 1949, 2230/M/3, both Cx T, ACLM, AHM.
45. Documentation comments throughout Cx T, 1948/1949, ACLM, AHM. See also OT, B. Navess, J. da Costa, S. Tembe.
46. The following is based on OT, G. Mabunda.
47. Marginal notes on registration fichas from the ACLM sample document resistance to wage increases, for example, Ficha 2304.
48. OT, G. Mabunda.
49. About two-thirds of the informants mentioned *palmatória* beatings or racist intimidation. All were very clear that challenging such situations usually resulted in more pain and suffering. The clearest statement of that aspect came from OT, F. Muando.
50. OT, S. Tembe.
51. Case study developed from OT, S. Miuanga.
52. USACLM, 151, 1955, for estimates; *Brado Africano*, 28 January 1950; Hélio Felgas, *Emigração Indígena de Moçambique para os Territórios Limítrofes* (Lisbon, 1955), 31; Correspondence regarding clandestine emigration by sting team formed by ACLM in 1949, ACLM to RCNI, 3822/B/17/1 19 September 1952, Cx NN, ACLM, AHM.
53. ACLM sample.
54. *Ibid.*
55. *Ibid.*
56. ACLM sample and ACLM documents 328/184, ACLM, AHM.
57. Quote from OT, S. Zuana and P. Faleca.
58. For examples of chronic offenders, workers inciting others to quit, or serious labor challenges ending in beatings and deportation see: ACLM sample fichas, 45141, 44161, 44201, 24661, 25421, 25581, 25381, 1001, 4821. Most of the chronic offenders were clearly arrested most often for drunkenness. Otherwise, neither informants nor the documentation revealed any sustained, serious, and overt labor challenge in this period.
59. ACLM sample and "Livros de Regísto de Presos Judiciais e Administrativos," for 1951 to 1961, ACLM, AHM.
60. OT, V. Mainga, G. Mabunda, J. Cossa, T. Comiche, E. Langa, and N. Macaringue.
61. The majority of informants who came to the city as uneducated, unskilled adults first worked as casual labor on construction or the waterfront. The exception was informants who came to sign on for mine labor.
62. ACLM sample.
63. *Ibid.*
64. Although this was especially true of local people in better jobs (OT, J. da Costa [a, b, and d]; R. Tembe [a, b]; J. Samora, M. Mafuane, and M. Tembe), it was also the broad consensus of informants as expressed by OT, D. Nhangumbe. People knew it was not their place to say

anything, and fear was at the base of that knowledge. Note also the general tenor of caution in the life history of Raul Bernardo Honwana, *The Life of Raul Honwana.*
65. Marvin Harris, "Raça, Conflito e Reforma," 34.
66. The paragraph below is based on the Choque/de Sousa investigation contained in "Informação," 16/B/7 of 17 May 1960, Fundo SNI, Cx 591, AHM.

CHAPTER 8
A Hierarchy of Struggles in the Port Sector

1. *Brado Africano,* 13 October 1934.
2. W. A. Hance and I. S. van Dongen, "Lourenço Marques in Delagoa Bay," *Economic Geography* 33 (1957), 238–56.
3. RPCFLM, 1948 and 1953.
4. This paragraph is based on the following: Hance and van Dongen, "Lourenço Marques;" Mendes, *Maputo,* 302ff; Rodrigues Junior, *Transportes de Moçambique* (Lisbon, 1956), 6–7, 155, 164, 189; and USACLM, Despatches 142 (1951), 151 (1952), 141 (1953), 136 (1954), 127 (1955), 148 (1957), 170 (1959), 147 (1960), 170 (1961), 276 (1962).
5. Pereira de Lima, *Historia dos CFLM,* III, 60; and USACLM throughout the period, with summaries, 127 (1955) and 170 (1961).
6. The impact of wartime demand for coal and the return of India to the coal-exporting market in the 1950s emerge clearly in the city's export figures. Rodrigues Junior, *Transporte de Moçambique,* 85–86.
7. Summary from statistics in RPCFLM, 1934–1935.
8. RPCFLM, 1934–1935 and 1950.
9. Statistics from RPCFLM, 1946–1950.
10. ACLM to RCNI, 26 September 1949, Cx E, ACLM; USACLM, 131 (1956).
11. *Brado Africano,* 12 and 15 December1953.
12. OT, J. da Costa (b), R. Tembe (b).
13. OT, former *shibalo* overseers T. Comiche and J. Cossa.
14. OT, Chefe de Zona, G. de Brito.
15. "Relatório dos Agentes do Curador e Delegacia de Saude," 141 (1952) AHM.
16. ACLM sample revealed most fines and *shibalo* among registered hod carriers for Article 39, Paragraph 10 of the RSTI.
17. USACLM, 105 (1951); OT, long-time port workers T. Comiche, J. Cossa, and E. Langa.
18. *Brado Africano,* 24 April 1948.
19. "Relatório dos Agentes do Curador e Delegacia de Saude," 141 (1952) AHM.
20. *Brado Africano,* 12 and 15 December 1953.
21. *Brado Africano,* 16 January 1954; USACLM, 42 (1953), 127 (1955), 148 (1957).
22. Riberio, *Sumários,* Dip. Leg. 9 June 1928; Dip. Leg. 291, 14 March 1939; Dip. Leg. 18 October 1939.
23. OT, G. de Brito.
24. The dispensation from the "moral obligation to work" freed Africans of the threat of *shibalo* for unemployment or tax default. It was usually only granted for uncurable or chronic grave disease. See, for example, ACLM Fichas 4661, 6261, 1121, 18001.
25. *Brado Africano,* 24 December 1932; Costa, *Cartas de Moçambique,* 196–203.
26. The following discussion of the *shibalo* food riot is based on OT, R. Tembe (a, b, and c), J. da Costa (b), and J. Cossa. The 1947 *shibalo* work stoppage is covered in David Hedges and Arlindo Chilundo, *História de Moçambique,* Ch. 5, published in *Cadernos de História* 7 (1988), 45–90, and Proposta 129 of 9 September 1947 and accompanying documentation, SNI Cx 576, AHM.
27. According the the list of those arrested, five of the seven leaders and twenty-three of those sentenced to correctional labor were Chopi and twenty-eight of those sentenced were Bitonga. See SNI Director A. Montanha's report of the incident, 7 July 1947, 2157/B/15/3,

"Confidencial, Urgent" in SNI Cx 576, AHM.

28. OT, F. Zavala.

29. The following is based on OT, R. Tembe (a, b, and c), J. da Costa, (b), and J. Cossa.

30. The "full belly" strategy kept the *shibalo* cafeteria calm for a decade, then a second riot occurred. According to Tembe, the problem at this juncture was quality, not quantity. An influential Portuguese had taken over the flour contract and was supplying inferior flour. After three days of being served rotten flour, *shibalo* rioted again. OT, R. Tembe (a, b, and c), J. da Costa (b), and J. Cossa.

31. *Brado Africano*, 3 March 1949.

32. This paragraph is based on Hedges and Chilundo, *História de Moçambique*, Ch. 5; *Brado Africano*, 26 March 1949; Notícias, 9 April 1949; USACLM, 105 (1951); OT, C. Macaneo, V. Macuacua, R. Tembe, J. da Costa.

33. The 1963 dock strike falls outside the scope of this study, but it too was a labor action designed to force an increase in the basic shift wage. It too was met with force, arrests, and deportations. The strike is detailed in the licenciatura thesis of Alexandrino Francisco José, "A Greve dos Carregadores de Estiva do Porto Comercial de Lourenço Marques em Agosto de 1963, no Contexto da Luta da Libertação Nacional de Moçambique e Alguns Problemas na Reconstrução de História do Operariado Moçambicano" (Licenciatura thesis, Universidade Eduardo Mondlane, 1987). See also USACLM Confidential A-32, 16 September 1963.

34. USACLM, 105 (1951) describes the new system nicely and includes a translation of the new labor legislation.

35. ACLM Fichas 141, 821, 3341, 4001, 6041, 6461, 6821,11261, 18021, 2251, 25581, 44161, 26941, 29561, 43921, 46441.

36. ACLM Ficha 44161 with note, 12 May 1955, and Note 2482. Predictions based on the sample also suggest as many as twenty men may have been deported in this case.

37. The most dramatic examples of upward mobility to enviable jobs occurred in the 1960s among well-educated young port workers. See OT, G. Mabunda, L. Bié, B. Chibindji, E. Langa, A. Sibia.

38. ACLM sample.

39. USACLM, 151, 1955; 105, 1960; 146, 1961; U.S. Consul to Secretary of State, Telegram 73, 31 January 1963, USNA.

40. *Brado Africano*, 24 January 1931, 27 March 1932, 25 June 1932, 30 March 1946; *Anuário de Lourenço Marques*, 1938.

41. This paragraph based on OT, S. Zuana, J. da Costa (a, b), B. Chibindji, M. Tembe, G. de Brito, J. Cuna, J. Júlio, G. Mabunda, and E. Matusse.

42. José Cutileiro, *A Portuguese Rural Society* (Oxford, 1971), 203–204.

43. *Ibid.*, 205.

44. This paragraph based on OT, B. Chibindji.

45. OT, G. de Brito (a).

46. Direcção dos Portos, *Boletim do Porto*, Supplemento (July, 1970).

47. *Ibid.*

48. Compare OT, M. Tembe, for example, with G. Mabunda and J. Júlio.

49. Quoting from Cutileiro, *Portuguese Rural Society*, 203–204.

50. OT, J. da Costa (a). For Joaquim da Costa's analysis of this period, see his quote in the conclusion.

CHAPTER 9

Accommodation, Mobility, and Survival

1. See below, "African Urban Wage Chart, Lourenço Marques, 1933–1962", p. 132.

2. Wage rates culled from the press, interviews, published and unpublished documents, and the ACLM sample.

3. *Brado Africano*, 27 August 1949.

4. Women with children had special reliance upon family networks, OT, L. Tembe.

5. Aunts and uncles were mentioned most frequently, but the author failed to ascertain whether these were maternal or paternal links. Those specifics could shed light on the relative strength of shifting family support networks.

6. Ribeiro, *Sumários*, 531.

7. Moçambique, *Relatório, Serviço de Saude . . . Anno de 1886*.

8. *O Progresso*, 17 November 1904.

9. *Actas da Câmara Municipal de Lourenço Marques* [Actas, CMLM], 1 February, 15 February, 8 March, and 26 April 1927.

10. *Brado Africano*, 22 February 1936; Postura 7 of 30 October 1937, *Ordem da Província*.

11. Saldanha in *Corréio de Lourenço Marques*, 18 February 1925.

12. *Brado Africano*, 1 February 1936.

13. From quota legislation: Desp. 10 January 1944; Desp. 30 June 1948, Desp. 24 November 1948; Desp. 30 November 1949, in Ribeiro, *Sumários*.

14. CMLM Edital, 3 January 1940; *Notícias*, March through April 1949.

15. OT, S. Chicango, A. Cumbe, P. Faleca, I. Jeque, A. Kuamba, C. Macaneo, M. Mafuane, S. Manhica, J. Marangue, F. Mondlane, J. Mondlane, F. Muando, E. Muianga, Z. Muianga, A. Nhalivilo, D. Nhangumbe, A. Nhaposse, I. Nuvunga, M. Paulo, A. Senete, and F. Tinga.

16. *Anais de CMLM* (1950), 138–40, and (1953), 312.

17. *Anais de CMLM* (1950), 20–21, 138–40.

18. *Anais de CMLM* (1950), 20–21; Santos, *Indústria*, 61; ACLM Fichas, 16621, 17461, 20881, 26541, 27141; RCNI Circular 929, B/15/12 of 27 March 1940, ACLM, AHM.

19. *Anais de CMLM* (1950), 20–21.

20. ACLM Ficha 20541, OT as in note 15 above.

21. ACLM Fichas 4681, 40081, 16561, 2701, 3821.

22. ACLM, 2706, 39461, 37161, 14021, 3061, 201, 16901.

23. Two groups self-identified as Bitonga/Xitswa with ten men and Chopi with nine. The rest of the group were Tsonga speakers.

24. The following is based on OT, M. Mafuane.

25. The following is based on OT, D. Nhangumbe.

26. OT, D. Nhanbumbe.

27. OT as in note 15 above.

28. USACLM, 105 (1960); Moçambique, Junta Bairro de Casas Populares, *Relatório, 1960–1963* (Lourenço Marques, 1964), 66.

29. ACLM to President CMLM, 5 Dec. 1950, 1861/B/1/3, Cx E, ACLM, AHM.

30. No informant had received the full benefit of the standard *shibalo* contracts. See esp. OT, F. Nhuache, V. Nhabanga, F. Chondela, and Z. Muianga.

31. Labor inspection reports are filed under B/15/2 throughout the period in Cx E, ACLM; see also RCNI to ACLM, 9 September 1948, 2901/B/15/2, ACLM, AHM.

32. Circular, Secretaria Geral to ACLM, 22 May 1950, 814/B/15, Cx HH, ACLM, AHM.

33. Pinto de Fonseca, "Relatório da Direcção," 25 June 1960, FGG, Rel. 721, AHM.

34. Circular, Secretaria Geral to ACLM, 22 May 1950, 814/B/15, Cx HH, ACLM, AHM.

35. "Inspecção," Delegado de Saude, 8 August 1947; ACLM to A. Coelho, Aviso 65, 6 August 1947, both ACLM Cx HH; ACLM to RCNI, 27 January 1950, 145/B/15, Cx CC, ACLM, AHM.

36. ACLM to contractor [P. S. Gil] of "Liceu Salazar," No. 36, 25 February 1950. Cx EE, ACLM, AHM.

37. Culled from *shibalo* contracts in Cx A, CC, G, FF, and JJ for 1930s to 1960s, ACLM, AHM.

38. See the chart for 1914 to 1946 in Chapter 6, p. 98.

39. Santos, *Indústria*, 61ff; ACLM Fichas 36461, 37161, 16621,12841.

40. Alfredo Pereira de Lima, "Para um Estudo da Evolução Urbana de Lourenço Marques,"

188 AFRICAN WORKERS AND COLONIAL RACISM

Boletim Municipal, 7 (31 December 1970), 7-16, see esp. 15; USACLM, 170 (1959); Mendes, *Maputo,* 95-99.

41. Mendes, *Maputo,* 95-99.

42. Some 1,277 construction and public works labors in 1940; 2,050 in 1950; 3,500 in 1960; and 3,750 in 1962. See Chart, Chapter 6, p.102.

43. I was unable to corroborate this allegation through press or municipal reports, but at least twenty informants mentioned it and provided similar details. For most detail, see OT, F. Tinga, A. Cumbe, E. Muianga, and B. Navess.

44. OT, E. Muianga. Twenty-seven informants specifically mentioned construction of the Sé cathedral in connection with urban labor abuse. Bento Navess, a Methodist minister referred to the Sé as a "monstrosity" due to its construction history. OT, B. Navess; see also Fuller, "An Ethnohistorical Study," 148 n4.

45. Letterhead on Paulino Santos Gil contracts for *shibalo* correspondence for the 1950s throughout ACLM Cx CC, ACLM, AHM.

46. Quote from interview with South African businessmen with companies in Mozambique; OT, B. LeMay, D. Spence. See also, OT, V. Mainga; ACLM Doc. 135/97, SNI Cx 72, both AHM; *Notícias,* 25 March 1949.

47. ACLM Caixas A, E, and CC, ACLM, AHM.

48. ACLM to Paulino Santos Gil, 7 February 1951, Cx JJ; SNI Cx 28, AHM.

49. OT, V. Mainga, I. Nuvunga.

50. OT, I. Nuvunga.

51. Santos Gil *shibalo* contract correspondence for 1949-51, ACLM Cx JJ, AHM.

52. ACLM Caixas A, JJ, and FF, AHM.

53. OT, V. Mainga.

54. For example, Guia 668/B/15/4, 1946 on complaint of 15 October 1945; SNI to ACLM, 4 September 1945 both ACLM Cx A, AHM.

55. "Diário de Serviço, 1937-1939," 1 April 1937, ACLM Doc. 92/78, AHM.

56. "Diário de Serviço, 1937-1939," 10 February 1939, ACLM Doc. 92/78, AHM; CMLM, *Anais, 1950,* 122; *Anais, 1952,* 180; *Anais, 1953-54,* 295, 305-306.

57. The following documented in RCNI, 22 November 1944, Guia 509/B/11/II, Guia 514/B/11/II; Paulino Santos Gil to RCNI, 20 November 1944; "Auto de Declarações," 25 November 1944, RCNI, Francisco António Sitoi, Oquisuo Zavala, Monotiana Inguana, Fainda Muianga, Toalofo Zandemela and Sabão Mapehane; A. Montanha to Paulino Santos Gil, 11 December 1944, all SNI Cx 713, AHM.

58. Montanha to P. Santos Gil, 11 December 1944, SNI Cx 713, AHM.

59. P. Santos Gil to SNI, 15 December 1944, SNI Cx 713, AHM.

60. Contracts culled from ACLM Cx A, CC, G, FF and JJ. Statistics for the 1950s and 1960s will undoubtedly be revised as these data are cataloged, ACLM, AHM.

61. ACLM to P. S. Gil, 7 February 1950, 170/B/15/2 Cx JJ, ACLM, AHM.

62. ACLM to P. S. Gil, 23 May 1950, 489/B/15/2, Obras Liceu Salazar, ACLM, AHM.

63. OT, M. Bucane, and worksongs in Annex II.

64. *Brado Africano,* 6 April 1946.

65. *Ibid.,* 24 February 1951.

66. In 1941 there was one African in secondary school and thirty-three mulattos. In 1960 there were five African women in secondary school and nine in commercial specialization. Anders Ehnmark and Per Wastberg, *Angola and Mozambique: The Case Against Portugal* (London, 1963), 141. *Anuário Estatístico* (1942); Silva, "As Missões Católicas Femininas," 37; David Hedges, "Educação, Missões e a Ideologia Política de Assimilação, 1930-1960," *Cadernos de História,* 1 (1985), 7-19.

CHAPTER 10
Accommodation and Mobility—Strategies
in the Private Sector

1. Caetano was minister of the overseas from 1944 to 1947, and subsequently minister of state in the Office of the Presidency, the equivalent of deputy premier of Portugal, second in command to Salazar during this period. Caetano, *Os Nativos na Economia Africana* (Coimbra, 1954), 33–34.
2. José, "A Greve dos Carregadores de Estiva," 12; OT, R. Tembe (b), and J. da Costa (b).
3. Harris, "Raça, Conflito, e Reforma."
4. Quotes from OT, R. Tembe (b), and José, "A Greve dos Carregadores de Estiva," 12, respectively.
5. Honwana, *Memórias*, note p. 76, in interview with Allen Isaacman, 20 May 1987; and OT, R. Tembe (b and c), and J. da Costa (b and c).
6. Dozens of informants responded precisely in this fashion, but R. Tembe (b and c) and J. da Costa (b and c) provided the most oral detail. See also Santos Oliveira, "Recordações sôbre Lourenço Marques."
7. Michel Cahen, "Corporatisme et colonialisme, II" is the essential study concerning Ferraz de Freitas's ordering of the urban informal sector, but see also Rita Ferreira, "Os Africanos de Lourenço Marques," 352ff; Rui Pereira, "Colonialismo e Antropologia: A Especulação Simbólica," *Revista International de Estudos Africanos [RIEA]* 10/11 (1989), 269–81.
8. From approximately 14,000 in the District of Lourenço Marques to 30,600; Rita Ferreira, *Evolução de Mão de Obra*, 80, 84, 89, 108.
9. Comparing the censuses of 1940, 1950, and 1960.
10. The 1940 census, for example, documented that 79 percent of African domestics were males under twenty, 48 percent of that group were between ten and fifteen, and 28 percent between fifteen and twenty.
11. See chart below from censuses of 1940, 1950, 1960, p. 143.
12. According to the 1940 Census, only 35 percent of female domestics were under twenty and 16 percent were between twenty-five and thirty.
13. ACLM survey 234/147, 1949, ACLM, AHM, and see Chapter 3.
14. The following paragraphs are based on M. Sofia Pomba Guerra, "O Problema dos Trabalhos Domésticos: Conferência Promovida pela Subsecção dos Estudos Femininos em 12 de Março de 1948," *BSEM* XVII, 59 (1948), 1–23.
15. ACLM sample.
16. ACLM survey 234/147, 1949, ACLM, AHM.
17. Compare census figures for 1940, 1950, and 1960. The census figures do not always differentiate between district and city of Lourenço Marques, but few domestic servants worked outside the city.
18. The changing situation for rural and urban Mozambican women in Sul do Save is the subject of the author's current research, "Women in the City—Women of the City, 1945–1975." Only the most basic factors are raised here.
19. *Brado Africano*, 12 March 1938.
20. *Ibid.*
21. ACLM to RCNI, 29 September 1949, 50/B/8, ACLM, AHM; Silva, "As Missões Católicas," 56.
22. ACLM to RCNI, 29 September 1949, 50/B/8, ACLM, AHM.
23. *Estatística Industrial*, 1947–1962; Santos Rufino, *Albuns Fotográficos e Descritivos*, IV, 13–16; Silva, "Missões Católicas," 56.
24. OT, A. Muiane and L. Tembe.
25. *Estatística Industrial*, 1945–1962, with statistics on personnel as well as production from 1956 to 1962.

26. Penvenne, "Here Everyone Walked with Fear," 148–53.
27. ACLM sample shows 92 percent of cashew workers between the early 1950s and 1960 were born outside the city.
28. ACLM sample.
29. Wage rates culled from interviews, newspapers, archival and ACLM sample data.
30. De Bettencourt, *Relatório*, I, 47.
31. OT, S. Zuana.
32. *Lourenço Marques Guardian*, 9 September 1943, 6 February 1946, 5 April 1948, 15 and 29 March, 1950.
33. *Anuário Estatístico*, 1935–1942, and "Relatório Annual, 1946," Doc. 352/21, Cx R, ACLM, AHM.
34. ACLM to PAM, Guia 22 October 1947, Cx S; DPAC to ACLM, Doc. 176/12, 741 of 22 March 1945; ACLM to RCNI, 8 March 1950, 251/B/8, Cx DD, all ACLM, AHM.
35. *Lourenço Marques Guardian* , 2 January 1947, 5 April 1948.
36. ACLM Documents 328/184, 390/206, and 448/226, "Registos da Aplicação de Castigos Corporais," according to Confidential Circular 1,139, B/11/1 of 22 Aug. 1951, Secretaria Geral to ACLM, for 1951–53, 1955–957, ACLM, AHM.
37. ACLM Docs. 328/184, 390/206, and 448/226, ACLM, AHM.
38. *Ibid.*
39. *Ibid.*
40. ACLM to RCNI, 23 October 1947, 1694/M4, ACLM, AHM.
41. ACLM to RCNI, 1030/B/7, October 1950, and all of File B/7 for 1950, R Cx II; File B/7 and M/4 for 1947–50, R Cx X, T, and DD, ACLM, AHM.
42. For overall corroboration, see deportation files in Fundo DSNI, Cx 577 to 591, 1947 to 1960, AHM.
43. De Bettencourt, *Relatório*, I, 48.
44. *Ibid.*
45. Quoted in *Brado Africano*, 11 November 1942.
46. *Brado Africano*, 23 May 1942, 11 March 1950. For African women's expression of this concern see OT, L. Tembe and A. Muiane, corroborated by Alves, "Destribalização da Mulher Indígena," 117–19, and Silva, "Missões Católicas," 55, 57. For Mozambican male corroboration of same see OT, especially J. Sumbane, A. Cumbe, and C. Macaneo.
47. Silva, "Missões Católicas," 55ff; Alves, "Destribalização da Mulher Indígena," 117–19.
48. ACLM sample. Just under half the female *criadas* in the sample experienced a wage drop, usually upon reentry after what appeared to be the birth of a child. See for example fichas 31601, 34161, 44061, 45061, 13281.
49. ACLM sample.
50. *Recenseamento Geral da População . . . 1960*, III, Vol. I, "Distrito de Lourenço Marques."
51. *Ibid.*
52. The following informants discussed their experience in domestic service: J. Cossa, J Gulele, S. Zuana, N. Macaringue, G. Mabunda, F. Simango, M. Tembe. J. da Costa, E. Langa, S. Chichango, M. Inguane, C. Macaneo, V. Macuacua, M. Mafuane, J. Mahumane, A. Mambiro, J. Manguese, S. Manhica, J. Mondlane, N. Machanga, E. Muianga, Z. Muianga, F. Nandje, V. Nhabanga, A. Nhalivilo, A. Nhaposse, and F. Tinga.
53. OT regarding evening school and useful networks, see especially C. Macaringue, G. Mabunda, M. Inguane, and E. Muianga.
54. Quote from E. Langa repeated by most of informants cited in note 51 above.
55. OT, M. Inguane.
56. OT, C. Macaneo.
57. OT, F. Simango, M. Tembe, J. Costa, A. Nhaposse, E. Muianga, Z. Muianga, and V. Nhabanga all report basically positive experiences.
58. OT, F. Tinga, A. Nhalivilo, and M. Mafuane, for example.

59. OT, S. Zuana.
60. ACLM sample.
61. OT, J. Macaringue.
62. *Ibid.*
63. OT, Z. Muianga.
64. ACLM sample.
65. Sexual and authority relationships for female domestics can only be adequately addressed through further research.
66. ACLM sample. Male informants, as in note 52 above, all recorded steady wage increases in domestic service up to a ceiling determined by the social class of the employer.
67. ACLM log, 24 January 1959 to 14 September 1962. For the calendar year 1959, of the 1,107 registered unemployed domestics, less than 3 percent were cooks and only 8 percent of the group were local people.

CONCLUSION
African Workers and Colonial Racism Images, Groups, and Individuals

1. OT, V. Nhabanga.
2. The phrase, "estavam bem," was usually used for whites, but it was also used for *assimilados.* Manuel Tembe used this phrase to refer to members of the Grêmio Africano, whom he considered to be a privileged group apart even though he was himself an *assimilado.* OT, M. Tembe.
3. OT, J. da Costa (a).
4. See Chapter 7, p. 116
5. OT, V. Nhabanga and "Basta," *Brado Africano,* 27 February 1932.
6. Fonseca, "Relatório . . . 25 Jan. 1960," 8, FGG, Relatório 722, AHM.
7. Hedges, "Educação, Missões e a Ideologia Política de Assimilação," 9.
8. The theme of preventing direct African competition with whites runs throughout the colonial documentation from Freire de Andrade's classic statement in his *Relatórios* to Montanha's reports in the 1940s, to Pinto de Fonseca's report in 1960. Freire de Andrade, *Relatório,* 2nd ed., I, 74; "Informação," 59/1a/5M AB/AC, Direcção dos Serviços de Administração Civil, 13 July 1948, Fundo DSNI, Cx 171; Fonseca, "Relatório . . . 25 Jan. 1960," FGG, Relatório 722, both AHM.
9. See Bill Freund, "Labor and Labor History in Africa; A Review of the Literature," *African Studies Review* 27 (1984):1–58; Freund, *The African Worker*; Frederick Cooper, "Urban Space, Industrial Time and Wage Labor in Africa," in Cooper, *Struggle for the City.* 7–50; Cooper, *On the African Waterfront*; Stichter, *Migrant Laborers.*

ANNEX II
Mozambican Work Songs

1. This is the most complete version of a song most Mozambicans knew, sung by João docanga Machanga, 15 July 1977, CMM.
2. Manuel Cossa, 12 July 1977, CMM.
3. Joaquim Hafo Kuamba, 7 July 1977, CMM.
4. Felizberto Zavala led this song and a half-dozen of his colleagues joined in, 13 July 1977, CMM.
5. Sung by Flor Fanequisso Muconto, 15 July 1977, CMM.
6. Joaquim Hafo Kuamba, 7 July 1977, CMM.

Sources and Bibliography

A Note on Sources

Archives

All of the documentation from the Administração do Concelho de Lourenço Marques [ACLM] used in this book was uncatalogued and uninventoried when used, and remains uncatalogued and only partially inventoried today. That obviously does not permit convenient references, so I have devised a makeshift system of identification to facilitate future research. The ACLM documentation was scattered through the attic of the former labor registration office; some papers were simply lying around loose and the rest were stacked on the floor in metal and paper boxes (*caixas*). I cite the reference numbers, dates, and signatories (if any) of specific documents and note those in the ACLM collection as ACLM, AHM.

Material in the *caixas* was clearly related, and when I wish to cite the whole collection or run of documents in a *caixa* , I use my own lettering system. I lettered the *caixas* as I went through them, penciling in A, B, etc., and then AA, BB under the metal lid. As of 1993 these materials remain uncataloged but preserved at the Arquivo Histórico de Moçambique. The *caixa* lettering is only useful to colleagues because I deposited carbon copies of all my notes on the documentation at the Centro de Estudos Africanos, Universidade Eduardo Mondlane. My notecards at the Centro are organized by my system of *caixa* letters. Since I copied out many of the documents in the notes, the letter organization at least provides access to the copied documents. The SNI *caixas* cited here were also extensively reorganized when the Arquivo Historico de Moçambique moved to its present location of Avenida Filipe Magaia. Only those *caixas* marked Fundo DSNI reflect the present archival organization.

With regard to the Freedom of Information material from the U.S. National Archives, this material was generated by my request for the annual economic and labor reports of the U.S. consul in Lourenço Marques for the period 1950 to 1974. The documents are now available at the African Studies Library at Boston University. They are organized by year, and within each year by the despatch number.

Mozambique

Câmara Municipal de Maputo, Maputo
Actas da Câmara Municipal de Lourenço Marques, 1902–1928
Livros de Registo de Correspondéncia Entrada . . . 1898–1933
Administração de Concelho de Maputo, Primeiro Bairro, Maputo
Uncatalogued Documentation, 1891 to 1962
Arquivo Histórico de Moçambique, Maputo
Secretaria de Negócios Indígenas
Correspondéncia Logs 3–48 through 3–464
Uncatalogued SNI Caixas, 1900–1933

Portugal

Arquivo Histórico Ultramarino, Lisbon
Moçambique, Primeira Repartição, 1898–1918
Moçambique, Segunda Repartição, 1897–1904
Direcção dos Caminhos de Ferro Ultramarino, 1897–1924
Junta Consultiva do Últramar, 1904–1906
Moçambique Miscelanae, Caixa 237
Biblioteca Pública Municipal do Porto
Letter books from Moçambique

United Kingdom

Public Record Office, London
Foreign Office Files, FO 2, FO 84, FO 367, FO 368, FO 371

United States of America

United States National Archives, Washington, D.C.
Diplomatic Branch, Record Groups 59 and 84
"Despatches from U.S. Consuls in Lourenço Marques, Mozambique, 1854–1906,"
Microcopy T-171
"Records of the Department of State Relating to the Internal Affairs of Portugal,
1910–1925," Microcopy 705
"OSS Research and Analysis," Report 771
Freedom of Information Act Documentation, 1950 to 1975
"Annual Economic Reports" and "Annual Labor Reports" for the colony of
Mozambique, 1950 to 1962 and "Annual Economic Reports", 1963 to 1974. Mis-
celaneous Documentation, 43 documents for the group 1950–1962 and 99 doc-
uments for the period 1963–1974.

Books, Articles, and Dissertations

Alpers, Edward A. "The Role of Culture in the Liberation of Mozambique." *Ufahamu*
12, 3 (1983), 143-90.
Alves, Judith Martins. "A Destribalização da Mulher Negra em Geral com Alguns
Apontamentos Sôbre o Problema Vivido em Moçambique." *Estudos Ultramarinos*
2 (1961), 99–129.

Associação Commercial de Lourenço Marques. *Relatório da Direcção 1891-1904.* Lourenço Marques, 1892-1905.

Berger, Iris. *Threads of Solidarity: Women in South African Industry 1900-1980.* Bloomington, 1991.

Boléo, José de Oliveira, "Geografia das Cidades—Lourenço Marques," Boletim da Sociedade de Geografia de Lisboa, 63 Ser. 5-6 (1945), 217-27.

Bovill, John H. *Natives under the Transvaal Flag.* London, 1910.

Bozzoli, Belinda, ed. and comp. *Class, Community and Conflict: South African Prospectives.* Johannesburg, 1987.

————. *Labour, Townships and Protest.* Johannesburg, 1978.

————. *Town and Countryside in the Transvaal: Capitalist Penetration and Popular Response.* Johannesburg, 1983.

Bozzoli, Belinda, with the assistance of Mmantho Nkotsoe. *Women of Phokeng: Consciousness, Life Strategy and Migrancy in South Africa, 1900-1983.* Portsmouth, NH, 1991.

Bulpin, T.V. *Lost Trails of the Transvaal.* 2nd ed., Cape Town, 1969.

Brock, Lisa Ann. "From Kingdom to Colonial District: A Political Economy of Social Change in Gazaland, Southern Mozambique, 1870-1930." Ph.D. thesis, Northwestern University, Evanston, Ill., 1989.

Cabral, J. R. P. *Relatório do Governador de Inhambane, Anno 1911-1912.* Lourenço Marques, 1913.

Caetano, Marcello. *Os Nativos na Economia Africana.* Coimbra, 1954.

Cahen, Michel. "Corporatisme et colonialisme: approche du cas mozambicain, 1933-1979, I: Une Genése difficile, un mouvement squelettique"; II: "Crise et survivance du corporatisme colonial, 1960-1979." *Cahiers d'Études Africaines* 92, XXIII, 4 (1983), 383-417; and 93, XXIV, 1 (1984), 5-24.

————. "Lénine, l'impérialisme portugais, Gervase Clarence-Smith," *Cahiers d' Études Africaines* 107-108, XXVII, 3/4 (1987), 435-42.

Câmara Municipal de Lourenço Marques. *Anais, 1950.* Lourenço Marques, 1951.

Capela, José. *A Burguêsia Mercantil do Porto e as Colónias (1834-1909).* Porto, 1975.

————. *O Movimento Operário em Lourenço Marques, 1898-1927.* Porto, 1981.

————. *O Vinho para o Preto: Notas e Textos Sôbre a Exportação do Vinho para Africa.* Porto, 1973.

Cardosa, José. "A Crise da Agricultura na Colónia de Moçambique," *Boletim da Sociedade de Estudos de Moçambique* I, 5 (October 1932), 9-36.

Carvalho, Tito de. *Les Colonies portugaises au point de vue commercial.* Paris, 1900.

Castilho, Augusto de. *O Distrito de Lourenco Marques, No Presente e No Futuro.* 2nd ed. Lisbon, 1881.

Castro, Governor Álvaro de. *Africa Oriental Portuguêsa, Notas e Impressões.* 1a serie, Lisbon, n.d.

Castro, Armando. *O Sistema Colonial Português em Africa (Meados do Século XX.* Lisbon, 1978.

Chamberlain, George Agnew. *African Hunting Among the Thongas.* New York, 1923.

Clarence-Smith, W. G. "The Myth of Uneconomic Imperialism: Portugal in Angola, 1836-1926." *Journal of Southern African Studies* 6 (1979), 165-80.

————. . *The Third Portuguese Empire, 1825-1975: A Study in Economic Imperialism.* Manchester, 1985.

Colson, Elizabeth. "African Society at the Time of the Scramble," in L. Gann and P. Duignan, eds., *Colonialism in Africa*, I, 27–65. Cambridge, 1968.

Comissão Organizadora das Comemorações do Primeiro Centenário de Mouzinho de Albuquerque em Mozambique. *Mouzinho: Governador de Lourenço Marques, 25 Setembro de 1890–4 de Janeiro de 1892: Compilação de Documentos Oficiais do Arquivo Histórico de Moçambique.* Lourenço Marques, 1956.

Cooper, Frederick. *On the African Waterfront: Urban Disorder and the Transformation of Work in Colonial Mombasa.* Yale, 1987.

Cooper, Fredreick. "Urban Space, Industrial Time and Wage Labor in Africa," in Frederick Cooper, editor. *Struggle for the City: Migrant Labor, Capital and the State in Urban Africa.* Beverly Hills, 1983.

Costa, Tenente Mário. *Cartas de Moçambique.* Lisbon, 1934.

Crush, Jonathan, David Yudelman, and Alan Jeeves. *South Africa's Labor Empire: A History of Black Migrancy to the Gold Mines.* Boulder, 1991.

Cruz, Daniel da. *Em Terras de Gaza.* Porto, 1910.

Cunha, J. M. da Silva. *O Trabalho Indígena: Estudo de Direito Colónial.* Lisbon, 1949.

Cutileiro, José. *A Portuguese Rural Society.* London, 1971.

Darch, Colin. "Notas sôbre Fontes Estatísticas Oficiais Referente á Economia Colonial Moçambicana: Uma Crítica Geral," *Estudos Moçambicanos,* 4 (1983–85), 103–125.

Delagação de Portugal á 6.a Assembleia da [Comissão Temporária da Escravatura da Sociedade das Nações.] "Algumas Observações ao Relatório do Professor Ross Apresentadas como Elemento da Informação á Comissão Temporária da Escravatura da Sociedade das Nações." *Boletim da Agência Geral das Colónias* Ano 1, 6 (December 1925), 179–190; Ano 2, 7 (January 1926), 149–62: Ano 2, 8 (February 1926), 152–64.

Dias, Raul Neves. *A Imprensa Periódica em Moçambique, 1854–1954...* Lourenço Marques, 1956.

——. *Quatro Centenários em Moçambique...* Lourenço Marques, 1954.

Duffy, James. *Portuguese Africa.* Cambridge, 1959.

——. *A Question of Slavery: Labour Policies in Portuguese Africa and the British Protest, 1850–1920.* Oxford, 1967.

Earthy, E. Dora. *Valenge Women: The Social and Economic Life of the Valenge Women of Portuguese East Africa: An Ethnographic Study.* London, 1933.

Egerö, Bertil. *Mozambique: A Dream Undone: The Political Economy of Democracy, 1975–1984.* Uppsala, 1990.

Ehnmark, Anders, and Per Wastberg. *Angola and Mozambique: The Case Against Portugal.* London, 1963.

Elton, Frederick. "Journal of an Exploration of the Limpopo River." *Journal of the Royal Geographical Society* 42 (June, 1873), 1–48.

Enes, António. *Moçambique: Relatório apresentado ao Governo.* Lisbon, 1946.

Erskine, St. Vincent. "Journey of Exploration to the Mouth of the River Limpopo." *Journal of the Royal Geographical Society* 39 (1869), 232–76.

——. "Journey to Umzila's, South-East Africa, in 1871–1872." *Journal of the Royal Geographical Society* 45 (1875), 45–128.

——. "Two Journeys of Mr. St. Vincent Erskine in Gaza Land, During the Years 1873, 1874 and 1875. Adapted from Mr. Erskine's Journals by R. Mann, Esq. M.D." *Proceedings of the Royal Geographical Society* 22 (1877–1878),126–37.

Felgas, Hélio Auguste Esteves. *Emigração Indígena de Moçambique para os Territórios Limítrofes.* Lisbon, 1955.

Fernandes, Roberto Saboia de Madeiros. "Portugal and Its Overseas Territories: Economic Structure and Policies, 1950-1957." Ph.D. thesis, Harvard University, Cambridge, 1960.

Fialho Feliciano, José. "Antropologia Económica dos Thonga do Sul de Moçambique." 3 vols. Ph.D. thesis, Universidade Técnica de Lisboa, Lisbon, 1989.

First, Ruth, et al. *Black Gold: The Mozambican Miner, Proletarian and Peasant.* New York, 1983.

Flegg, H., and W. Lutz. "Report on an African Demographic Survey." *Journal of Social Research* [South Africa]. 10 (1959), 1-24.

Freire de Andrade, Alfredo Augusto. *Colonisação de Lourenço Marques: Conferencia feita em 13 Março de 1897 pelo sócio honorário A.A. Freire de Andrade.* Porto, 1897.

———. *Relatórios sôbre Moçambique.* 4 vols. Lourenço Marques, 1907-1910.

———. "As Terras da Coroa." In Eduardo Borges de Castro, *Africa Oriental: Portugal em Africa.* Porto, 1895.

Freund, William. *The African Worker.* Cambridge, 1988.

———. "Labor and Labor History in Africa: A Review of the Literature," *African Studies Review* 27 (1984), 1-58.

Fuller, Charles E. "An Ethnohistorical Study of Continuity and Change in Gwambe Culture." Ph.D. thesis, Northwestern University, Evanston, Ill., 1955.

Gomes da Costa, Manuel. *Gaza, 1897-1898.* Lisbon, 1899.

Gool, Selim. *Mining Capitalism and Black Labour in the Early Industrial Period in South Africa: A Critique of the New Historiography.* Lund, 1983.

Guerra, M. Sofia Pomba. "O Problema dos Trabalhos Domésticos: Conferência Promovida pela Subsecção dos Estudos Femininos em 12 de Março de 1948." *Boletim da Sociedade de Estudos de Moçambique* 8, 59 (1948), 1-23.

Guimarães, Angela. *O Corrente do Colonialismo Português: A Sociedade de Geografia de Lisboa, 1875-1895.* Lisbon, 1984.

Guyer, Jane. "The Raw, The Cooked and the Half-Baked: A Note on the Division of Labor by Sex," *African Studies Center Working Paper* No. 48, Boston, 1981.

———, and Pauline E. Peters. "Conceptualizing the Household: Issues of Theory and Policy in Africa," *Development and Change* 18, 2 (April 1987), 197-213.

Haley, J. W. *Life in Mozambique and South Africa.* Chicago, 1926.

Hance, W. A., and I. S. van Dongen. "Lourenço Marques in Delagoa Bay." *Economic Geography* 33 (1957), 238-56.

Harries, Patrick. "The Anthropologist as Historian and Liberal: H.-A. Junod and the Thonga." *Journal of Southern African Studies* 8 (1981), 37-50.

———. "Exclusion, Classification, and Internal Colonialism: The Emergence of Ethnicity Among the Tsonga-Speakers of South Africa." In Leroy Vail, ed., *The Creation of Tribalism in Southern Africa*, 82-117. Berkeley, 1989.

———. "Kinship, Ideology and the Nature of Pre-colonial Labour Migration: Labour Migration from the Delagoa Bay Hinterland to South Africa up to 1895." In Shula Marks and Richard Rathbone, eds., *Industrialisation and Social Change in South Africa: African Class Formation, Culture and Consciousness, 1870-1930.* London, 1982.

———. "Labour Migration from Mozambique to South Africa: With Special Reference to the Delagoa Bay Hinterland." Ph.D. thesis, University of London, 1982.

————. "Production, Trade and Labour Migration from the Delagoa Bay Hinterland in the Second Half of the Nineteenth Century," [University of Cape Town] *Africa Seminar: Collected Papers*, I (1978), 28–39.

————. "The Roots of Ethnicity: Discourse and the Politics of Language Construction in South East Africa." *African Affairs*, 87 (January 1988), 25–52.

————. "Slavery, Social Incorporation and Surplus Extraction: The Nature of Free and Unfree Labour in South-East Africa." *Journal of African History* 22 (1981), 309–330.

————. "Slavery Amongst the Gaza Nguni: Its Changing Shape and Function and Its Relationship to Other Forms of Exploitation." In J. B. Peires, ed. *Before and After Shaka: Papers in Nguni History*, 210–29. Grahamstown, 1981.

Harris, Marvin. "Labour Emigration Among the Moçambique Thonga: Culture and Political Factors." *Africa* 29 (1959), 50–66.

————. "Labour Emigration Among the Moçambique Thonga: A Reply to Sr. Rita-Ferreira." *Africa* 30 (1960), 243–45.

————. "Raça, Conflito e Reforma em Moçambique," *Politica Exterior Independente* 1 (1966), 9–39.

————. "Race, Conflict and Reform in Mozambique." In Stanley Diamond and Fred G. Burke, eds., *The Transformation of East Africa: Studies in Political Anthropology*, 157–83. New York, 1966.

Hedges, David. "Educação, Missões e a Ideologia Política de Assimilação, 1930–1960." *Cadernos de História: Boletim do Departamento de História da Universidade Eduardo Mondlane* [hereafter, *Cadernos de História*] 1 (June 1985), 7–18.

————, and Aurélio Rocha, "Moçambique Durante o Apogéu do Colonialismo Português, 1945–1961: A Economia e a Estrutura Social." *Cadernos de História* 6 (1987), 29–64.

————, and Arlindo Chilundo, "História de Moçambique, Vol. III, Capítula 5: A Luta dos Camponeses e Trabalhadores a Contestação da Situação Colonial, 1945–1961." *Cadernos de História* 7 (1988), 45–90.

Heisel, Donald F. "The Indigenous Populations of the Portuguese African Territories." Ph.D. thesis, University of Michigan, Ann Arbor, 1966.

Henriksen, Thomas H. *Revolution and Counter-revolution: Mozambique's War of Independence, 1964–1974*. Westport, Conn., 1983.

Hermele, Kenneth. *Contemporary Land Struggles on the Limpopo: A Case Study of Chokwe Mozambique, 1950–1985* [AKUT, 34]. Uppsala, 1986.

Honwana, Raúl. *The Life of Raúl Honwana: An Insider's View of Mozambique: From Colonialism to Independence, 1905–1975*. Edited with an introduction by Allen F. Isaacman; translated by Tamara L. Bender. Boulder, Colo., 1988.

————. *Memórias*. Rio Tinto, 1989.

Hunt, Nancy Rose. "Placing African Women's History and Locating Gender," *Social History* 14 (1989):359–379.

Iliffe, John. "The Creation of Group Consciousness among the Dockworkers of Dar es Salaam, 1929–1950." In R. Sandbrook and R. Cohen, eds., *Development of an African Working Class*. Toronto, 1975.

"Inquerito Habitacional Realizado no Bairro da Munhuana." *Estudos de Ciências Políticas e Sociais* 72 (1964).

Isaacman, Allen F. *The Tradition of Resistance in Mozambique: Anti-Colonial Activity in the Zambesi Valley, 1850–1921* Berkeley, 1976.

Isaacman, Allen F., Michael Stephen, et al. "Cotton is the Mother of Poverty: Peasant Resistance against Forced Cotton Production, 1938–1961." *International Journal of African Historical Studies* 13, 4 (1980), 581–615.

Jeeves, Alan H. *Migrant Labour in South Africa's Mining Economy: The Struggle for the Gold Mines' Labour Supply, 1890–1920.* Kingston, 1985.

Jessett, Montague George. *The Key to South Africa: Delagoa Bay.* London,1899.

Johnson-Odim, Cheryl and Margaret Strobel. "Conceptualizing the History of Women in Africa, Asia, Latin America, the Caribbean and the Middle East." *Journal of Women's History* 1 (Spring 1989).

Johnstone, Frederick. *Race, Class and Gold: A Study in Class Relations and Racial Discrimination in South Africa.* London, 1977.

José, Alexandrino Francisco. "A Greve dos Carregadores de Estiva do Porto Commercial de Lourenço Marques em Agosto de 1963, no Contexto da Luta de Libertação Nacional de Moçambique e Alguns Problemas na Reconstrução de História do Operário Moçambicano." Licenciatura thesis, Universidade Eduardo Mondland, Maputo, 1987.

Junod, Henri A. *Les Chantes et les contes des BaRonga de la Baie de Delagoa.* Lausanne, 1897.

––––––. "The Fate of the Widows Amongst the Ba-Ronga." *Annual Report of the South African Association for the Advancement of Science.* Grahamestown, 1909.

––––––. *Grammaire Ronga, suivie d'un manuel de conversation et d'un vocabulaire Ronga-Portugais-Français-Anglais. . . .* Lausanne, 1896.

––––––. *The Life of a South African Tribe.* 2 vols. New York, 1962.

Junod, Henri-Philippe, and Alexandre A. Jaques. *Vutlhari Bya Vatsonga (Machangana): The Wisdom of the Tsonga-Shangana People.* 2nd ed. Johannesburg, 1957.

Katzenellenbogen, Simon E. *South Africa and Southern Mozambique: Labour, Railways and Trade in the Making of a Relationship.* Manchester, 1982.

Keegan, Tim. *Facing the Storm: Portaraits of Black Lives in Rural South Africa.* Athens, 1988.

Lacerda, Francisco Gavincho de. "O Trabalho Indígena em Moçambique." *Boletim da Agência Geral das Colónias* 5 (1926), 9–14.

Liesegang, Gerhard. "A First Look at the Import and Export Trade of Mozambique, 1800–1914." In G. Liesegang, H. Pasch, and A. Jones, eds., *Figuring African Trade: Proceedings of the Symposium on the Quantification and Structure of the Import and Export and Long Distance Trade of Africa in the 19th Century, (1800- 1913).* Berlin, 1987.

––––––. "Notes on the Internal Structure of the Gaza Kingdom of Southern Mozambique, 1840–1895." In J.B. Peires, ed., *Before and After Shaka: Papers in Nguni History,* 178–209. Grahamstown, 1981.

––––––. *Vassalagem ou Tratado de Amizade? História de Vassalagem de Ngungunyane nas Relações Externas de Gaza* [Estudos do Arquivo Histórico de Moçambique, 1]. Maputo, 1986.

Lobato, Alexandre. *Lourenço Marques, Xilunguíne: Biografia da Cidade. I—A Parte Antiga.* Lisbon, 1970.

––––––. "Lourenço Marques, Xilunguíne: Pequena Monografia da Cidade." *Boletim Municipal [Lourenço Marques]* 3 (1968), 7–19.

Lopes, Manuel Barnabe. "Panorama Económico e Político dos Caminhos de Ferro de Moçambique." *Revista do Gabinete de Estudos Ultramarinos* 1 (1951), 7–15.

Lopes Galvão, J. A. "O Regime de Mão de Obra Indígena em Moçambique." *Boletim de Agência Geral das Colónias*, 3 (1925), 116–28.

Lopo, Constantino de Castro. *Câmara do Comércio de Lourenço Marques, 1891–1966.* Lourenço Marques, 1966.

Lowth, Alys, ed. *Doreen Coasting.* London, 1912.

Machado, J. J. "Lourenço Marques á Pretória." *Boletim da Sociedade de Geografia de Lisboa* 11/12 (1885), 647–725.

Mackay, Wallis. *The Prisoner of Chiloane: or, with the Portuguese in South East Africa.* London, 1890.

Maia, Carlos Roma Machado de Faria e. *Guerra Anglo-Boer de 1899–1902 na Fronteira de Lourenço Marques e de Gaza.* Coimbra, 1943.

Manghezi, Alpheus. "Ku Thekela: Estratégia de Sôbre-vivência Contra a Fome no Sul de Moçambique." *Estudos Moçambicanos* 4 (1983), 19–29.

Martins, Ferreira. *João Albasini e a Colónia de S. Luis: Subsídio para a História da Província de Moçambique e as Suas Relações com o Transvaal.* Lisbon, 1957.

McLeod, Lyons. *Travels in Eastern Africa, with the Narrative of a Residence in Mozambique.* London, 1860.

Medeiros, Eduardo. "A Evolução Demográfica da Cidade de Lourenço Marques (1895–1975), Estudo Bibliográfico." *Revista Internacional de Estudos Africanos* [RIEA] 3 (1985), 231–39.

Mendes, Maria Clara. *Maputo antes da Independência: Geografia de uma Cidade Colonial.* Lisbon, 1985.

Mendonça, Fatima. *Literatura Moçambicana: A História e as Escritas.* Maputo, 1988.

Middlemas, Robert Keith. *Cabora Bassa: Engineering and Politics in Southern Africa.* London, 1975.

———. "Twentieth Century White Society in Moçâmbique." *Tarikh* 6, 2 (1979), 30–45.

Mondlane, Eduardo. *The Struggle for Mozambique.* Baltimore, 1969.

Monteiro, Rose. *Delagoa Bay: Its Natives and Natural History.* London, 1891.

Moreira, José da Silva. "A Imprensa dos Albasinis." licenciatura thesis, Universidade Eduardo Mondlane, 1982.

Morris, Martha Binford. "Rjonga Settlement Patterns, Meaning and Implications." *Anthropological Quarterly* 45 (1972), 217–31.

Moser, Gerald, and Manuel Ferreira. *Bibliografia das Literaturas Africanas de Expressão Portuguesa.* Lisbon, 1983.

Neves, Diocleciano Fernandes das. *Itinerário de Uma Viagem á Caça dos Elephantes.* Lisbon, 1878.

Neves, Olga Maria Lopes Serrão Inglesias. "Em Defesa da Causa Africana: Intervenção do Grêmio Africano na Sociedade de Lourenço Marques, 1908–1938." Master's thesis, Universidade Novado Lisboa, 1989.

Newitt, M. D. D. "Mine Labour and the Development of Mozambique." *Societies of Southern Africa in the 19th and 20th Centuries* 4 (1974), 67–76.

———. *Portugal in Africa: The Last Hundred Years.* Essex, 1981.

Northey, Margaret Elizabeth. *General Joaquim José Machado: A Selective Bibliography.* Johannesburg, 1970.

Noronha, Eduardo de. *O Distrito de Lourenço Marques e a Africa do Sul.* Lisbon, 1895.

———. *A Rebellião dos Indígenas de Lourenço Marques.* Lisbon, 1894.

Pacheco, António. "Lourenço Marques—Dificuldades do Passado—Responsabilidades de Hoje—Problemas do Futuro." [*Collected Papers of the*] *Congresso da Sociedade de Estudos da Colónia de Moçambique* 3 (1947).

————. "Lourenço Marques na Última Década du Século XIX." *Boletim da Sociedade de Estudos de Moçambique* 31 (1962), 7–58.

Pélissier, René. *Naissance du Mozambique: Résistance et Révoltes Anticoloniales (1854-1918).* 2 vols. Orgeval, 1984.

Penvenne, Jeanne Marie. "'Here Everyone Walked with Fear!' The Mozambican Labor System and the Workers of Lourenço Marques, 1945–1962." In Frederick Cooper, ed., *Struggle for the City: Migrant Labor, Capital, and the State in Urban Africa,* 131–66. Berkeley, 1983.

————. "Labor Struggles at the Port of Lourenço Marques, 1900–1933." *Review* 8 (1984), 249–85.

————. "Principles and Passion: Capturing the Legacy of João dos Santos Albasini." Boston University *Discussion Papers in the African Humanities,* 12 (Boston, 1991).

————. "'We are all Portuguese!' Challenging the Political Economy of Assimilation, Lourenço Marques, 1870–1933." In Leroy Vail, ed., *The Creation of Tribalism in Southern Africa,* 255–88. Berkeley, 1989.

Pereira, Rui. "Colonialismo e Antropologia: A Especulação Simbólica." *RIEA,* 10/11 (1989), 269–81.

Pereira Leite, Joana. "La Formation de l'Économie Coloniale au Mozambique; Pacte Colonial et Industrialisation; du Colonialisme Portugias aux Réseaux Informels de Sujétion Marchande, 1930–1974." Doctorat, Ecole des Uautes Etudes en Sciences Sociales, Paris, 1989.

Pereira de Lima, Alfredo. *Edifícios Históricos de Lourenço Marques.* Lourenço Marques, 1966.

————. *História dos Caminhos de Ferro de Moçambique.* 3 vols. Lourenço Marques, 1971.

————. *O Palácio Municipal de Lourenço Marques.* Lourenço Marques, 1967.

————. "Para um Estudo da Evolução Urbana de Lourenço Marques." *Boletim Municipal* 7 (1967).

Personal Narratives Group. *Interpreting Women's Lives; Feminist Theory and Personal Narratives.* Bloomington, 1989.

Pirio, Gregory. "Commerce, Industry and Empire: The Making of Modern Portuguese Colonialism in Angola and Mozambique, 1890–1914." Ph.D. thesis, University of California at Los Angeles, 1982.

Pitcher, Ann. "Sewing the Seeds of Failure: Early Portuguese Cotton Cultivation in Angola and Mozambique, 1820–1936." *JSAS* 17, 1 (1991), 43–70.

"Portuguese Colonies." *Annuaire de Documentation Coloniale Comparée,* 1 (1928), 469–775.

Quintinha, Julião, and Francisco Toscano. *A Derrocado do Império Vátua e Mousinho d'Albuquerque.* 3rd ed. Lisbon, 1935.

Ranger, T. O. "Audiences and Alliances." *Southern African Review of Books* (May/June, 1991): 4–5.

Reis, Carlos Santos. *A População de Lourenço Marques em 1894: Um Censo Inédito.* Lisbon, 1973.

República Popular de Moçambique, Ministério de Educação. *Atlas Geográfico,* Vol. 1, 2nd ed. Stockholm, 1986.

Ribeiro, José Caramona. *Sumários do Boletim Oficial de Moçambique, 1855–1965.* Lourenço Marques, n.d.

Rita Ferreira, António. "Os Africanos de Lourenço Marques." *Memórias do Instituto de Investigações Científicas de Moçambique* 9, C (1967–1968), 95–491.

————. "Demografia da População Africana de Lourenço Marques." *Indústria de Moçambique* II, 5 (May 1969), 143–74.

"The Ethno-History and the Ethnic Groupings of the Peoples of Moçambique." *South African Journal of African Affairs* 3 (1973), 56–76.

————. *Evolução de Mão de Obra e das Remunerações no Sector Privado em Moçambique desde 1950 á 1970: Análise da Situação Cambial de Moçambique.* Lourenço Marques, 1971.

————. "Labour Emigration among the Moçambique Thonga: Comments on a Study by Marvin Harris." *Africa* 30 (1960), 141–42.

————. "Labour Emigration among the Moçambique Thonga: Comments on Marvin Harris's Reply." *Africa* 31 (1961), 75–77.

————. "A Oscilação do Trabalhador Africano entre o Meio Rural e o Meio Urbano." *Indústria de Moçambique* 2 (March 1969), 96–99.

Rocha, Ilídio. *Catálogo dos Periódicos e Principais Seriados de Moçambique. . . .* Lisbon, 1985.

————. *Das Terras do Império Vátua as Praças da Republica Boer.* Lisbon, 1987.

Rodrigues Júnior. *Transportes de Moçambique.* Lisbon, 1956.

Roesch, Otto. "Migrant Labour and Forced Rice Production in Southern Mozambique: The Colonial Peasantry of the Lower Limpopo Valley." *JSAS* 17, 2 (June 1991), 239–70.

Ross, Edward Alsworth. *Report on the Employment of Native Labor in Portuguese Africa.* New York, 1925.

Sá Nogueira, Rodrigo de. *Dicionário Ronga Português.* Lisbon, 1960.

Saldanha, Eduardo d'Almeida. *O Problema de Moçambique: Artigos Publicados pelo Journal de Commércio e das Colónias de Setembro á Novembro 1923.* Lisbon, 1923.

————. *Questões Nacionais: O Sul do Save.* Lisbon,1928.

Santos, Manuel Pimental Pereira dos. *A Indústria em Moçambique.* Lourenço Marques, 1956.

Santos, Rui Martins dos. *Uma Contribuição para a Análise de Economia de Moçambique.* Lisbon, 1959.

Santos Rufino, José dos. *Albuns Fotográficos e Descritivos da Colónia de Moçambique.* Hamburg, 1929.

Scott, James C. *The Moral Economy of the Peasant: Rebellion and Subsistence in Southeast Asia.* New Haven, 1976.

————. *The Weapons of the Weak: Everyday Forms of Peasant Resistance.* New Haven, 1985.

Sheldon, Kathleen E. "Sewing Clothes and Sorting Cashew Nuts: Factories, Families and Women in Beira, Mozambique." *Women's Studies International Forum* 14, 1/2 (1991), 27–35.

Silva, Alfredo Henrique de. *Um Error de Justiça de que se tem sido Víctima Roberto Ndevu Mashaba. . . .* Porto, 1897.

Silva, Clemente Nunes. *Lourenço Marques: Escandalos da Administração Municipal por um Municipe.* n.p., 1897.

Silva, Maria da Conceição Tavares Lourenço da Silva. "As Missões Católicas Femininas." *Estudos de Ciências Políticas e Sociais* 37 (1960), 49–77.

Soares, Paulo, and Valdemir Zamparoni. "Antologia de Textos do Jornal 'O Africano'

(1908-1919)." *Estudos Afro-Asiaticos* 22 (September 1992), 127-78.

Sopa, António Jorge Diniz. "Catálogo dos Periódicos Moçambicanos Procedide de uma Pequena Notícia Histórica: 1854-1954."licenciatura thesis. Universidade Eduardo Mondlane, 1985.

Stichter, Sharon. *Migrant Laborers.* Cambridge, 1985.

Tristão de Bettencourt, José. *Relatório do Governador Geral de Moçambique: Respeitante ao Período de 20 Março de 1940 á 31 de Dezembro, 1942.* 2 vols. Lisbon, 1945.

Tullner, Mathias. "Apontamentos sobre a Greve de 1917 no Porto e Caminhos de Ferro de Lourenço Marques." *Arquívo* 9 (April 1991), 45-58.

Urdang, Stephanie. "Rural Transformation and Peasant Women in Mozambique. *International Laboour Office Working Paper.* Geneva, 1986.

Vail, Leroy, ed. *The Creation of Tribalism in Southern Africa.* Berkeley, 1988.

Vail, Leroy, and Landeg White. *Capitalism and Colonialism in Mozambique: A Study of Quelimane District.* Minneapolis, 1980.

———. *Power and the Praise Poem: Southern African Voices in History.* Charlottesville, 1991.

van Butselaar, Jan. *Africains, Missionnaires et Colonialistes: Les Origines de l'Église Presbytérienne du Mozambique (Mission suisse) 1880-1896.* Leiden, 1984.

van Onselen, Charles. *Chibaro: African Mine Labour in Southern Rhodesia, 1900-1930.* London, 1976.

———. *Studies in the Social and Economic History of the Witwatersrand, 1886-1914.* 2 vols. London, 1982.

Vaughan, G. Edgar. *Portuguese East Africa: Economic and Commercial Conditions in Portuguese East Africa [Mozambique], October, 1951.* London, 1952.

Vaughan, Megan. *The Story of an African Famine.* Cambridge, 1987.

Vieira, Salamão. "Os Electricos de Lourenço Marques I: 1900-1920." *Arquivo* 9 (April 1991), 5-44.

Walker, Cherryl, ed. *Women and Gender in Southern Africa to 1945.* London, 1990.

Warhurst, Philip R. *Anglo-Portuguese Relations in South-Central Africa, 1890-1900.*

Webster, David. "Migrant Labour, Social Formations and the Proletarianization of the Chopi of Southern Mozambique." *African Perspectives,* 1 (1978), 156-63.

Wheeler, Douglas L. "Gungunhana." In Norman R. Bennett, ed., *Leadership in Eastern Africa: Six Political Biographies.* Boston, 1968.

White, Luise. *The Comforts of Home: Prostitution in Colonial Nairobi.* Chicago, 1990.

Young, Sherilynn J. "Changes in Diet and Production in Southern Mozambique, 1855-1960," paper presented at the [British] African Studies Association Conference, Edinburgh, 1976.

———. "Fertility and Famine: Women's Agricultural History in Southern Mozambique." In Robin Palmer and Neal Parsons, eds., *The Roots of Rural Poverty in Central and Southern Africa,* 66-81. Berkeley, 1977.

———. "What Have They Done With The Rain?: 20th Century Transformations in Southern Mozambique with Particular Reference to Rain Prayers." Paper presented at the [U.S.] African Studies Association Annual Meeting, Baltimore, 1978.

———. "Women in Transition: Southern Mozambique, 1875-1976." Paper presented at the Conference on the History of Women, St. Paul, Minnesota, 1977.

Yudelman, David, and Alan Jeeves, "New Labour Frontiers for Old: Black Migrants to the South African Gold Mines, 1920-1985." *JSAS* 13 (1986), 101-124.

Zamparoni, Valdemir D. "A Imprensa Negra em Moçambique: A Trajectoria de 'O

Africano' 1908–1920." *Africa: Revista do Centro de Estudos Africanos* [São Paulo] II, 1 (1988), 73–86.

Published Documents

Câmara Municipal de Lourenço Marques. *Actas da Câmara Municipal de Lourenço Marques*. Lourenço Marques, 1890-1930.

"Casos de Peste em Lourenço Marques, 10 Dezembro 1907." *Relatórios e Investigações Anexxo ao Boletim Official*. Lourenço Marques, 1908.

Circumscrições de Lourenço Marques. *Relatórios das Circunscrições: Distrito de Lourenço Marques, 1909-1910, 1911-1912, 1912-1913*. Lourenço Marques, 1911, 1912, 1915.

———. *Respostas aos Quesitos Feitos pelo Secretaria de Negócios Indígenas, Dr. Francisco Ferrão para a Confecção do Relatório Sôbre o Distrito de Lourenço Marques*. Lourenço Marques, 1909.

Comissão Provincial de Nutrição. "Inquerito Nutricional e Alimental á 292 Operários Indígenas da Fábrica de Cimentos da Matola e Suas Famílias." Lourenço Marques, 1960.

Compilation of Legislation Affecting Labour . . . Immigration. Lourenço Marques, 1939.

Conselho do Governo. *Actas do Conselho do Governo*.

Curador dos Indígenas Portuguêsas no Transvaal. *Relatório do Curador dos Indígenas Portuguêsas no Transvaal, 1924-1925*. Lisbon, 1926.

Direcção Conselho da Administração do Porto e dos Caminhos de Ferro de Lourenço Marques. *Ano Económico, 1926 through 1935*. Lourenço Marques, 1928-1936.

Direcção do Porto e Caminho de Ferro de Lourenço Marques. *Relatório da Direcção do Porto e Caminho de Ferro de Lourenço Marques*. 1906–1908, 1910,1912, 1936–1960, incomplete.

———. *Estatística dos Caminhos de Ferro de 1888 á 1910*. Lourenço Marques, 1912.

———. *Relatório Anual dos Serviços da Exploração do Caminho de Ferro e do Porto*. Louenço Marques, 1914.

Direcção dos Portos, Caminhos de Ferro e Transportes de Moçambique. *Boletim do Porto, Caminhos de Ferro e Transportes de Moçambique*. [Supplemento, July 1970].

Ordem da Província do Sul do Save. Incomplete collection, Lourenço Marques.

Regulamento do Trabalho dos Indígenas na Colónia de Moçambique: Aprovado por Portaria no. 1,180 de 4 de Setembro de 1930. Lourenço Marques, 1930.

Relatório da Inspecção das Circunscrições do Distrito de Louenço Marques, Ano 1914- 1915. Lourenço Marques, 1916.

Relatórios e Informações Anexxo ao Boletim Oficial, 1908. Lourenço Marques, 1908.

Repatrição Técnica de Estatística. *Anuário Estatística, 1926/27-1962*. Lourenço Marques, 1928-1963.

———. *Censo da População em 1940*. Lourenço Marques, 1944.

———. *Estatística Indústrial, 1947-1965*. Lourenço Marques, 1950–1966.

———. *Inquérito Estatístico de 1937-1938*. Lourenço Marques, 1941.

———. *Recenseamento Geral da População em 1950, III: População Não Civilizada*. Lourenço Marques 1955.

———. *Recenseamento Geral da População na Província de Moçambique, 1960, I: Distrito de Lourenço Marques*. Lourenço Marques, 1960.

Secretária Geral do Governo Geral da Província de Moçambique. *Recenseamento da População e das Habitações da Cidade de Lourenço Marques e Seus Subúrbios. Referidos*

á 1 de Dezembro de 1912. Lourenço Marques, 1913.
Secretaria Geral de Moçambique. *Relatório da Secretaria Geral de Moçambique, 1910.* Lourenço Marques, 1911.
Serviços de Saude de Lourenço Marques. "Relatório do Serviço de Saude de Lourenço Marques ao Anno de 1886." *Archivos Médicos Coloniães* 1 (1890), 45–86.

Yearbooks and Newspapers

O Africano, 1908–1919
O Africano, Almanaque Humoristico e Ilustrado, 1910–1919
Anuário de Lourenço Marques [formerly *Delagoa Directory*], 1914–1940
O Brado Africano, 1918–1963
A Cidade, 1919
O Commércio de Lourenço Marques, 1893
Correio de Lourenço Marques, 1925–1926
Delagoa Directory [becomes *Anuário de Lourenço Marques*], 1899–1913
O Diário, 1943
Diário de Notícias, 1906–1910
O Distrito, 1905
Distrito de Lourenço Marques, 1888, 1899, and 1904–05
O Emancipador, 1919–1927, 1933–1934
O Futuro, 1894–1909
O Heraldo, 1910
O Incondicional, 1910–1920
O Intransigente, 1911
Journal das Colónias, 1880–1882
Jornal de Commércio [becomes *Jornal de Comércio*], 1920–1923
Lourenço Marques Guardian, 1905–1933, 1947–1962
O Mignon, 1902–1905
Mozambique Gazette, 1907–1913
Notícias, 1947–1962
O Progresso, 1901–1905
O Simples, 1911
Transvaal Leader, 1910
A Tribuna, 1907
União, 1933–1938
A Vanguarda, 1903

Annex I
Oral Interview Material

Port and Railway Formal Interviews

Name, Date and Place of Birth, Date of Interview
All Port and Railway Interviews Conducted at Secção dos Cais, Maputo

Baza, Raul Carlos. Lourenço Marques, 1930. 15 June 1977.
Bié, Amossé Lazaro. Mchopes, 1944. 21 June 1977.
Brito, Francisco Guilherme de. Lourenço Marques, 1915. 27 June (a), 5 July 1977 (b).
Chibindji, Bandi Albasini. Chibuto, 1910. 16 June 1977.
Comiché, Timóteo. Inharrime, 1917. 18 June 1977.
Cossa, José Mahandulane. Xai-Xai, 1913. 18 June 1977.
Costa, Joaquim da. Lourenço Marques, 1899. 15 June (a), 16 June (b), 5 July (c), 24 August (d) 25 August (e), 11 Nov. 1977 (f).
Cuna, José. Manjacaze, 1937. 15 June 1977.
Grazina, João Rodrigues da Silva. Portugal, 1895, 16 July 1977.
Gulele, Juta Vane. Inharrime, 1936. 15 June 1977.
Júlio, João. Beira, 1917. 16 June 1977.
Langa, Eugénio. Manjacaze, 1921. 18 June 1977.
Mabunda, Gabriel. Chibuto, 1934. 10 June 1977.
Macaringue, Njone Boavida. Gaza, 1931. 18 June 1977.
Matusse, Eugénio André. Manjacaze, 1922. 16 June 1977.
Novunga, Ananias Daniel. Manjacaze, 1932. 17 June 1977.
Sibia, Arrone Justino. Zavala, 1923. 21 June 1977.
Simango, Francisco Matequeza. 1922, Moamba. 17 June 1977.
Tembe, Manuel João dos Santos. Matola, 1913. 18 June 1977.
Tembe, Roberto. Catembe, 1896. 15 June (a), 16 June (b), 5 July (c), 24 August (d), 25

August (e), 12 November (f) 1977.
Zuana, Silvestre José. Chibuto, 1920. 17 June 1977.

Informal Interviews at Port

Muhate, Isaíhas. 9 June 1977.
Santos, Alexandre Vitor. 9 June 1977.

Câmara Municipal de Maputo Formal Interviews

All Câmara interviews were conducted at Câmara Municipal de Maputo. Gaspar Salamão Guevende, grupo dinimizador da Câmara Municipal de Maputo, assisted in organizing these interviews. He personally conducted about ten and assisted in translation and analysis of difficult translations.

Name, Date and Place of Birth, Date of Interview

Bucane, Magumane Jojo. Chibuto, 1906, 7 July 1977.
Capitine, Cirilo. Inharrime, 1913. 6 July 1977.
Chichango, Sianai Lakene. Morrumbene, 1914. 1 July 1977.
Chondela, Francisco Tovele. Manjacaze, 1918. 14 July 1977.
Cossa, Manuel. Xai-Xai, 1910. 12 July 1977.
Cumbe, Alfeu Tualofo. Zavala, 1914. 4 July 1977.
Faleca, Pedro Palechane. Inharrime, 1929. 7 July 1977.
Guambe, Andela Faduco. Inharrime, 1909. 15 July 1977.
Inguane, Manuel Sihalo. Manjacaze, 1917. 13 July 1977.
Jeque, Inácio dos Santos. Inharrime, 1922. 5 July 1977.
Kuamba, Arnaldo Tombane. Morrumbene, 1916. 5 July 1977.
Kuamba, Joaquim Hafo. Panda, 1926. 7 July 1977.
Macaneo, Cumbiane José. Chibuto, 1917. 5 July 1977.
Machanga, João Ndoconga. Beira, 1891. 15 July 1977.
Macuacua, Valente Mucocuane. Manjacaze, 1909. 7 July 1977.
Mafuane, Marcelino Welamo. Homoine, 1910. 1 July 1977.
Mahumane, Julião Mangane. Manhica 1902. 6 July 1977.
Maluane, Benjamin Mavimbe. Maputo, ca. 1900. 1 July 1977.
Mambiro, António Menete. Morrumbene, 1912. 2 July 1977.
Manguese, Januário Pene. Morrumbene, 1914. 14 July 1977.
Manhica, Sozinho Jelene. Xai-Xai, 1907. 1 July 1977.
Marangue, João Bande. Panda, 1918. 6 July 1977.
Mondlane, Fausto Chekefane. Manjacaze, 1921. 4 July 1977.
Mondlane, Jacinto Bobo. Manjacaze, 1922. 1 July 1977.
Muando, Francisco Machambana. Inhambane, 1910. 4 July 1977.
Muconto, Flor Fanequisso. Manjacaze 1910. 15 July 1977.
Muchanga, Muzuamfo Tiago. Chibuto, 1908. 2 July 1977.
Mufana, Pequenino Langa. Homoine, 1913. 4 July 1977.

Muianga, Ernesto Machalucuane. Xai-Xai, 1923. 4 July 1977.
Muianga, Samuel Chipoco. Lourenco Marques 1930. 19 July 1977.
Muianga, Zagueu Uaziweiane. Manjacaze, ca. 1910, 1 July 1977.
Mussana, Mussongueia Samuel. Chibuto, ca. 1874. 4 July (a), 3 October 1977 (b).
Nandje, Fernando Mussuaze. Manhica, 1908. 2 July 1977.
Nguenha, Magumane Pequenino. Maxixe, 1922. 15 July 1977.
Nhabanga, Valente Pande. Marracuene, 1910. 11 July 1977.
Nhalivilo, Alberto Toume. Inharrime, 1926. 7 July 1977.
Nhangumbe, Daniel Tene. Inharrime, 1909. 1 July 1977.
Nhaposse, Augusto Muando. Inhambane, 1925. 6 July 1977.
Nhuache, Fernando. Inhambane, 1909. 8 July 1977.
Nuvunga, Issaca Seteteane. Zavala, 1899. 1 July 1977.
Paulo, Mussengane Titosse Neves. Massinga, ca. 1925. 6 July 1977.
Samora, Joaquim Francisco. Maputo, 1919. 11 July 1977.
Setete, António José. Inharrime, 1930. 7 July 1977.
Sumbane, Joaquim. Macia, 1906. 4 July 1977.
Tambajam, Castigo Mahache Tambajam. Zavala, 1910. 2 July 1977.
Tembe, António Gabriel. Catembe, 1913. 6 and 11 July 1977.
Tembe, Saul. Catembe, 1924. 7 June 1977.
Tinga, Francisco Muange. Maxixe, 1922. 6 July 1977.
Uinge, Sechene Romisene. Homoine, 1900. 8 July 1977.
Zavala, Enoque Samboco. Inharrime, 1907. 2 July 1977.
Zavala, Felisberto Guiliche. Inharrime, 1918. 13 July 1977.
Zonda, Machuza. Chibuto, 1905. 15 July 1977.

Other Informants—Formal and Informal Interviews

Name, Place of Birth (if mentioned), Date and Place of Interview

Albasini, Ambrosia Crisostomo Pacheco. 30 July (a), 4 August 1989 (b), Porto, Portugal.
Albasini, Lucas Francisco. 7 August 1989, Lisbon, Portugal.
Albasini, Rudolfo da Silva. Lourenço Marques, 1932. 30 July (a), 4 August 1989 (b), Porto, Portugal.
Banze, Júlio. 10 October 1977, Maputo.
Chande, Ana Paulo Crisostomo Albasini. 30 July (a), 4 August (b),1989, Porto, Portugal.
Chande, Gulamo. 4 August 1989, Porto, Portugal.
Chamisso, Alfredo. 30 May 1977, Câmara de Comércio de Maputo.
Fernanda, Emília Ochoa Avêz. 7 August 1989, Lisbon, Portugal.
Fonseca, João Távares de. 4 August 1989, Porto, Portugal.
Hoffman, Andrée. 31 May 1977, Swiss Missions Complex, Maputo.
LeMay, Basil. Republic of South Africa, 9 May 1977, Polana section of Maputo.
Mainga, Vicente Pande. Chibuto 1917. 11 November (a), 12 November (b) 1977, Arquivo Histórico de Moçambique.
Manhica, João António. 10 October 1977, Administração do Concelho de Maputo.
Moreira, Josê da Silva. 10 November 1977, Maputo.

Muiane, Amélia Alfredo. Lourenço Marques, 1931. 13 September 1977, Câmara Municipal de Maputo.

Mulimua, Abel. 7 June (a), 10 September (b) 1977, Maputo.

Navesse, Bento T. 1 June 1977, Alto Mahé section of Maputo.

Nhaca, Nicodemus Salamão. Lourenço Marques, 1914. 11 October 1977, Arquivo Histórico de Moçambique.

Sarna, Dona. 2 November 1977, Maternidade de Matola.

Spence, David. Republic of South Africa, 9 May 1977, Polana section of Maputo.

Serra Ventosa, Sr. 7 June (a), 29 June (b) 1977, Câmara Municipal de Maputo.

Tembe, Lídia Felizmina. Lourenço Marques, 1917. 2 November 1977, Maternidade de Matola.

Zombole, Paulo. 9 September 1977, Maputo.

Annex II
Mozambican Worksongs

The worksong component of oral data collection was conducted in conjunction with the Câmara Municipal de Maputo group, and was assisted by Gaspar Salamão Guevende. Guevende and Paulo Zombole both worked on original language translation into Portuguese. The original translation was Guevende's, and Zombole corroborated the work. My translations into English are intended to convey the sense of the song, with apologies to the elegance of the original language. All songs were taped and the tapes were deposited at the Arquivo Histórico de Moçambique and the language laboratory of Harvard University in Cambridge, Massachusetts.

Shibalo muni magandana[1]

Shibalo muni magandana, ho . . .
   ho magandana, ho . . .
Shibalo muni magandana, ho . . .
   Shibalo muni magandana ho . . .
Xa kukhoma ni vavasati, ho . . .
   nafa babooo, ho . . .
Shibalo muni magandana, ho . . .
   niku wisa ahi sikoti, ho . . .
Shibalo muni magandana, ho . . .
   xa kukhoma ni vavasati, ho . . .
Xa kukhoma ni vakokhuana, ho . .
   xa ku tirha ni vamamana, ho . . .
Shibalo muni magandana, ho . . .
   si kolonhi sa hidlaya, ho . . .
Shibalo muni magandana, ho . . .
   xa kukhoma ni vakokhuana, ho . . .
Xa kukhoma ni vo vavovo, ho . . .

Shibalo muni magandana, ho . . .
Shibalo muni magandana, ho . . .
ni ku wisa ahi sikoti, ho . . .
Hi ta wisa mukama muni, ho . . .
Shibalo muni magandana ho . . .
A mu fambi muya kanwina, ho . . .
Hi ta fa hina magandana, ho . . .
Shibalo muni magandana, ho . . .
xa ku tirha na vapapai, ho . . .
Xa ku tirha ni vamamana, ho . . .
xa ku tirha ni vamakueenu, ho . . .
Xa ku tirha na vamamana, ho . . .

What Kind of Shibalo Is This of Magandana?*
*Magandana is an evil person

What kind of *shibalo* is this of Magandana, ho . . .
Ho . . . Magandana, ho . . .
What kind of *shibalo* is this of Magandana ho . . .
It catches everyone, even the women, ho . . .
What kind of *shibalo* is this of Magandana, ho . . .
It catches everyone, even the women, ho . . .
I am dying, my father, ho . . .
What kind of *shibalo* is this of Magandana, ho . . .
They don't even let us rest, ho . . .
What kind of *shibalo* is this of Magandana, ho . . .
It catches everyone, even the women, ho . . .
It catches everyone, even the grandparents, ho . . .
We are put to [road] work with our mothers, ho . . .
What kind of *shibalo* is this of Magandana, ho . . .
The settlers are trying to kill us, ho . . .
What kind of *shibalo* is this of Magandana, ho . . .
It catches everyone, even our grandparents, ho . . .
What kind of *shibalo* is this of Magandana, ho . . .
What kind of *shibalo* is this of Magandana, ho . . .
They don't even let us rest, ho . . .
When will we be allowed to rest, ho . . .
What kind of *shibalo* is this of Magandana, ho . . .
Why don't you go back to your country, ho . . .
We are killing ourselves, Magandana, ho . . .
What kind of *shibalo* is this of Magandana, ho . . .
We are put to [road] work with our parents, ho . . .
We are put to work with our mothers, ho . . .
We are put to work with our sisters and brothers, ho . . .
We are put to work with our mothers, ho . . .

Some alternate versions also include laments about *magaiça* (migrant mineworkers) who return to their homeland and court the wives of absent *shibalo* workers. The *magaiça* allegedly take advantage of the absent man's hospitality. The *magaiça* entertain with gifts and money, while *shibalo* return home empty-handed.

Kamanuel Mendes[2]

Kamanuel Mendes siyambala masaka ngululene
Ayi, Mende-Bo, ia wo muthandha kajane

Kamanuel Mendes, siyambala masaka ngululene
Kamanuel Mendes, ia wo muthandha kajane
Wo muthandha. . .
Kamanuel Mendes, ia . . . wo muthandha kanjane
Siyambala masaka nugululene
Kamanuel Mendes, ia . . . wo muthandha kanjane

Wo muthandha . . . wo muthandha
Kamanuel Mendes, ia wo muthandha kanjane
Siyambala masaka ngululene,
Kamanuel Mendes, ia wo muthandha kanjane.

Manuel Mendes

Oh Manuel Mendes, dresses us in pig sacks.
Ah Mendes, old boy, you enjoy doing it, don't you Mendes!

Oh Manuel Mendes, dresses us in pig sacks.
Ah Mendes, old boy, you enjoy doing it, don't you Mendes!

You enjoy it . . .
Manuel Mendes . . . you enjoy it!
Dress us in pig sacks.
Manuel Mendes . . . you enjoy it, don't you, Mendes!

You enjoy it!
Enjoy it!
Manuel Mendes, you enjoy it!
Dressing us in pig sacks, how you enjoy doing it, Mendes!

Manuel Mendes was an important Portuguese settler/trader, headquartered in Xai-Xai. He was in the import/export business, handling agricultural products, wines, building materials, and all sorts of retail goods. He also had his own water and land transportation businesses by World War I. He employed *shibalo* workers on his farms and dressed them in the burlap sack cloth from the animal fodder he handled in his trade.

Xiphukuphuku xa Mulunguana[3]

Xiphukuphuku xa mulunguana xi fana na mani, xamulunguana
Xiphukuphuku xa mulunguana xi fana na mani, xamulunguana
Khale hiku sevendzela a wu na themba, xamulunguana
Xiphukuphuku xa mulunguana, hayi . . . hayi . . . xamulunguana

Khale hiku sevendzela a wu na themba, xamulunguana
Xiphukuphuku xamulunguana, hayi . . . hayi . . . xamulunguana
Ah xamulunguana hayi . . . hayi . . . xamulunguana
Khale hiku sevendzela a wu na themba, xamulunguana
Xiphukuphuku xa mulunguana hayi . . . hayi . . . xamulunguana
Xiphukuphuku xa mulunguana xi khale na themba, xamulunguana

Khale hiku sevendzela a wu na themba, xamulunguana
Xiphukuphuku xa mulunguana sevendze kanjani, xamulunguana
Ah xamulunguana, a wu na themba, xamulunguana

Xiphukuphuku xa mulunguana sevendze kanjani, xamulunguana
Xiphukuphuku xa mulunguana sevendze kanjani, xamulunguana
Khale hiku sevendzela a wu na themba, xamulunguana

Crazy Little Whiteman

You crazy little whiteman, you are seeing ghosts, little whiteman
You crazy little whiteman, you are seeing ghosts, little whiteman
We've worked for you for a long time, but you don't dare trust us, little
    whiteman
You crazy little whiteman, hayi . . . hayi . . . little whiteman.
We've worked for you a long time, but you don't dare trust us, little white-
    man.

You crazy little whiteman, hayi . . . hayi . . . little whiteman
You little whiteman, hayi . . . hayi . . . little whiteman
You crazy little whiteman, hayi . . . hayi . . . little whiteman
We've worked for you a long time, but you don't dare trust us, little white-
    man.

You crazy little whiteman, how can you work like that, little whiteman?
We've worked for you a long time, but you don't dare trust us, little white-
    man
You crazy little whiteman, how can you work like that, little whiteman?
You little whiteman, you don't dare trust us, little whiteman.

You crazy little whiteman, how can you work like that, little whiteman?
You crazy little whiteman, how can you work like that, little whiteman?
We've worked for you a long time, but you don't dare trust us, little white-
    man.

This song was sung by Mozambican prison laborers on São Tomé. The workers mock
the authoritarian, but frightened little white overseer who bullies them around, but
still does not dare to turn his back on them.

Lokuvaku Lanja[4]

Loku vaku lanja, lanja ka wena—lanja
Loku vaku lanja, lanja ka wena—lanja
Loku vaku lanja, lanja ka wena —lanja

Maputukezi i male mi baku leyi— lanja
Maputukezi i male ma Ntxontxaku leyi —lanja
Maputukezi i male ma Ntxontxaku leyi— lanja

Loku vaku lanja, lanja ka wena —lanja
Loku vaku xhova, xhova ka wena— xhova
Loku vaku lanja, lanja ka wena— lanja

Maputukezi i male mintxo ntxaku leyi— lanja
Maputukezi i male miyivaku leyi —lanja

When They Say "Heave That Shovel"—Heave

When they say "Heave that shovel," shovel— heave
When they say "Heave that shovel," shovel— heave
When they say "Heave that shovel," shovel— heave

The Portuguese live by stealing our wages— heave
The Portuguese live by stealing our wages— heave
The Portuguese live by stealing our wages— heave

The song is timed to accompany shovelling coal or sand, with the refrain, lanja, similar to the English word heave. The sharp sounds and rhythm combine so well, one can almost smell the coal dust and sweat.

Wayiwona[5]

Wayiwona wa koka misava hiyoleyi nwananga . . . Wayiwona
 koka misava hiyoleyi Baba . . .
Wayiwona wa koka misava hiyoleyi
 Rhuala! . . . Rhuala! . . . Satanhoca ndziwena!
Wayiwona wa koka misava hiyoleyi nwananga . . . Wayiwona
 koka misava hileyo nwananga.

Wayiwona yo koka misava phumela nwanda. . . Wayiwona
 Wayiwona . . . Tirha! . . . Tirha! . . . Wufa! . . . Tirha Wufa!
Wayiwona yo koka misava miyela nwananga . . . Wayiwona
 Koka misava miyela nwananga . . .
Wayiwona wa koka misava hileyo nwananga . . . Wayiwona

You Will See, My Son

You will see, you are shovelling sand, you are here my son. . . .
 You will see.
 I am shovelling sand here, my father
You will see, you are here shovelling sand, you are here. . . .
 Get Going! Get Going! . . . Devil snake Ndziwena!
You will see, you are shovelling sand, my son . . . you will see.
 Shovel sand since you are here, my son.
You will see, shovelling sand, accept it my son . . . you will see.

You will see, you . . . Work! Work! . . . Die! . . . Work to Death!
You will see, you are shovelling sand, be calm my son . . . you will see.
  Shovel sand, be calm my son.
You will see, you are shovelling sand, you are here my son . . . you will see.

This is sung to roadwork. The older workers, the fathers, warn the inexperienced, their sons–either literally or figuratively–to work calmly despite the insults
and the demands so that they will survive the hard work without permanent injury.

Celina[6]

Wawuya Celina . . . wawuya Celina
Wawuya satiwamina ho . . . Celina.

Ho Celina . . . ha Celina . . . ahe Celi . . . ho Celina
Ndzi xavela zikatawa ndzi xavela satiwamina
kasi lingualavani . . . ho Celina.

Khume ga malembe ndzi lowola satiwamina
kasi ligueleguele . . . ho Celina
Va kufamba Celina . . . ho Celina . . . ahe Celi . . . ho Celina
Va kuho Celi . . . e Celi . . . ahe Celi . . . ho Celina.

Ndzi xavela nwamanarhu ndxi xavela satiwamina
kasi lingualavani ho . . . Celina
Ndzi xavela zikatawu ndzi xavela satiwamina
Kasi ligueleguele . . . ho Celina.

Khume gamalembe ndzi lowola satiwamina . . . ahe Celi . . . ho Celina
Ntlanu wa malembe ndzi lowola Celi, ahe Celi . . . ho Celina
Ho kufamba saina ooo . . . Celina . . . ahe Celi . . . ho Celina
Vari famba Celina . . . Celina . . . ahe Celi . . . .ho Celina

Ndxi xavele nwamanarhu ndxi savela Celi . . . Kasi lingualho . . . ho Celi
Ndzi xavele zikatawu ndxi xavela satiwamina, kasi ligueleguele . . . ho
    Celina
Khume gatipondo ndzi lowola Celi . . . ahe Celi . . . ho Celina
Ho kufamba saina oooCelina . . . ahe Celi . . . ho Celina
Hiku wawuya Celina . . . wawuya sidimela satiwanguavavani . . . ho
    Celina
Wawuya Celina oooo Wawuya Celina satiwagueleguele . . . ho Celina
Ndzi xavele nwamanarhu ndzi xavela Celi . . . ahe Celi . . . ho Celina.

Here Comes Celina

Here comes Celina, here comes Celi
Here comes my wife, Oh Celina.
Ho Celina, Ha Celina, Ahe Celi, Ho Celina
I bought blouses, I bought them them for my wife,
But in the end she is a whore . . . Ho Celina.

Ten years to lobolo my wife
In the end she is a whore. . . . Ho Celina
They say you are leaving Celina. . . . Ho Celina, Ahe Celi, Ho Celina
They say , Ho Celina, Ha Celi, Ahe Celi, Ho Celina

I bought a first-class *capulana*, I bought it for my wife
But in the end she is a whore. . . . Ho Celina
I bought blouses, I bought them for my wife
But in the end she is a whore . . . Ho Celina

Ten years to *lobolo* my wife. . . . Ahe Celi . . . Ho Celina
Five years to *lobolo* Celi, Ahe Celi Ho Celina
We say you will sign [divorce papers], Oh Celina, Ahe Celi Ho Celina.
They say that you are going, Celina, Oh Celina, Ahe Celi, Ho Celina

I bought a first-class *capulana* I bought it for my wife . . .
   in the end she is clever, Ho Celi . . .
Ten notes of one hundred *escudos* to *lobolo* Celi . . . Ahe Celi Ho Celina
We say that you will sign, Oh Celina, Ahe Celi, Ho Celina.

We say you will go back [to your parents], Celina,
   Oh, you will return as a wife disgraced by prostitution
You will go back, Celina, Oh you will go back, Celina,
   a wife disgraced by prostitution, Ho Celina
I bought a first-class *capulana*, I bought it for Celi
   Ahe Celi, Ho Celina.

The song was explained as the three phases of love in the life of a youth. He was happy to have the bride coming to his home. He became disillusioned after having given her all the appropriate gifts to assure her love (blouses, fine *capulanas*, *lobolo*), but she is unfaithful, she is a prostitute. After discovering his wife's infidelity, he demands she sign for divorce, entitling him to the return of his *lobolo*. She is sent off to her parents as a disgraced woman.

INDEX

Ticket system, in domestic service, 58
Time bargaining, 122
Tobacco factories, 144
Toscano, Francisco, 167n.3, 179n.8, 179n.10,
   179n.15
Tourism, 38, 44, 102, 142
Trade, 17
Transportation projects, postwar, 106
Transvaal, 16–17
   municipal beer system of, 42
Tsonga, 20, 22, 27, 164n.23
Tswa, 20
Tullner, 177n.38–177n.39

U

Umbeluzi, 75
Unemployment, 98t, 101
   during Depression, 97–99, 98t
   Portuguese, in postwar era, 101
   shibalo as punishment for, 107
União Africana, 82–83
União Ferroviário, 82
   African support for, 85
   strike of 1917, 84–85
   strike of 1925-26, 87
Unions
   African, 82–83
   Portuguese, 82
University of the Witwatersrand, 11, 160n.31
Uputsu (millet beer), 25, 40–41
Urdang, Stephanie, 166n.49

V

Vail, Leroy, 11, 20, 159n.6, 159n.14, 160n.31,
   160n.34, 160n.36, 161n.45–161n.46, 163n.3,
   163n.6, 164n.21–164n.22, 171n.26,
   175n.66, 179n.2–179n.3, 180n.37, 181n.76,
   183n.23, 183n.30
van Butselaar, Jan, 167n.5
van Dongen, I. S., 185n.2, 185n.4
Van Onselen, Charles, 10, 41, 161n.41, 163n.3,
   170n.57–170n.58, 170n.62, 173n.57
Vaughan, G. Edgar, 182n.82
Vaughan, Megan, 165n.30
Vieira, Salamão, 163n.6, 168n.9, 168n.14
Viticulture, 31
"Vozes de Burro" (The Braying of an Ass)
   newspaper column (João Albasini), 65
Vucuzana, Valente M., 125

W

Wack, Charles, 30
Wage labor
   conditions in, 155
   as escape from shibalo, 75
   as protection from shibalo, 72
Wages
   for African males in Lourenço Marques,
      1933-1962, 132t, 132
   for African office workers, 126
   African versus European, 5
   after indigenato, 116
   of casual labor, 51
      at port complex, 80
   for civil service jobs, 134
   decline in, 17
   differentials among Africans, 131, 134
   of domestic servants, postwar, 143
   in domestic service, 55–57, 60, 149, 152
   effects of registration system on, 105
   factories, 145t
   for native professionals and assimilados,
      110, 134
   for police, 134
   at port, postwar, 121–122
   at port complex, 80, 83, 85t–86t, 85–86, 120
   in postwar era, 100
   for railway, 134
   raises in, 85
      strikes to force, 83–85
   for shibalo, 134
      1933-1962, 136, 136t
   of shibalo, at port complex, 80
   of slaughterhouse workers, 133–134
   withheld by bureaucracy, 74
   for women, 143, 145t
Wage savings, reliance on, 25
Walker, Cheryl, 161n.42
Warhurst, Philip R., 163n.3, 169n.31, 169n.36,
   169n.39
Wastberg, Per, 188n.66
Weapons of the Weak: Everyday Forms of Resistance (Scott), 9–10
Webster, David, 165n.32–165n.33
Wenela (Witwatersrand Native Labour Association), 25–26, 30
   drop in contracts with, 96, 96t
   system, 25
   trade agreement with Portugal, 17
Wharf cargo handling, state takeover of, 81–
   82, 87–88
Wheeler, Douglas L., 162–163n.1, 166n.39